The
LION'S PRIDE

The LION'S PRIDE

THEODORE ROOSEVELT
AND HIS FAMILY
IN PEACE AND WAR

Edward J. Renehan Jr.

OXFORD
UNIVERSITY PRESS

OXFORD
UNIVERSITY PRESS

Athens   Aukland   Bangkok   Bogotá   Buenos Aires   Calcutta
Cape Town   Chennai   Dar es Salaam   Delhi   Florence   Hong Kong   Istanbul
Karachi   Kuala Lumpur   Madrid   Melbourne   Mexico City   Mumbai
Nairobi   Paris   São Paulo   Singapore   Taipei   Tokyo   Toronto   Warsaw

and associated companies in

Berlin   Ibadan

First published by Oxford University Press, Inc., 1998

First issued in 1999 as an Oxford University Press paperback
198 Madison Avenue, New York, New York 10016

Oxford is a registered trademark of Oxford University Press

Library of Congress Cataloging-in-Publication Data
Renehan, Edward, 1956–
The lion's pride : Theodore Roosevelt and his family in peace and
war / Edward J. Renehan Jr.
p.   cm.
Includes bibliographical references and index.
ISBN 0-19-512719-6
ISBN 0-19-513424-9 (Pbk.)
1. Roosevelt, Theodore, 1858–1919—Family. 2. Presidents—United
States—Family relationships.   3. Roosevelt, Theodore, 1858–1919.
4. United States—Politics and government—1913–1921.   5. World War,
1914–1918—Influence.   I. Title
E757.3.R46   1998
973.91'1'0922—dc21   98-23998

1 3 5 7 9 10 8 6 4 2

Printed in the United States of America
on acid-free paper

This book is dedicated to my son

WILLIAM JAMES RENEHAN

and to the memory of his beloved "Poppy"

WILLIAM AUGUST BARTKOVICK

who left us on 16 February 1998

The young lions roar after their prey, and seek their meat from God.

PSALMS 104:21

Contents

Acknowledgments   xi

Part One: ROOSEVELT FORM

1   Mementoes   3

2   Roots   9

3   Crowded Hour   21

Part Two: THE LION'S PRIDE

4   The Uninvited   37

5   A Rather Enlarged Football Game   51

6   All the Kinds of Boys There Are   71

7   The Kaleidoscope Shaken   87

8   Too Proud to Fight   99

9   Equal Billing with Woodrow   110

10   Dust in a Windy Street   123

11   Everybody Works But Father   138

12   Rue de Villejust   148

13   Issoudun   155

14   Pater Familias   168

15   Dark Harbor   186

16   The Capital of the World   204

17   The Old Lion Is Dead   212

18   War Once More   226

19   Epilogue   241

Notes   247

Selected Bibliography   267

Index   273

Acknowledgments

My friend and agent, Julian Bach, was among the first to have faith in this project. M. S. "Buz" Wyeth Jr.—longtime editor at HarperCollins—was next in line. Then my old friend and editor, Peter Ginna, newly ensconced at Oxford University Press, came along and gave the book a most excellent home. Every writer should have such accomplices as these.

William H. Harbaugh, Emeritus Professor of History at the University of Virginia, Charlottesville, provided indispensable criticism that made the book all the better. I cannot overstate my obligation to Bill, who is the dean of Theodore Roosevelt scholars. His *Power and Responsibility: The Life and Times of Theodore Roosevelt* is the very best one-volume life of TR ever published.

My friend Tweed Roosevelt, great-grandson of Theodore Roosevelt and grandson of Archibald B. Roosevelt, provided information, criticism, and—on a more practical plane—a welcoming place to stay in Boston while I pursued research in the Theodore Roosevelt Collection at Harvard's Houghton Library. Wallace Finley Dailey, Curator of the Harvard Roosevelt Collection, proved an invaluable and expert guide to the vast riches to be found there. Wallace was always available, always energetically and pleasantly so, and gave generously of his precise knowledge.

Dr. John Gable, Ph.D., a noted Roosevelt scholar and Executive Director of the Theodore Roosevelt Association, critiqued several chapters and, when I came up dry, even supplied a title: *The Lion's Pride*. P. James Roosevelt of Oyster Bay spoke with me at length on several occasions about his family and their story.

For various other aids, comforts, and courtesies, I am indebted to Bill and Eleanor Bartkovick, Douglas Brinkley, Ben Cheever, Evelyn Cherpak, Arthur Goldwag, John LeBoutillier, Stephen and Rogina Jeffries, Christa Renehan, Joan Renehan, James Renehan, J. West Roosevelt, Jamie Ruby, Geoffrey C. Ward, Edith Derby Williams, the late Hamilton Fish, and the late Henry Serrano Villard.

I would be lost without the outstanding staff at Oxford University Press. In particular, I would like to thank production editor Kimberly Torre-Tasso, copy editor Barbara Coeyman Hults, and editorial assistant Isabella Robertson.

As usual, my wife, Christa, and our two children—Billy and Katherine—have good-naturedly put up with a house full of ghosts. In this instance, the spooks were all Rooseveltian and thoroughly pleasant to have around. We shall miss them.

Edward J. Renehan Jr.
Wickford, North Kingstown, RI
6 January 1998
The Feast of the Epiphany

The LION'S PRIDE

Part One

ROOSEVELT FORM

Chapter 1

MEMENTOES

*A*t one o'clock in the afternoon of 1 July 1898, Colonel Theodore Roosevelt led his Rough Riders in two daring charges up Kettle Hill and the adjacent San Juan Ridge, just outside the city of Santiago, Cuba, in a pivotal battle of the Spanish-American War. Their object was to dislodge the Spanish from these two heavily defended positions, and thus pave the way for the capture of Santiago. The only mounted officer in the battle, the bespectacled 39-year-old Roosevelt seemed an easy target for the Spanish guns firing from the top of each promontory. "Are you afraid to stand up when I am on horseback?" he shouted at the start of the first charge, rallying his troopers to run behind him as he turned, at a gallop, toward the Spanish. "No man," wrote journalist Richard Harding Davis, "who saw Roosevelt take that ride expected he would finish it alive." Davis said it was the bravest thing he'd ever seen, and the most foolhardy.

In the evening, Roosevelt stalked happily back and forth across the brow of San Juan Hill, the highest peak of the San Juan Ridge. The trenches below him were filled to capacity with cadavers. Roosevelt seemed to take a grim satisfaction in contemplating the day's carnage.

As his close friend and fellow Rough Rider, Bob Ferguson, wrote, "no hunting trip so far has equalled it in Theodore's eyes. . . . T. was just revelling in victory and gore."[1]

Throughout the evening he stood high on the crest of the ridge in range of firing Spanish guns, just so he could get a good view back at all the "damned Spanish dead." At one point a shell landed so close it singed him. The same shell killed several men standing nearby. At least one observer commented that Roosevelt seemed to think himself invulnerable. The only time he bent low was to collect spent cartridges he thought his young sons would like as souvenirs.

Roosevelt personally brought down one Spaniard that day—the first and only time he ever killed a man. The events at the San Juan Ridge made him a celebrity and primed his political career to take off like a rocket upon his return to the States. Yet, as he told one of his closest confidants, the most important thing about his charge at San Juan was that it would serve forever for his children "as an apology for my having existed . . . should the worst come to the worst I am quite content to go now and to leave my children at least an honorable name."[2] To another friend he wrote that the war against Spain was his "one chance to cut my little notch in the stick that stands as a measuring rod in every family. I know now that I would have turned from my wife's death bed to answer that call."[3]

ॐ ॐ

All the children of Theodore Roosevelt—most especially his four boys—grew up in the light of his great martial example. Each came of age sharing Roosevelt's Kiplingesque view of the battlefield as a place of honor, fulfillment, and robust democracy. All of them realized that their father had found a political fortune in his dashing charge up the battle-scarred slopes of the San Juan Ridge. And each was forever infused with Roosevelt's passion for righteous battle. Yet they also saw that romantic vision of armed conflict tarnished by the first great war they encountered as adults, and the tragedies it inflicted on their family.

"Quentin's death is always going to be the greatest thing in any of our lives. . . ." Theodore Roosevelt Jr. wrote his sister Ethel in 1918, not long after the youngest of the family was blown from the sky in aerial combat over Chaméry, France.[4] Ethel, who had seen the painful results of battle close-up when she served with her husband in a Paris military hospital, perceived clearly that the European war experience she and Teddy had undergone would forever separate the happiness of their youth from the sad longing and retrospection of their maturities. "I sometimes just cannot believe," she wrote, "that all this has come to us and that never again will we be happy and young as we were, and that always there will be the pain beneath the laughter."[5] Alice Roosevelt Longworth—the eldest of Theodore Roosevelt's brood— spoke not only for herself but for her sister and brothers when she wrote: "All our lives before and after have just been bookends for the heroic, tragic volume of the Great War."[6]

Heroic and tragic indeed. By the time of the Armistice (11 November 1918), Theodore Roosevelt Jr. (the eldest of Theodore Roosevelt's four boys) and Archie Roosevelt (the second-youngest) were both gravely wounded, and Archie showed disturbing signs of the profound mental depression that was to haunt him, on and off, till the end of his life. Quentin, the baby of the family, was dead. So too was the Roosevelts' good friend—Quentin's fellow aviator and boon companion from Groton and Harvard—Hamilton Coolidge, who was shot down near the Argonne Forest on Theodore Roosevelt's sixtieth (and last) birthday, within weeks of the Armistice. Among Theodore Roosevelt's immediate family, his second-oldest son, Kermit, was the only uniformed male to survive the war relatively unscathed.

For all their losses, family members expressed few regrets. Instead they assured one another that as a clan they'd done what was necessary in their time. "You are drifting into a family," Archie had written Quentin's fiancée in 1917, "that is doing the right thing as well as it knows how, and you will never have to make any excuses for any of your future in-laws not sacrificing themselves for the cause."[7]

The Roosevelt who came closest to expressing regret was the one among them who was most free to do so. "To feel that one has inspired a boy to conduct that has resulted in his death, has a pretty serious side for a father," Theodore Roosevelt wrote of Quentin. However, he did not publicly question the usefulness of the losses suffered by his and so many other families. How could he? He had, after all, been the high priest of American interventionism since early 1915. The war in which his youngest son died and his other sons suffered was one for which he'd lobbied with a vengeance. "Honor, highest honor," the sickly and dispirited ex-President editorialized after Quentin's last flight, "to those who fearlessly face death for a good cause; no life is so honorable or so fruitful as such a death. Unless men are willing to fight and die for great ideals, including love of country, ideals will vanish, and the world will become one huge sty of materialism."[8]

The family clung to this credo after Roosevelt himself died on 6 January 1919. In the decades that followed, they commemorated the sad events of the war years with the same gusto as they had the happier moments in their shared history. At Sagamore Hill, the home on Long Island where Quentin Roosevelt was once a boy and Theodore Roosevelt a robust young father, the mementoes and memorabilia of their deaths took equal places beside the mementoes and memorabilia of the family's joyous life together before the war. Trophies of great victories and accomplishments rested side by side with symbols—artifacts—of mortal pain bravely borne, which were themselves taken as tokens of more subtle victories and accomplishments.[9]

In the North Room, which was Theodore Roosevelt's trophy room, the heads of beasts slain in Kenya, the Far West, and Maine gazed dumbly at visitors. Beside these were hung Roosevelt's Nobel Prize medal and his hat and sword from Rough Riders days. Then there was his death mask. Among moose and bear and buffalo, the startled guest came across the white plaster face of the hunter, with closed eyes, as he'd looked at his death. On another wall of the same room hung the twisted, mutilated axle of the Nieuport plane in which Quentin Roosevelt died in 1918.

After Quentin was killed, German photographs of his battered corpse mysteriously found their way to Sagamore Hill. The anonymous sender was probably malicious. There was most likely a wish to offend, wound, or horrify. But the photographs did not offend. They were instead cherished as further evidence of Quentin's gallant ending. Prints were placed in family scrapbooks, copies sent to relatives.[10] Nearly thirty years later, after Quentin's body had been exhumed from the field at Chaméry and taken to an American military cemetery at Normandy, his Chaméry headstone was carried to Sagamore and installed in a place of honor beneath the flagpole. Here his elderly mother—Edith, widow of Theodore Roosevelt—could see it and be daily reminded of her youngest child's brave sacrifice.

ॐ ॐ

Both Ted Jr. and Kermit died in uniform during World War II, though not from enemy fire. Their mother, Edith, died in 1948. Sagamore Hill was opened to the public five years later. The tourists swarmed in. Among them—anonymous and silent—was Archie, Theodore Roosevelt's lone surviving son, who lived only a few miles away. In line with the other sightseers, he would stand behind the ropes and stare into all the rooms he remembered so well from childhood.[11]

He was annoyed, on one such visit, to see both the death mask and the axle gone from the North Room. The items, he learned, had been placed in storage in the basement vault.[12] Under stern questioning, a nervous National Park Service guide explained that the pieces were thought too disturbing for some of the sightseers who came through the house—so many of them young children. The removal, complained Archie, was the act of people who "do not understand the Roosevelts and do not understand what we did in the war, who we were before the war, or who we were after."[13] His mother, he was sure, would want the relics left where she had kept them for nearly thirty years and where they remained on the day she died. It was, after all, _her_ home.

In his charming yet guarded memoir _All in the Family_, Ted Jr. said Sagamore Hill was a product of the years "as surely as is a reef of coral."[14] Each room and niche, each table and chair seemed to be associated with some choice bit of family lore. Every item was a keepsake, such as the footstool of the children's great-grandfather Roosevelt. To understand a family, said Ted, it was important to understand the stories held in the items that made up the furnishings and decorations of their house.

There are marvelous stories contained in Sagamore Hill's cherished trophies of World War I. The stories go a long way toward helping us, paraphrasing Archie, to understand the Roosevelts, what they did in the war, why they did it, who they were before the war, and who they were after. But the stories do not begin with the war. In fact, they long predate the period when the six remarkable Roosevelt children—particularly the four sons who served in the fighting ranks—were sent to encounter the destiny at which they'd been aimed, like bullets shot by an expert marksman, since birth.

Chapter 2
ROOTS

The spacious yet austere house called Sagamore Hill rises high above the placid, protected harbor of Oyster Bay on the north shore of Long Island. The bay's outlet into Long Island Sound cannot be seen from this vantage point; thus the view from the porch is of something that looks very much like a lake. Every element of the scene—the lake that is not a lake, the wooded hills rolling up from the Sound, and the welcoming old home itself—conspire today as they have for decades to define a unique stretch of geography Theodore Roosevelt once described as "the ideal landscape for childhood."[1]

It is still, in many ways, the ideal landscape for childhood. Indeed, children by the thousands come here each year to roam the house and grounds. Clutching their schoolbags and lunch boxes, they stare in amazement at the stuffed beasts lining the halls of the mansion, the guns and sabers that seem to be everywhere, and the toys and bedrooms of the boys and girls, now dust, who once called this remarkable place home.

Children have always sensed Roosevelt's good-natured presence here in this most special of spots. Roosevelt's grandson, Archibald Roosevelt Jr., who was an infant when Roosevelt died, believed Roosevelt's spirit permeated the house and grounds. The ghost who haunted Sagamore, wrote Archie Jr., was "a kindly one who kept a jolly and benevolent eye" on the children who came after him. "He was our hero and our playmate," wrote the grandson. "He just had too much vitality to die and leave all those grandchildren deprived of his companionship."[2]

The house in which Roosevelt's spirit moved and moves is a massive, lumbering battleship of a place. Its foundations are twenty inches thick. The joists and rafters and roof boards are of equivalent heft. In the words of Roosevelt scholar Herman Hagedorn, the house exudes "solidity . . . dignity, hospitality, comfort, the social stability of the owner, and permanence." Yet there is no ostentation. Sagamore Hill is less a mansion than simply a very large family home. Its design is wholly utilitarian. Of its twenty-three rooms, twelve are bedrooms.

Roosevelt specified the number of bedrooms in 1883. At the time he was a 25-year-old newlywed. His wife, Alice Hathaway Lee, was pregnant with their first child. His plans for family, just like all the other plans he made in life, were large from the start. (Once, when hearing tell of an Italian cabby who fathered twenty children in twenty-five years of marriage, Alice Roosevelt Longworth commented, "How father would love that man!"[3])

In Roosevelt's time no other houses were visible from Sagamore. "We have no one looking into our pantry and there is no need to close a shutter," he wrote. He did not "live in a neighbor's pocket." Even the neighbors he could not see—those nearest to the property line of Sagamore—were fellow Roosevelts: his cousins Emlen and West.[4] Here at Sagamore Hill, surrounded by friendly cousins and comfortable seclusion, Theodore Roosevelt's children would—as he wrote his friend Owen Wister—be able to run barefoot and bare-chested with friends and cousins, shouting "screams of savage joy," and reaping "every benefit of the freedom of wild places."[5]

Roosevelt's dream of an ecstatic and confident tribe storming up and down the beach must have seemed very remote just before the house on the hill was completed in 1884. In February of that year, young Alice Lee—for whom Roosevelt built the mansion—had died in Manhattan of complications from Bright's disease. She expired just hours after giving birth to a daughter, her namesake. In another room of the same house, on the same day, Theodore Roosevelt's mother passed away.

For a time the world looked black. He wrote that his life—his happiness—was over. He did not go anywhere near the new house on the hill. Instead he went to the Badlands of North Dakota where he roped and ranched and tried to lose himself, leaving Baby Alice in the care of one of his sisters in the East. At first it seemed he would never emerge from his malaise, never connect with his young daughter, never again embrace and acknowledge the life he'd known before his great tragedy. But then he pulled himself together and carried on.

With his second wife, Edith Carow, he populated the beaches and woods of Sagamore in the manner he'd always intended. Edith made him the father of five more children: four boys and a girl. Ted Jr. was born in 1887, Kermit in 1889, Ethel in 1891, Archie in 1894, and Quentin in 1897. With the daughter of the first marriage—the girl born in 1884 who was called "Sister" within the family because of the unspeakable memories associated with her given name—they made a precocious and rambunctious band of happy and confident youths.

Roosevelt doted on the children without spoiling them. He delighted in their delights, took great interest in their adventures, and always—*always*—did everything possible to prompt their imaginations. "I love all these children and have great fun with them," he wrote in a letter to his sister-in-law, "and I am touched by the way in which they feel I am their special friend, champion, and companion."[6] He was their most valued playmate, with whom they rode horseback, ran races, hiked, swam, hunted, and climbed. He was likewise their role model. The message of his vigorous example was a straightforward one. If the children were to be like him—and they dearly wished to be exactly like him—they must be ever active, embrace life, overcome all obstacles, and, above all, never complain.

తా తా

A significant part of what Roosevelt conveyed to his children was
the same gospel of confident, happy, adventurous life he'd absorbed
from his own father, the first Theodore Roosevelt.[7] As a youth, Teddy
Roosevelt had been a weak and wilting asthmatic: a sufferer, a victim.
He remained so until the day his father—"the greatest man I ever knew,
and the only man I ever feared"—issued the stern and uncompromising
injunction that he must, through force of will, stop gasping for air and
start taking control of his destiny by building his body. Only then would
he have strength and health to match the superb agility of his mind.

Ever after, he forced himself to persevere. Ever after, he refused to
give in to, or even acknowledge, any physical discomfort or pain or
weakness. By the time he started spending summers at Oyster Bay—
when he was 16 years old in 1874—his days were routinely ones of
ecstatic physical triumph. Here he ran, hiked, boxed, and hunted. He
did so inexhaustibly—constantly challenging himself to become ever
stronger, braver, and more confident. He was known to row twenty
miles in a day. He was tireless. He knew no bounds.

తా తా

Roosevelt liked to tell his children stories. Ghost stories were his
specialty, and his ghost stories were legend. They linger to this day,
handed down through succeeding generations of the clan he never
really left. In addition to the ghost stories, there were also tales of family
and shared heritage: of illustrious ancestors whom his children and their
cousins were challenged to prove themselves worthy of.

In 1911, his nephew William Sheffield Cowles Jr.—son of his sister
Anna Roosevelt Cowles and her husband, Rear Admiral William Sheffield Cowles—was struggling at Groton School to overcome the trauma of his first separation from his mother. Roosevelt encouraged the
boy while at the same time lecturing him sternly on his duty to his
forebears. "I know well how homesick you are, and what a hard experience these first months at school are for you. . . ." wrote Roosevelt,

"I have always admired you and believed in you; you are brave, you have grit and resolution; and now you are undergoing your first real test, you are for the first time doing something that is hard and disagreeable; *and you must make good* . . . Sheffield, a gentleman *must* be educated, *must* be able to hold his own among other gentlemen; a boy with your ancestry *must* be worthy of his ancestry."[8]

Among the ancestors to live up to were two war-hero brothers of Theodore Roosevelt's mother: Mittie Bulloch of Roswell, Georgia. The eldest, James Dunwody Bulloch—"Uncle Jimmy"—was an admiral in the Confederate Navy. Posted secretly to Liverpool during the Civil War, Bulloch masterminded clandestine ship construction of Confederate commerce raiders—among them the *Florida* and *Alabama*—that became notorious for destroying significant amounts of Union shipping on the high seas. Bulloch's younger brother, Irvine, served as a midshipman on the *Alabama* and, legend has it, fired the last shot in the famous fight with the Union corvette *Kearsarge* off Cherbourg, sticking to his post as the *Alabama* sunk beneath him on 19 June 1864. Subsequently, Irvine served on the commerce raider *Shenandoah*, harassing New England whalers in the Bering Strait.

The economic impact of the commerce raiders was significant, so much so that historian Philip Van Doren Stern considers James Bulloch's contribution to the Confederacy second only to that of Robert E. Lee.[9] The *Alabama* alone destroyed or captured no fewer than fifty-seven American merchant ships (with a total estimated value of $6,547,000) before being sunk herself by the *Kearsarge*. In the process, the *Alabama* and its fellow commerce raiders diverted numerous Union naval ships from the blockade of Confederate harbors, nearly destroyed the American merchant marine (which never again recovered the world dominance it had enjoyed before the Civil War), and inflated American maritime insurance rates to such an extent as to drive more than one New England shipowner into bankruptcy. (Four years after the surrender of the Confederacy, Senator Charles Sumner of Massachusetts proposed that the United States demand damages of Great Britain in excess of $100 million, on the grounds that Britain's involvement with the

Alabama had doubled the length of the war and in so doing cost the federal government at least that much.[10])

Because of their association with the commerce raiders, both Bulloch brothers were excluded from the general amnesty after the war, and wound up as exiles. They spent the remainder of their lives in Liverpool, where they raised families and pursued lucrative careers as cotton merchants. Although Irvine made at least one surreptitious trip back to the States, James never again returned. When he died in early 1901, he left an instruction that his gravestone be inscribed with the words: "American by birth, Englishman by choice."[11]

The Bulloch brothers' relations with their nephew Teddy were always affectionate. When 11-year-old Teddy met his Bulloch uncles during a family trip to Europe in 1869, he was nothing less than awestruck. More than a decade later, Teddy came off the success of his first book, *The Naval War of 1812*, insisting that his uncle Jimmy write up his memoirs of the days of the commerce raiders. The result was Bulloch's memoir, *The Secret Service of the Confederate States in Europe,* published in two volumes in London in 1883.

ॐ ॐ

Teddy's paternal ancestors—the Roosevelts of New York—were significantly less glamorous than the dashing Bullochs of Georgia. Virtually all the Roosevelts for generations were upstanding men of business and worthy citizens of Manhattan, but few were colorful.

The most romantic figure of the Roosevelt clan—singularly so, for his generation—was Robert Barnwell Roosevelt.[12] "Uncle Barnwell," whom Teddy's children had occasion to meet when he was an old man, was a person of many parts: a politician, a swashbuckling gentleman adventurer, a pioneering conservationist, and a great hunter and fisherman. He was also a writer of books on the themes of hunting and conservation, and a veteran of the Union Army.

Unlike the other Manhattan Roosevelts, Barnwell was a Democrat. Still, he was a thoroughly Rooseveltian Democrat. He was anti-Tammany and as such stood staunchly against what many—Democrat and Republican alike—considered the backbone of the Democratic Party: graft. Although he accepted the support of party boss William Tweed for a successful Congressional bid in 1870, he subsequently turned on Tweed and denounced Tammany election-tampering in a much-publicized speech at Cooper Union. After the speech, he joined other reform Democrats (among them Abram Hewitt and Samuel Tilden) in the bipartisan "Committee of Seventy" that removed Tweed from power. Barnwell said the sacrifice of Tweed was necessary in order that the party might fulfill its destiny and do great things to relieve the suffering of the poor.

Barnwell lived next door to the Manhattan brownstone on 20th Street where Teddy was born and raised. There, throughout the 1860s and 1870s, Barnwell and his wife, Elizabeth, not only kept several children but also a small menagerie of pets including a parrot, a monkey, guinea pigs, and pigeons. Barnwell also owned a cow, which, on one memorable day of Teddy's childhood, was led to the backyard via the main floor of the townhouse. It took more than an hour for the confused and terrified animal to be dragged and pushed through the ornate halls of the opulent brownstone.[13]

Unknown to any of the other Roosevelts, Uncle Barnwell kept a mistress and several more children—though no animals—in another house just a few short blocks away from his zoo on 20th Street. Nor was Barnwell's womanizing restricted to his mistress. Indeed, Barnwell was one of the most energetic and voracious philanderers in New York. When his family eventually found out about his outlandish double life, the revelation led to more than two decades of tension between him and his outraged brothers, nephews, and nieces. Teddy was one of the few family members who kept in touch with Barnwell during the 1880s. He briefly read law in Barnwell's office and was glad to have Barnwell's encouragement—amid a sea of criticism from other uncles and cousins—when he decided to enter politics. In 1898, one of Barnwell's sons by his mistress rode with the Rough Riders. Thus did relations remain warm between Teddy and the uncle who had so influenced him as a politician, outdoorsman, and author.[14]

ॐ ॐ

Barnwell was born in 1829, three years after the death of Thomas Jefferson. He lived to the age of 77, dying in 1906, while his nephew was in the White House. His younger brother, Theodore, two years Barnwell's junior, did not enjoy such longevity. Nevertheless, Teddy Roosevelt's children knew Theodore Sr.—the grandfather they never met—even better than they knew their exotic, Bohemian great-uncle Barnwell. Indeed, through dozens of oft-repeated, inspiring tales of selfless goodness, Teddy Roosevelt transformed Theodore Sr. into a near-mythic figure revered to this day by his many descendants.

When Teddy Roosevelt and Teddy's two sisters and brother were growing up, Theodore Sr. was associated with the family firm of Roosevelt & Son. One of Theodore Sr.'s four older brothers, James Alfred Roosevelt, was senior partner.[15]

Their father, old Cornelius Van Schaack Roosevelt (known as CVS within the family), retired in the 1850s after a career during which he made himself into one of New York's first millionaires. Although he inherited Roosevelt & Son from his own father and grandfather, CVS was the man who really built the firm and secured the family's fortune. It was CVS who redirected the business from the moderately profitable retailing of hardware to the enormously profitable importing of plate glass. And it was CVS who, during the financial panic of 1837, went about Manhattan buying up vast tracts of land at bargain prices: a wise investment that paid off one hundred-fold over time via the family-owned Broadway Improvement Association. As of 1876, when the plate-glass business was sold to a British firm, Roosevelt & Son became primarily concerned with private banking and investment. The offices were moved from Maiden Lane to Pine Street. James Alfred remained at the helm of both Roosevelt & Son and the Broadway Improvement Association, with his younger brother, Theodore, loyally—if unenthusiastically—carrying out whatever tasks were assigned him.

Theodore's real interest was charity. As a son of wealth—as someone

who had been blessed with the gifts of both a fortune and a career—
Theodore Roosevelt Sr. was afflicted with what he called a "trouble-
some conscience." To keep it from troubling him too much, he engaged in a flurry of good works. Together with the pioneering social
worker Charles Loring Brace, he created the Children's Aid Society
and the Newsboys' Lodging House. He went on to help found the
New York Orthopedic Hospital and the American Museum of Natural
History. The charter of the latter was drawn up and signed in Theodore
Sr.'s Manhattan parlor. He donated the land upon which the museum
was built. Later on, with Joseph Choate and Pierpont Morgan, he
helped found the Metropolitan Museum of Art.

He was possessed by what family friend John Hay called a "maniacal
benevolence." Not content to simply let his money do his work for
him, he spent every Sunday evening at the Newsboys' Lodging House.
There he talked with the homeless youngsters, gave them advice, and
provided them the benefit of his affection, wisdom, and example. He
knew each of the boys—and there were hundreds of them—by name.
He took the time to study their histories and understand their problems.
"They would gather around him," remembered Brace, "and he would
question each one as to what he was doing, and give him advice and
sympathy and direction. You felt the moment Mr. Roosevelt was in
the room that he was a help to those poor fellows."[16]

When he could, Theodore arranged to have some of the boys sent
to new homes in the Western territories. Years later, in 1900, Governor
Theodore Roosevelt of New York was approached at a conference by
Governor James Brady of the Alaska territory. Reaching out his hand,
Brady said he did not seek to meet the up-and-coming governor of
New York. Nor did he wish to greet the Rough Riding hero of the
Spanish-American War. No, Brady simply wished to shake hands with
the son of the first Theodore Roosevelt. With great emotion, Brady
told Roosevelt how, as a boy, he'd been picked up off the streets of
New York by Theodore Sr., who placed him in a home on the Pacific
coast. Not only had Theodore Sr. found Brady new parents and paid

his way west, he also periodically checked up on the boy and wrote him letters of encouragement. "Your father," Governor Brady told Roosevelt, "made me who I am today."[17]

One contemporary dubbed Theodore Sr. "Greatheart" after the heroic character in *The Pilgrim's Progress* who provided safe passage for innocents making the journey of life. "Come now, and follow me," the brave Puritan told the children in Bunyan's classic tale, "and no hurt shall happen to you. . . ."

In 1876, when the scandals of the Grant administration made headlines, Theodore Sr. became active in reform politics. He helped organize the Republican Reform Club and joined with other distinguished citizens (among them Henry Adams, Frederick Law Olmstead, William Graham Sumner, William Cullen Bryant, Peter Cooper, and young Henry Cabot Lodge) in demanding an end to corruption in government—*Republican* government, that was. (Democratic graft, said Adams, was natural as the tide, and just as impossible to repress despite all the best efforts of Theodore's brother Barnwell.)

George William Curtis, editor of *Harper's Weekly*, was one of Theodore's close colleagues in the reform movement. Curtis had been raised in Concord, Massachusetts, and as a boy had helped Thoreau build his cabin at Walden Pond. Significantly more social than his hero Thoreau, Curtis was boisterously active in New York politics—a tireless advocate for women's suffrage, civil service reform, and improved public education. In this connection, he preached a gospel that said government was too important to leave to those who currently dominated it: men whom Curtis characterized as corrupt ward captains poor enough to be manipulated by wealthy industrialists, trusts, and other business interests.

So far as Curtis was concerned, the educated classes had an obligation to take back government for the good of the people. He criticized affluent, learned men who sat at home "not knowing there is anything to be done, not caring to know; cultivating a feeling that politics are tiresome and dirty, and politicians vulgar bullies and bravoes; half persuaded that a republic is the contemptible rule of a mob, and secretly longing for a splendid and vigorous despotism." Curtis challenged these "armchair citizens" to pause and reflect. Was theirs really a government mastered by ignorance? Or was it simply one betrayed by lazy intelligence?[18]

Curtis insisted it was essential that gentlemen—men of refinement, breeding, and high ideals—enter and dominate the political arena. If not, then other, less-desirable elements would surely do the same. The educated class had a duty to rise and govern in the American democracy, offering inspired, selfless, incorruptible leadership to the common run of people who would otherwise be left victims to the political manipulations of capital and its operatives. Theodore Roosevelt Sr.— who, wrote Curtis, "walked these streets the image and figure of the citizen which every American should hope to be"—was just the type he wished to see active in public life.[19]

In 1876, Theodore Sr. traveled to the Republican Convention, where he joined Curtis and other reformers in successfully blocking the nomination of the corrupt Roscoe Conkling for president. Largely because of the agitation of reform elements, the Republican endorsement went to Rutherford B. Hayes instead.

In 1877, when President Hayes nominated Theodore to replace Conkling's protégé, Chester A. Arthur, as collector of customs for the Port of New York, Theodore told his family he secretly hoped he would not get the appointment. It would be an enormous and perhaps impossible job to clean up the graft in the Customhouse. If approved by the Senate, he would most definitely take the position and serve with diligence, as was his responsibility, but his "great wish" was that he would not need to do so. Senator Conkling, who chaired the Commerce Committee in the Senate, viewed Theodore's nomination as a direct slap against him by President Hayes. He saw to it Theodore's great wish was granted.

To Curtis's unhappiness, Theodore never ran for office himself. Perhaps he might have, if given time. Stomach cancer killed him in early 1878. On the day he died—9 February—a crowd of his fellow New Yorkers stood a deathwatch outside his house. Many of them were ragged children: the newsboys and orphans he helped so tirelessly, who knew him so well, and who loved him. On the day of his funeral, more than two thousand people crowded into the Fifth Avenue Presbyterian Church for the service. Editorials in every leading newspaper and preachers in pulpits across the city praised Theodore's energetic, high-minded, selfless citizenship, and called others to similar service.

As we know, one who heard this call loudly was a 19-year-old Harvard student dressed for mourning who sat in the first row of the church: Theodore Roosevelt, the younger. It was a call and a heritage he passed on to his own children, along with the heritage of so many other fascinating ancestors, not the least of whom were the courageous Uncles Bulloch and the irrepressible adventurer and politico, Uncle Barnwell.

Chapter 3

CROWDED HOUR

*O*ne of Archie Roosevelt's earliest memories was of a day long gone when he stood on the lawn at Sagamore Hill with Sister, Ted, Kermit, Ethel, and Father. It was the spring of 1898. Quentin, a babe in arms, was safe inside the house. Archie was just 4 years old. Sister—the eldest—was 14. Ted was 11, Kermit 9, and Ethel 7. Their father—Theodore Roosevelt—was 39, trim and robust. He lay flat on the ground, squinting through his thick pince-nez glasses, taking practice with his rifle. His target was a life-size paper figure tacked to a tree, behind which was the beautiful blue of Oyster Bay.

The children took turns peering over their father's shoulder, down the rifle barrel, and past it to the target and the Sound. They were eager not to distract him, but they were also fascinated. When Ted broke the silence to make an exclamation after an excellent shot, Father shushed him sternly: "Bunnies mustn't talk!"[1] Father needed to concentrate if he was to kill enough Spaniards to win the war. He'd traded his austere job as assistant secretary of the navy for a commission as a lowly lieutenant colonel in the cavalry. He and his good friend Colonel Leonard Wood—a West Pointer who had won the Congressional Medal of

Honor for his exploits pursuing the Apache chief Geronimo—had just wrapped up the exhausting business of raising the elite cavalry regiment soon to be known as the *Rough Riders*.[2] With both a war and a cavalry conveniently at his disposal, it would be a pity if Father got to the fighting line and proved too inept to hit anything.

That, the children knew, was hardly likely. The many stuffed beasts in the halls of Sagamore Hill bore witness to the excellence of their father's marksmanship. Cougars and buffalo, bear and jaguars—many shot in the Dakotas where Roosevelt ranched and hunted for long stretches throughout the 1880s—all testified to his prowess with the gun and his willingness to kill.

Throughout his life, he'd always forced himself out of the narrow, safe confines of cloistered affluence. He'd regularly courted rough and dangerous experiences: boxing and hunting and ranching with an absolutely reckless abandon upon which many commented. There was a distinctive, flagrant selflessness with which he confronted every obstacle and risk. When he boxed, he sought out the toughest opponents he could find. When he ranched, he did it in the harshest, most punishing landscape available: the Badlands. In hunting, his preference was wild game—grizzly bear, buffalo, and mountain lion—the quest for which exposed the hunter to mortal danger. When the time came, he urged his sons to court the same types of adventure. "I am one of those fortunate ones who had a father who took the time and made the effort to instill in his sons a love of the great outdoors," remembered Archie. "He taught us to accept the discomforts and hardships that attend sport in the open fields and wilderness, and accept them as a challenge to our manhood."[3]

Through the years, the scars on Roosevelt's body accumulated, as did the animals in his trophy room, but still he felt that his manhood had not been tested enough. He yearned for the glory of battle. It appeared to some—including his wife—that he was running toward the sound of Spanish guns with a frantic, delighted urgency that was hard to understand. "I am not acting in a spirit of recklessness or levity, or purely for my own selfish enjoyment," he insisted to a friend when announcing his plan to form the Rough Riders.[4] One particularly observant associate said Roosevelt had always surrendered himself to dangers with a "wanton abandonment." Why should he do anything other than that now?[5] Another suggested that Roosevelt would not think himself worthy of life until he succeeded in killing himself.

ॐ ॐ

By tradition, Roosevelts were merchants, not warriors. Teddy's paternal forebears had successfully avoided service in both the Revolution and the War of 1812. Only Uncle Barnwell, alone among all the Roosevelts of his generation, had volunteered to don a uniform during the Civil War. In order to avoid being drafted under the terms of the 1863 Conscription Bill, Theodore Roosevelt Sr. employed a young German immigrant by the name of Abraham Graf as his replacement. The broker who found Graf was paid $1,000. Graf himself received a grand total of $38 to enlist in the 7th New York Infantry. After being captured by the Confederates and paroled, he died of fever and scurvy in a Union hospital at Point Lookout, Maryland, on 31 March 1865. Graf and his employer, Roosevelt, never laid eyes on each other. It is doubtful Theodore Roosevelt the younger ever knew the name of the man who was hired as his father's replacement, or what had happened to him.[6]

Early in the Civil War, before the start of conscription, Theodore Roosevelt Sr. believed that he, like his brother Barnwell, should volunteer to fight for the Union. However, his wife, Mittie, was dedicated to the cause of the Confederacy and insistent that her husband not take up arms against her family. Acceding to his family, Theodore instead served the Union by working without compensation as Civilian Allotment Commissioner. In this role he established an eminently paternalistic program whereby federal soldiers set aside a portion of their pay for their families back home. He was surprised to have his first real success among the men of the New York regiment who, he said, represented "the scum of our city."[7]

Theodore Roosevelt Sr. and his family were safely out of town during the summer of 1863 when draft riots broke out in Manhattan. While the men of New York's working class rebelled against conscription in the only meaningful way they could, the Roosevelts, among them five-year-old Teddy, enjoyed the beach at fashionable Long Branch, New Jersey. "I do not wonder that the poor mechanics oppose conscription," wrote Mittie Roosevelt at the time. "It certainly favors the rich at the expense of the poor."[8]

Although there is no record of his ever mentioning it, Theodore Roosevelt the younger could not have been pleased to look back on his father's hiring a substitute during the Civil War. (Indeed, Theodore Sr. himself is on record as thinking his conduct shameful. "He always afterward felt that he had done a very great wrong in not having put every other feeling aside and joined the fighting forces," recalled one of his daughters.[9]) In later years, both Theodore Roosevelt's daughter, Alice, and his sister, Corinne, suggested that the memory of Theodore Sr.'s lapse was Teddy's prime inspiration in always trudging recklessly toward any battle that beckoned. More probably, the recollection of his father was but one element in a mix of memories and influences turning Teddy toward war.

Teddy came of age in a time when there was a tendency among the educated classes to greatly romanticize most aspects of warfare. During the 1890s, the philosophical militarist Brooks Adams—a friend of Roosevelt's—never missed a chance to extoll the purifying glories of righteous battle. Another Harvard man, Oliver Wendell Holmes Jr., called war "divine" and insisted the United States (a "snug, over-safe corner of the world") needed a treacherous life-or-death fight every generation or so, in order that people might realize "our comfortable routine is no eternal necessity of things. . . ." Playing into this sentiment was the general Brahmin infatuation with all things British, including the general British extollment of warfare. There was approval all around when Britain's Lord Wolseley wrote, "All other pleasures pale before the intense, the maddening delight of leading men into the midst of an enemy, or to the assault of some well-defended place." It was the era

of Alfred, Lord Tennyson's "Charge of the Light Brigade" and Rudyard Kipling's *Barrack-Room Ballads*.[10]

Just a year before the Spanish-American War, Assistant Secretary of
the Navy Theodore Roosevelt paraphrased Lord Wolseley in a speech
at the Naval War College, Newport, when he confidently and enthusiastically told a thousand listeners "no triumph of peace is quite so
great as the supreme triumphs of war."[11] Like his friend and fellow
naval historian Alfred Thayer Mahan, Roosevelt saw in war an element
of Christian duty. Roosevelt endorsed Mahan's view of history as "the
plan of Providence," a divine drama orchestrated by God in which
military force played an undeniable role. Roosevelt and Mahan concurred that the power to wield force successfully was a gift God granted
to those who would serve His purposes. Since humanity was "far removed from perfection," wrote Mahan, war was a "necessary evil" and
"a remedy for greater evils, especially moral evils."[12] It was no accident
that "Onward Christian Soldiers" was the favorite hymn of both Mahan
and Roosevelt. The anti-imperialist Mark Twain commented after
meeting Roosevelt that Teddy was "clearly insane . . . and insanest
upon [the subject of] war and its supreme glories."[13] But Teddy was
no more insane about war than many others of his day—among them
Holmes, Brooks Adams, Kipling, and Mahan.

On some level at least, Roosevelt's embrace of warfare was a reaction against his merchant roots. Throughout his life, Roosevelt tended
to be scornful of business interests and their focus on the vulgar concerns
of trade. He stated plainly that he wished to see the United States
become something more than a nation of tradesmen and manufacturers.
He sometimes wished out loud for war, simply so as to give the American people something to think about other than material gain. War,
he told a friend, was perhaps most valuable as a device whereby the
mission of the United States could escape the risk of appearing trivial.

As he said in his Naval War College speech, there had been and
always would be moments in history when war was the only alternative
to a wilderness that only tyrants and oppressors could call "peace."

Roosevelt insisted that at moments when war was inevitable, it should be seized upon as a purifying, unifying moment in the life of a country and a people. Out of the deadly fire of battle, the metal of nationhood would emerge stronger and more resilient than before. Without the occasional trial and trauma of war, a country would grow too fat, too smug, and too complacent for its own good, its citizens totally caught up in the self-centered concerns of commercialism and pampered modern living. Then nothing but a degenerate, self-absorbed bourgeois culture would prevail, dominated by "commercial classes" who were "too selfish to be willing to undergo any trouble for the sake of abstract duty."[14]

Wishing to see that Brahmin, commercial, and working classes all tasted the renewing fruit of democratic militarism, Roosevelt was an early and enthusiastic advocate of universal military training and universal military service. His ideal was a peace- and wartime draft that would conscript farmer, machinist, and Ivy Leaguer alike early in life, casting them together side by side and inspiring in them a sense of *égalité et fraternité* that would last a lifetime. This, he said, would be the fundamental building block of democratic nationhood.

৵ ৵

The war with the Spanish was one for which Roosevelt, as Assistant Secretary of the Navy, strenuously lobbied. Taking the Monroe Doctrine as his inspiration, he said he wanted nothing less than "to drive the Spaniard from the New World." He made the point, repeatedly, to President McKinley, to every member of the Cabinet he could buttonhole, to Naval Secretary Long, to his battle-hungry friend Leonard Wood, and to anyone else who might effectively fan the fires of war. When presented with the prospect of a joint Spanish–American inquiry into the causes of the sinking of the battleship *Maine* in Havana harbor on 15 February 1898, he urged against it lest it produce a finding that the Spanish were not culpable (and they probably weren't). Finally, with public opinion pressuring him from all sides, President McKinley surrendered to the war fever of Roosevelt and his cohorts. On 11 April he sent a militant war message to an equally militant Congress. War was declared on 19 April.[15]

Just as the war began, Roosevelt's wife, Edith, was, in his words, "crawling back to life" after a serious illness. Two months earlier, in February, the Canadian surgeon William Osler had diagnosed an abdominal tumor. There was surgery, and then "for two weeks we could not tell whether she would live or die," recalled Roosevelt. "Sometimes one seemed likely, sometimes the other . . ." Then Edith made the turn for the better and Roosevelt felt free to leave. He would, however, have gone to battle whether she lived or died. "I made up my mind," he told a friend after he returned from Cuba, "that I would not allow even a death to stand in my way; that it was my one chance to do something for my country and for my family . . ."[16]

ॐ ॐ

"And is my father going to war?" little Archie asked Father as he prepared to depart. "And will he bring back a bear?" At school, Kermit knocked down and bloodied a boy who said Roosevelt would be killed. Fifty years later, Alice ("Sister") wrote vividly of the surge of apprehension she had felt when Father said good-bye. Ted and Kermit broke down and buried their heads in their mother's lap as she read them a letter in which their father coldly calculated his chances of survival at two in three, and instructed her to give the two oldest boys his sword and revolver should he be killed. Tiny Ethel spent entire days sitting on the back steps of the porch at Sagamore, sewing and folding bandages she said were for the Rough Riders. Archie, pushing his wooden trains across the floor, said he was not playing "choo-choo" at all but rather "Father come home."[17]

ॐ ॐ

It seemed everyone wanted to be a Rough Rider. In total, more than twenty-three thousand applications arrived from volunteers across the country. So many applications flowed in from Harvard that Roosevelt accepted only one out of every ten lest he be accused of favoritism. Among the Crimson men were Woodbury Kane, a world-class yachtsman who was cousin to John Jacob Astor, and Joseph Sampson Stevens, then generally considered the world's greatest polo player. Roosevelt's regiment also included football star Dudley Dean along with Bob Wrenn, tennis champion of the United States. Among the assorted pole-vaulters and football players from Princeton, Yale, and Columbia were Will Tiffany and Hamilton Fish.[18]

To this mix of approximately 50 clubmen and Ivy Leaguers were added some 430 Native Americans, cowboys, ranchers, Texas Rangers, and lumberjacks. Buffalo Bill Cody—then aged 52—was asked to serve as head of scouts. Cody wanted to do it but could not get out of contracts for performances booked long in advance. Instead, he signaled his approval of the enterprise by allowing several of his show's best riders and "shootists," as he called them, to join Roosevelt's regiment.

Lieutenant Colonel Roosevelt's letters to his children from the regiment's San Antonio training camp provided vivid descriptions of life in the rough. From his remote outpost near the Alamo, Roosevelt reported that the blue bloods and cowboys were working together splendidly. It seemed that the experience of army life, and the shared challenge of war, was a great democratizing exercise. He told his children there was no hierarchy in the camp other than that imposed by the military. Some cowboys were officers; some Brahmins were not. Each member of the unit was judged solely by what he contributed rather than by how much money he had or who his forebears were.[19] The Rough Riders, Roosevelt wrote his children, were "obedient and yet thoroughly self-reliant and self-helpful, not afraid of anything and able to take care of themselves under all circumstances."[20] They were very brave and never complained—not even when they had hardly anything to eat, were worn out, or had to sleep on the bare ground in their wet clothes.[21]

In the beginning, at least, there was a certain element of stagecraft to the democracy of the Rough Riders. While it is indeed true that some cowboys were officers and some Brahmins were privates, only rarely was any Brahmin put into a situation where he would report directly to anyone who was not another northeasterner. The vast majority of the college men wound up as lieutenants, sergeants, and corporals. Furthermore, the largest concentration of northeasterners was found in Troop K under Captain Woodbury Kane. Cowboys predominated in other troops both as officers and enlisted men. Early in his days with the Rough Riders, Roosevelt himself was not without certain patrician airs, most of which—to his credit—he shed by the end of the campaign in Cuba.

However, on board the *Yucatan*, the boat that carried the Rough Riders to Cuba in June, conditions and accommodations were hardly equal. Officers paid a dollar a day to the owners, the Ward Line, for three fine meals consisting of hot soup, meat, vegetables, bread and butter. They ate these feasts on fine, cloth-covered tables in a luxurious dining saloon. By contrast, enlisted men sat on the deck eating hardtack, beef jerky, and cans of beans that were shared eight men to a can. Rank, of course, has always had its privileges, and there were no complaints about the officers' comforts. Problems arose, however, when Roosevelt invited "gentleman troopers" to dine with the officers. The western troopers protested, and Roosevelt's ill-considered invitation was quickly withdrawn. Still, those privates with money were welcome to buy all the food they wished from the officers' kitchen. Those who could afford it—such as privates who twelve months before had been summering at Newport—certainly did so.[22] By the end of the Cuban campaign, a wiser and fairer Roosevelt (he was always a quick study) would spend his own money to see that *all* the Rough Riders had good food on their plates.

So far as Roosevelt was concerned, the great common attribute of the Fifth Avenue crowd and the cowboys was that none of them were regular army. As his letters reveal, he thought every regular army officer he encountered was a buffoon—except for his friend Leonard Wood and John Pershing, a white officer with the black Tenth Cavalry. Years later, he still had not changed his mind. "In '98 . . . I was better than any colonel save one in the regulars before Santiago. . . . ," he wrote Archie in 1917. "In the army it is only the exceptional men who can conquer the unfavorable conditions . . . [few army regulars] go on improving after they become majors; and as soon as a man ceases to improve he goes backward."[23] The majority of the regular officers he met during the Spanish-American War seemed to Roosevelt to be in a backward mode. He had no respect for them, and he let his disrespect show both in the field and in the book he eventually wrote about his Cuban exploits entitled *The Rough Riders*. Given his prejudice against professional career soldiers, it is not surprising that in his few months of service he became notorious for stubborn and righteous insubordination.

Once the Rough Riders got into action, their history was brief and violent. Sergeant Hamilton Fish was one of the first to fall. He and sixteen others died at the battle of Las Guásimas in late June. After the fight, as the Rough Riders buried their dead in a single hastily dug hole, Roosevelt commented that he found in the common grave a metaphor for all that was best about America. Here, together, would lie "Indian and cowboy, miner, packer, and college athlete, the man of unknown ancestry from the lonely Western plains, and the man who carried on his watch the crest of the Stuyvesants and the Fishes."[24]

After sharing the first battle with the Rough Riders, after seeing the reality of death seize both socialite and cowboy regardless of class, Roosevelt's egalitarian rhetoric rang truer and seems to have become more real and more sincere. He said Sergeant Fish reminded him of another Brahmin, Robert Gould Shaw. As the white commander of a black unit, the 54th Massachusetts, Shaw died with many of his men in their famous, and suicidal, assault on Fort Wagoner in the summer of 1862. After the battle, Shaw was stripped of everything except undervest and buried in a shallow ditch beside fifty of the enlisted men he'd led to death. "Let him be buried with his niggers," said a Confederate general, intending it as an affront. Later, when Shaw's father, Judge Francis Shaw of Boston, was offered the opportunity to recover his son's corpse, he refused to do so. He said Robert was meant to rest side by side with his men. There was no higher honor that could be afforded him.

Two results of the events at Las Guásimas were Wood's promotion to general in command of the entire 2nd Cavalry Brigade, and Roosevelt's to full colonel with sole immediate command of the Rough Riders. Roosevelt's bold charge at Kettle Hill, near the summit of the San Juan Ridge, came on 1 July, just a few days after the promotions. It was a charge the Rough Riders shared with some of the most experienced regular-army soldiers in the Cuban campaign: the dismounted black "buffalo soldiers" of the Ninth and Tenth Cavalry, all of them fearless veterans of the Indian Wars. In Roosevelt's subsequent account of the adventure, he applauded the black regulars with whom the Rough Riders had taken the hill. Once Kettle Hill had been conquered, the black regulars and the Rough Riders converged with the Twenty-Fourth Infantry, another black regiment, to take the adjacent San Juan Hill, the highest promontory on the San Juan Ridge. Theodore Roosevelt was conspicuously brave throughout every stage of the battle, rallying not only his own men but also the "buffalo soldiers" to victory. The battle, said Teddy, represented his finest moment—a moment when he "rose above those regular army officers like a balloon." It was his "crowded hour" that changed the color and context of every hour, month, and year to follow it.[25]

Along with "the damned Spanish dead," there were also more than one thousand American corpses. Eighty-nine of these fatalities were from the Rough Riders, the balance coming from other units. A full 20 percent of the men and 50 percent of the officers of the Ninth and Tenth Cavalry died that day. Nevertheless, the victors were ecstatic. "It was glorious," wrote John Pershing. "For the moment every thought was forgotten but victory. We officers of the Tenth Cavalry could have taken our black heroes in our arms." Pershing also wrote glowingly of Roosevelt, applauding his fearless leadership in the field and calling it "indispensable" to the day's success.[26]

Subsequently, once press accounts of the battle were published, Theodore Roosevelt emerged as the unmitigated hero of the hour. Still, Roosevelt was disliked by prominent members of the military establishment, among them Secretary of the Army Russell Alger, whom Roosevelt had embarrassed when he publicly criticized the army's inept response to a malarial outbreak among the troops. Not long after the end of the war, five Medals of Honor were awarded to members of the Tenth Cavalry. At the same time, Roosevelt was denied a similar honor.

৵ ৵

Roosevelt and his men returned from Cuba in August and disembarked at remote Montauk Point on the extreme eastern end of Long Island. Leaving his men behind at Montauk, Roosevelt took a brief leave and was soon back at Oyster Bay, where he was honored by a tumultuous celebration staged by the townspeople. Following the celebration, he luxuriated in the comforts of home. When not spending time with his children, he gave interviews to the press, whose representatives were swarming all over Sagamore Hill. ("Where is the Colonel?" one reporter demanded of Archie. "I don't know where the Colonel is but father is having a bath," replied Arch.[27])

Roosevelt returned to the Montauk camp in mid-September, shortly before the regiment disbanded. He brought his children with him.[28] "I was fourteen and a half years old," remembered Sister, "and I felt every inch the 'Colonel's daughter,' . . . if I was in love with one Rough Rider, I was in love with twenty, even though I did have a pigtail and short dresses." Ted and Kermit spent a night with their father in his tent. Ted took the cot, and Kermit an air mattress. Father, in singularly uncolonel-like fashion, stretched out on the table that doubled as his desk.[29]

On the day the regiment disbanded, Roosevelt personally said good-bye to each of the more than three hundred surviving members. Roosevelt cried at the parting. Many of his men cried as well. The men presented Roosevelt with a Frederic Remington statuette. Then Roosevelt gave a long and heartfelt speech in which he promised them all his undying allegiance and friendship—a promise he kept—and likewise paid a moving tribute to the black heros of the Twenty-Fourth, Ninth, and Tenth who had shared equally in the Rough Riders' triumph.

"A great many of [my men] have been killed," he wrote young Ted shortly after the fight at San Juan Ridge. "Of those that come back you will see some at my house often."[30] In addition to the Ivy Leaguers, a number of crusty Dakota wranglers wound up as guests at the White House and Sagamore. During Roosevelt's presidency, a newspaper editorial complained about Roosevelt's penchant for inviting "thugs and assassins of Idaho and Montana to be his guests in the White House."[31] When a guard refused admission to one old Rough Rider whom Roosevelt considered a particularly close friend, the president made no secret of his annoyance. "The next time they don't let you in, Sylvane," he told the Rough Rider in the presence of the guard, "you just shoot through the windows."[32]

The Rough Riders marched in Roosevelt's inaugural parade and attended Ted Jr.'s posh wedding in a Fifth Avenue church. As president, Roosevelt sometimes interrupted his busy schedule during speaking tours of the West to share meals and visits with cowboys who had served in '98.[33] When Roosevelt died in January of 1919, not a few graying Rough Riders came to Oyster Bay, squeezed into their old uniforms, and served as guards of honor at his funeral. Their old Colonel would have wanted no one else.

༄ ༄

Teddy Roosevelt's children grew up in the glow of Roosevelt's crowded hour. (In his father's office at the White House, 10-year-old Quentin Roosevelt brandished his father's sword from the Cuban campaign, shouting "Step up and see the i-d-e-n-t-i-c-a-l sword carried by Colonel Thee-a-dore Roos-e-velt in the capture of San Juan Hill. See it! See it!" Swinging the sword through the air, the boy opened a cut on the cheek of his friend Charlie Taft, son of Theodore Roosevelt's Secretary of War William Howard Taft.[34]) All of the boys in their time tromped the grounds of Sagamore Hill and the White House, re-enacting the battle at San Juan Ridge.

All the Roosevelt children—most especially the sons—either absorbed or inherited his reckless, all-or-nothing approach to hazards. As David McCullough reminds us with reference to the Roosevelts, the pediatric psychologist Margaret McPharland says attitudes are caught more than they are taught.[35] With this in mind, we may say Theodore Roosevelt's sons most certainly caught both his attraction to warfare and his egalitarian ethic.

Throughout World War I, Ted Jr. would be alternately praised and criticized as an officer who routinely and boldly moved ahead of the line in battle after battle. In each of the world wars, he was at once idolized by his men, with whom he shared all dangers, and criticized by career officers, who respected Ted's bravery more than they did his judgment. The same officers also sometimes found themselves reprimanding him for insubordination, reminiscent of his father's in '98. Patton, who admired Ted Jr. in many ways, wrote of him: "Great courage. But no soldier."[36]

Archie was the same way. So were Kermit and Quentin. One contemporary from the Great War called Arch "an absolutely selfless gladiator who insisted on being the first to smell the enemy's bad breath, regardless of the risk."[37] Arch earned a similar reputation yet again in the South Pacific during World War II. During World War I Kermit was lightly reprimanded while fighting with the British in the Middle East. Some victories, said Kermit's British colonel, could very well be had *without* full frontal assaults into the gaping mouths of enemy guns. (Even Theodore Roosevelt himself was concerned about Kermit. "He is a little too reckless and keeps my heart in my throat," he remarked during their African safari in 1910.[38])

As for Quentin, his friend Hamilton Coolidge wrote that "his daring was difficult to understand." He was possessed by an "utter fearlessness" that "perhaps caused his death."[39] Just three days before Quentin's death in 1918, the *New York Sun* congratulated him editorially for "attacking three enemy airplanes single-handed and shooting one of them down." In so doing, said the newspaper, Quentin was "running true to Roosevelt form." The editorial concluded by noting "each of the vigorous Colonel's four sons is out to make a record worthy of their father. . . ."[40]

No truer words have ever been written.

Part Two

THE LION'S PRIDE

Chapter 4

THE UNINVITED

The Manhattan office of the New York Progressive Party was dingy and unkempt. In the unseasonable, scorching heat of mid-September 1914, it also stank. The scent reminded Theodore Roosevelt, the 56-year-old ex-president and titular head of the Progressive Party, of a boxing gym. A ceiling fan circled slowly above Roosevelt's head. The fan did something to circulate the stench but nothing to cool the air. Thus Roosevelt sweated profusely as he urgently and angrily scrawled line after hasty line across a yellow pad. His perspiration stained his white collar. More beads of sweat dripped down from his face to stain the paper on which he focused his energies, letting loose a barrage of notes and letters and telegrams full of queries and instructions for Progressive comrades far and near. Many of his communiqués were meant to convey reassurance: the normally bellicose Roosevelt promised he would do nothing to upset the chances for Progressive victory in the autumn elections. He swore he would refrain from being provocative on the subject of Europe.

Weeks earlier—at the beginning of August—two million German infantrymen had swept through Belgium into France. In ordering the move, the German government ignored the Treaty of 1839, which guaranteed the neutrality of Belgium in case of conflicts in which Great Britain, France, and Germany were involved. At first, Belgian General Gérard Mathieu Leman struggled to hold on to the forts at Liège, but all in vain. For a time it seemed that not only was Belgium doomed, but France with her, and quite possibly England as well. Now, with autumn coming on, the situation had improved, if only slightly. The push of German forces was stalled at the river Marne. Paris appeared safe for the moment.

So far as Roosevelt was concerned, the whole extravaganza could not have been more terribly timed. If Roosevelt hated the Kaiser at the moment, it was less for what the German emperor was doing to Belgium and France than for what he was doing to Roosevelt's immediate political plans.

What would happen to the autumn campaign? All bets were off. Roosevelt had hoped to bolster Progressive Congressional candidates by embarking on a prolonged attack of Woodrow Wilson's foreign policy. The "schoolmaster," as Roosevelt often called him, had seemed a sitting duck with his pacifist secretary of state, his naive hopes for global disarmament, and his inept handling of problems stemming from the political unrest in Mexico. Before the outbreak in Europe, Roosevelt anticipated a campaign focused on criticizing Secretary of State William Jennings Bryan and his cooling-off treaties. The treaties, said Roosevelt, effectively nullified the Monroe Doctrine by implying an abdication of sovereignty while providing no deterrent to European aggrandizement in the Western hemisphere. All of this, said Roosevelt, added up to "the abandonment of the interest and honor of America."[1] So too did the administration's refusal to maintain a viable navy and fortify the Panama Canal.

Roosevelt earnestly believed there were no more important issues than these. Thus it was tragic, he told his son Kermit, that the American imagination—the fickle and often-limited interest of the public mind— had been drawn and was being held by one thing only: the conflict in Europe and how to stay out of it. The country had closed ranks in an overwhelming endorsement of Wilsonian neutrality, and Roosevelt had no choice but to announce that the Progressive Party would cooperate with the president during the crisis. To do anything else would have been political suicide.

It was a pity the Progressives had lost the chance to capitalize on the thorny problem of Mexico, on arbitration, and the decline of the navy, for there were not many other issues on which they could build a campaign platform. What was there for Roosevelt to fault in Wilson's domestic reform agenda? Not much. Two years earlier, during the presidential elections of 1912, Wilson co-opted much of Roosevelt's Bull Moose platform, cleverly cutting ground out from under Roosevelt and his rambunctious third party. How could Roosevelt criticize programs he was on record as having proposed in the first place?

All told, the situation was a frustrating one for the naturally combative Roosevelt. As his friends well knew, a restrained Roosevelt was usually also a combustible Roosevelt. Thus he was something more than his usual bundle of nervous energy that day at Progressive Party headquarters. He was, instead, a significantly dangerous concoction of pent-up action and anger. This was the Roosevelt his unexpected, uninvited guest found at a small desk in a hot corner, below a slow-moving fan, passionately knocking out missives designed to assure distant colleagues of his passivity.

His visitor walked into the long, open office without being announced. Spying Roosevelt, he made straight for him. The man, impeccably dressed, walked with a precise Prussian military gait. Roosevelt saw the German coming and recognized him. He did not recall the name, but he knew the man to be an attaché posted to the German consulate in New York.

The attaché stopped in front of the desk where Roosevelt worked, stood at attention, and saluted smartly. Roosevelt remained seated, stone-faced, as the courier produced two letters. One was from the German ambassador. The other was from the head of a German steamship line on which Roosevelt had traveled. Leaving the letters where the messenger laid them down on the desk, Roosevelt announced he would read them later, when he had time. He was occupied with urgent business at the moment and could not be disturbed.

The attaché said he had one more thing to deliver: a personal message from His Imperial Majesty, Kaiser Wilhelm. The Kaiser wanted to remind Roosevelt of the good times they'd shared four years earlier when Roosevelt was the Kaiser's guest in Berlin and Potsdam. Given those fond memories, the Kaiser was sure he could count on Roosevelt's sympathetic understanding of Germany's current position and action against the Allied powers.

At this, Roosevelt stood and, by his own account, answered: "Pray thank His Imperial Majesty from me for his courteous message; and assure him that I was deeply conscious of the honors done to me in Germany, and that I shall never forget the way in which His Majesty the Emperor received me in Berlin, *nor the way in which His Majesty King Albert of Belgium received me in Brussels.*"[2]

The German probably expected a more encouraging response based on what he'd been reading under Roosevelt's by-line in *The Outlook*. The German gathered himself, however. If he was surprised, he did not allow his surprise to show. No emotion registered on his face. He simply clicked his heels, bowed, and withdrew. He had his answer. Theodore Roosevelt was making no promises. He was supporting American neutrality today, but he might not do the same tomorrow.

ﾟ ﾟ

For all his love of Oyster Bay, Theodore Roosevelt was no yachtsman. The sailboats favored by his North Shore neighbors, not to mention at least one of his sons, were not for him. Roosevelt's vessel of choice was something quite different: a simple wooden rowboat which these days he guided through the water slowly—too slowly to suit him—with what he deprecatingly called "the stroke of Methusala." He could no longer rush across the water as he once did, sometimes rowing twenty miles or more in a single day, two oars flailing in violent haste. He got into trouble when he pushed himself. He tired easily. He was occasionally harassed by ringing in his ears. He also suffered from vertigo and often (too often) found himself short of breath after small exertion. He did not complain. He grit his teeth and trudged onward through a life that was becoming harder and harder to deal with.

He had nearly died a few months before, in the spring of 1914, during a punishing expedition to explore Brazil's unchartered River of Doubt. He came down with malaria in the midst of the prolonged and somewhat ill-planned, thousand-mile journey. He was infected with tropical parasites and dysentery, and suffered a suppurating wound on his leg. At one point he told his fellow explorers to leave him behind in the jungle. Once they were gone, he'd take care of himself with the fatal dose of morphine he'd brought along in case of such an emergency. His traveling companion and second-oldest son, 25-year-old Kermit, saved his life by refusing to leave him. If Roosevelt killed himself, declared Kermit, then he would insist on carrying the body out, even though he might die himself in the process.

After suffering weeks of malarial fever in the bow of a dugout canoe coasting slowly through bug-ridden jungles on piranha-filled waters, Roosevelt finally emerged from the South American wilderness thirty-five pounds lighter than when he went in. Returning from the River of Doubt in the late spring, he announced to his family that he was now, officially, an old man. Residual ailments stemming from his tropical fevers were to stay with him throughout his remaining four-and-a-half years. Roosevelt was also blind in his left eye: the result of a cataract.[3]

The old man's daily voyage on Oyster Bay usually took place just before dinner. His wife, Edith—his childhood sweetheart, three years his junior, to whom he'd returned nearly thirty years before following the tragic death of his first wife—almost always came along. Edith enjoyed the quiet times alone with him on the bay. She sensed his need for the peace and tranquility he found there, and she realized the placid water and beautiful shorebirds removed him from a world he found increasing ridiculous and annoying. Left in his study, with newspapers and telegrams delivering news of deeds and statements he found either foolish or reprehensible, he would fulminate and excite himself. On shore, he was frustrated by his inability to shape and change events as he once had. Out on the bay with her, he was relaxed, at rest.

Edith was Roosevelt's touchstone, advocate, and most-trusted adviser and supporter. As the historian David Burton has written, while Roosevelt was "exuberant, quixotic, and quick to judge; Edith was clear-eyed, restrained and wary. Her influence on her politician husband mirrored her outlook. During their life together, TR became more disciplined and more cautious; he was less likely to be beguiled by the prospects of immediate advantage. Under his wife's urging he learned, slowly and incompletely no doubt, to calculate his position, no matter how much he might bluster."[4] As first lady, Edith dazzled Washington and restored the shabby White House to its original elegance. She also lured many of the world's great intellects to the presidential dinner table where, it was said, they listened to Roosevelt but talked to Edith.

She had known him all her life. Born in 1861 in New York City, she was raised in a house on Livingston Place, just a few blocks from the Union Square mansion of Cornelius van Schaak Roosevelt, Theodore's grandfather. As a ten-year-old she was a school chum of Theodore's sister Corinne at Miss Comstock's School for Girls on West 40th Street. She'd watched him come of age and grow into manhood during long summers at Oyster Bay in the early 1870s. Whatever romance there was, however, faded when Theodore went away to Harvard and found another love in nearby Chestnut Hill. But then, after the death of Roosevelt's first wife, it was only a matter of time before they discovered each other once again.

Edith loved Roosevelt totally and devotedly. She always backed him in whatever challenges he took up, no matter what her reservations. She did not rebel, for example, in 1898 when he resigned his prestigious job as assistant secretary of the navy and left her, still recovering from major surgery, with a large, young family in order to fight a war that did not require his attendance. She stood by him in his third-party presidential candidacy of 1912, which she privately believed to be doomed from the start. She supported him in that crusade, even though she realized it was nothing but a march to the lonesome and barren political wilderness where they found themselves exiled today. She did not even raise her voice to stop Roosevelt from voyaging on the River of Doubt. Yet it was she who, with a dark sense of foreboding, insisted Kermit go along and take care of his father.

Now she did her best to help Roosevelt heal his broken body and restore his broken spirits. Whenever he wished to, she would let him rant about how the war in Europe had taken all of the wind out of his plans for a Progressive victory in the off-year elections. She did not contradict or nay-say. She let him think she believed what he did not: that the Progressive Party had a future, that there had ever been a real hope for significant Progressive success, that the whole thing had not been one huge mistake from the outset.

ॐ ॐ

Roosevelt was just 50 years old when he left the White House in March of 1909. Hearty and healthy, full of hyperactive curiosity and nervous energy, he looked forward to one of the most energetic post-presidencies in history.

He began it with a lengthy African safari and a triumphant European tour. Roosevelt was greeted by large, enthusiastic crowds in capitals that included Berlin, Rome, Copenhagen, and Budapest. In Berlin, the Kaiser received Roosevelt with what William Roscoe Thayer called "ostentatious friendliness." As a special token of respect, Wilhelm allowed Roosevelt to join him in the inspection of twelve thousand troops. Roosevelt was the only civilian to whom such an honor had ever been accorded. At Christiana, Norway, Roosevelt paid his respects to the Nobel committee, which had awarded him its Peace Prize several years before in recognition of his success in bringing an end to the Russo-Japanese War. Some weeks later, in May of 1910, Roosevelt represented the United States as special envoy to the funeral of King Edward VII.[5]

His thoughts, however, were of home. Sitting by his fire at night in the Kenyan hinterland, dining with the heads of ancient dynasties

soon to crumble beneath the weight of war, Roosevelt stayed attuned
to the subtle and sometimes not so subtle ebb and flow of domestic
political opinion. From his various outposts on the far side of the Atlantic, he tracked the decline of his hand-chosen successor, William
Howard Taft, and grew concerned as the delicate yet vital alliance
between progressive and conservative Republicans came apart under
Taft's inept management.

Returning to the United States in the summer of 1910, Roosevelt
quickly became embroiled in the factional fights within his party. As
had long been his habit, he took the side of progressive reformers against
party conservatives. In the process he became estranged from Taft. The
last vestiges of Republican Party unity collapsed in the off-year elections
of 1910, when the weakened Taft unsuccessfully opposed several progressive Republicans endorsed by Roosevelt. The Democrats saw big
gains in state offices nationwide as well as in the Congress. Commentators read these results—combined with small progressive Republican
gains here and there—as a repudiation of Taft and his policies.

Such was the setting in 1912 when Roosevelt challenged Taft for
the Republican presidential nomination. Although Roosevelt swept the
primaries, he lost the Republican endorsement in backroom bargaining
at the Chicago convention. Charging a "steal," Roosevelt stormed out
of the convention, taking his supporters with him, and formed the
Progressive Party (popularly known as the Bull Moose Party). As the
Progressives' nominee for president, the irrepressible Roosevelt led a
ragtag army of Republican defectors in a bruising, bare-knuckled campaign. He dashed back and forth across the country, attracting large
crowds wherever he went. He gave dozens of speeches, including one
delivered in Milwaukee immediately after being shot in the chest by a
would-be assassin.

Every talk Roosevelt gave was a lacerating attack on Taft and other
conservative Republicans, whom he branded as hollow stooges of
wealth. Roosevelt proposed a "New Nationalism" of greatly expanded
government, including federal conservation measures, votes for wom-
en, federal regulation of the economy and big business, and a full wel-

fare state. (The social welfare programs advanced by Theodore Roosevelt in 1912 were in many ways far more drastic and called for much
larger government than the programs enacted by his young cousin and
nephew-in-law, the Democrat Franklin Delano Roosevelt, in the
1930s. Theodore Roosevelt's domestic program while in the White
House was dubbed "the Square Deal." His Progressive Party platform
of 1912 was called the "New Nationalism." It was no accident that the
second Roosevelt to sit in the White House wound up borrowing from
both these catch phrases when coming up with one of his own: the
New Deal.)

Taft knew he was less popular than Theodore Roosevelt. He realized Roosevelt would outpoll him. He likewise understood that together he and Roosevelt would vastly outpoll the Democrat candidate,
Woodrow Wilson. Nevertheless Taft stayed in the race without hope
of winning simply to be a spoiler against Roosevelt, whom he and other
conservative Republicans had come to view as a dangerous radical and
something of a demagogue. Meanwhile, as has already been noted,
Wilson shrewdly folded large portions of the Bull Moose platform into
his own—robbing Roosevelt not only of his ideas, but also his base.

With the Republican vote divided, Wilson was elected president.
Taft came in third behind Roosevelt in the popular vote. In addition
to winning the White House, the Democrats reaped huge gains in
Congress, where they already dominated. The majority of Roosevelt's
fellow Republicans blamed him for the disaster. Not only had he handed the presidency to the Democrats, he'd assaulted the good names of
his fellow members of the G.O.P. in the process. Many never forgave
him.

Roosevelt's rhetoric of 1912, and the enemies it made him, were
nothing new. Throughout his public career, there was one consistent
flaw in his public utterances. Many of Roosevelt's most noble and
notable speeches were marred by name-calling. Conservatives who
lobbied against his civic reforms were "conscienceless speculators."
Peace advocates were "naive idealists" suffering from "ignorant indifference" to their nation's international interests. The liberal wing of

the Progressive Party housed a "lunatic fringe." It seems no one ever held a view contrary to Theodore Roosevelt who was not, according to his rhetoric, either stupid, insane, or a scoundrel. Taft received his share of name-calling in 1912, just as did Woodrow Wilson then and later.

৵৵

Some of the fence-mending Theodore Roosevelt had to do was in his own family. Roosevelt's daughter Alice (aged 30) was married to 45-year-old Nicholas Longworth, a five-term Republican congressman from Cincinnati who lost his seat in the 1912 election. It was a humiliating loss for Nick, especially since his own wife opposed him in favor of the Bull Moose candidate endorsed by her father. Even more frustrating, the difference between success and failure had been a mere ninety-seven votes. Now, in the autumn of 1914, Nick was running for his old seat once more, this time with his wife's support, for she was anxious to get out of "unlovely" Ohio and back to her favorite city in the world: Washington, D.C.

Alice—*Sister*—was a vibrant and vivacious woman. Much like her father, she had a quick mind, was a voracious reader, and was highly quotable. She was by far the brightest and most complex of all Roosevelt's generally bright and complex children. And at heart she was, like Roosevelt, a political animal. By 1914 they were getting on famously, although it had not always been so.

She'd been an exasperating teenager. She took every opportunity to rebel, whether by smoking cigarettes in the White House pantry, visiting notorious Washington bookies to place illegal bets on sporting events, or smuggling flasks of liquor into supposedly "dry" White House receptions. At one particularly dull White House event, she whipped out a cap pistol and commenced shooting at the surprised guests. When Roosevelt as president encouraged every American woman to have at least four children in order to avoid "race suicide," Sister formed a secret society that she called "The Race Suicide Club" for the exchange of birth-control information between her friends.

Sister shared her room in the White House with a blue macaw named Eli Yale, which she often carried around on her arm and introduced to visiting heads of state. She also had a garter snake named *Emily Spinach*. (The snake was named after her stepmother's sister Emily, a very thin and very tiresome spinster who lived in Italy.) One day, after seeing Alice stroll hautily through a White House reception with the snake coiled about her arm, Roosevelt's friend Owen "Dan" Wister asked him why he did not control his outlandish daughter. "Dan," said Roosevelt, "I can do one of two things. I can be President of the United States or I can control Sister. I can't possibly do both."

Unlike her father, Sister was rich. Her Lee grandparents cared for all her material wants, paying Roosevelt a steady allowance for her upkeep throughout her childhood. At times when Roosevelt's personal budget was strained, and his wife and children had to economize, Sister was the only one of the bunch who had everything she needed. "We should be nice to Sister," Roosevelt once said, half in jest. "We may need her money someday." When she came of age, while her father was still in the White House, she began to socialize with other young men and ladies of means. While her father made speeches criticizing the "malefactors of great wealth," Alice went to parties with the amorphous "Four Hundred," the self-defined "best" of society at the time whom the president and Edith viewed as nothing more than a self-indulgent collection of elitist snobs. "Alice has been at home very little," Roosevelt wrote his sister Corinne during one of Alice's stays with the Vanderbilts. "[She is] spending most of her time in Newport and elsewhere associating with the Four Hundred—individuals with whom other members of the family have exceedingly few affiliations."

She'd always been both rebellious and unorthodox. When Roosevelt was governor of New York and the family lived in Albany at the turn of the century, she won a major battle with her father and stepmother when she put her foot down about attending a conservative school for girls in Manhattan. "If you send me I will humiliate you," she wrote. "I will do something that will shame you. I tell you I will." Attending the inauguration ceremonies for McKinley as president and her father as vice president in 1901, she confided to her brother Ted that she hoped something "interesting" would happen at the otherwise "dull" affair. More precisely, her hope was that McKinley's wife would have one of her famous epileptic fits.

On a hiking trip with her family in the Adirondacks in the autumn of 1901, the 17-year-old put on a sorrowful face for reporters when word came that McKinley had died and her father was president. As soon as she was away from the journalists, however, she performed a joyous jig. At her coming-out party held in the East Room of the White House, she refused to dance with her young cousin Franklin, saying she preferred older men "like the Rough Riders."[6]

Like her father, Alice was politically savvy and personally daring. She loved and hated passionately; and any enemy of her father's was, by definition, a special enemy of hers.

ॐ ॐ

When she was a youngster, Sister's birthday was never celebrated at Sagamore Hill. A party was out of the question. After all, her birthday was the anniversary of the blackest day in her father's life. No one dared suggest that streamers, cake, and ice cream added up to an appropriate way for Father to commemorate the nearly simultaneous deaths of the two women he loved most in the world. To add an extra touch of painful irony, the date in question was 14 February: Valentine's Day.

Roosevelt's first wife, Sister's mother, was but a phantom at Sagamore, the house she had not lived long enough to see finished. Her place in the tribal memory of the Roosevelts had been painted over. She lingered but lightly, with no greater resonance than any other pentimento. Sister would have known no details of her at all had she not as a child spent several weeks every year with her Lee grandparents. In the autumn she visited them at their home on Beacon Street in Boston, overlooking the Back Bay. In the spring she joined them at their country house in Chestnut Hill. From the Lees, Sister learned a great deal about the delicate, blond, Victorian beauty who so captivated her father when he was a young Harvard student in the late 1870s. In the old Lee home on Beacon Street she read her mother's childhood diaries and dressed and cuddled her mother's dolls. Late in life, Sister said she wondered what her mother would have become if allowed to mature. Would she have turned out dynamic and vital, or simply sedate and trivial?

The slim written record of Alice's brief life—she was just 22 when she died—hinted to Sister that her mother may have been a dullard. It was said by some who knew her that she lacked depth. Others suggested she was sweet but uninteresting. One contemporary called her dormant and unimaginative and said she would have driven the ever-active, ever-inquisitive Roosevelt to suicide out of sheer boredom had she lived. Sister took this last scathing appraisal with a grain of salt, for she realized Edith Roosevelt was the last person to turn to for a balanced appraisal of Alice Lee.

Inevitably, there was always tension between Sister and Edith. After all, Sister was a chronic, often loud reminder of the one aspect of her past Edith most wanted to forget. Sister was living, indisputable evidence of the fact that when it came to wives, Edith was Theodore's second choice, even though Edith—who hailed from an old New York family—and he had known each other since childhood. Despite the many tensions, a complicated, sometimes ironic love grew in the space between the two women, for they did have one great shared passion. Both Edith and Alice were absolutely and unconditionally devoted to Theodore. In the autumn of 1914, they were also worried about him.

ॐ ॐ

Roosevelt's temperament fluctuated wildly from day to day that autumn of 1914. His outlook oscillated between despair and hope that he could recoup his political fortunes which, in some moods, he condemned himself for having squandered. His confidence was shaken. He worked aggressively to consolidate and expand the base of the Progressive Party. Yet there was, uncharacteristically, an air of futility about his effort. He wrote his son Kermit that the Party was "hopeless."[7]

At least one good, close friend was concerned about Roosevelt's condition in a sense more profound than the mere political. Owen Wister wrote Edith in the late summer of 1914 to point out some salient facts. Roosevelt had refused medical attention after being shot in the chest in 1912—bravely going on with a campaign speech in Milwaukee, seeming not to care about the consequences. Then he'd tried to lose himself in the rain forest, urging his companions to leave him to the mercies of the jungle, malaria, and morphine. Given these facts, had Edith ever considered that "the Colonel"—as he now insisted on being called—might have a death wish?

Edith dismissed the idea as absurd. Theodore's talk about his future being behind him was a lot of nonsense. She just wished he would stop bringing it up. It was good that people were starting to court his opinion on the war in Europe. It would serve to get his mind off all his recent setbacks, and to push his thoughts in creative directions. Theodore needed a challenge.[8]

The truth was, Roosevelt needed the world crisis as much as he needed a reason to live, and no less.

Chapter 5

A RATHER ENLARGED
FOOTBALL GAME

*T*hose who knew Roosevelt best were surprised by his initial reaction to the advent of war in Europe. Roosevelt appeared at first to be remarkably unconcerned with the Allied cause. In an article published in *The Outlook* of 22 August 1914, TR endorsed the traditional notion of American neutrality and, unlike several other "neutral" commentators, refused to make a judgment on British accusations of German treaty violations.[1] In a second piece, written near the end of August but published in late September, he took a remote, amoral, Darwinian perspective when considering the European carnage and the causes behind it. In struggles for existence between great nations, he said, "there was no such thing as abstract right or wrong."[2] Writing to a well-placed German friend, Dr. Hugo Munsterberg of Harvard University, Roosevelt indicated his belief that no single nation was responsible for the conflict and that each "from its own standpoint" was "right under the existing conditions of civilization and international relations."[3]

In his disengaged analysis, Roosevelt appeared to be in sympathy with the mildly pro-Allies yet stridently isolationist, antiwar mood that was prevalent across the country. From the outset of hostilities in Europe, American opinion on the war had been largely divided along ethnic lines. The one area of the country in which pro-German sentiment dominated was the Middle West, where the German-American population was proportionally larger than elsewhere. While generally sympathetic to the Allies, overwhelming numbers of Americans were nevertheless unwilling to risk U.S. involvement in what was called, using the vernacular of isolationism, *the European War*. In the autumn of 1914, the prospect for the United States taking the unprecedented step of active intervention between warring European nations seemed as remote as the prospect of Theodore Roosevelt sitting once more in the White House.

ᴔ ᴔ

Roosevelt's fiercely pragmatic neutrality was at odds with many others of his class and many of his longtime political allies. Unlike Roosevelt, who always emphasized his Dutch ancestry over the British blood he'd inherited through his mother, the majority of the nation's ruling class traced its lineage to Great Britain. Also unlike Roosevelt, the majority of the ruling class were staunch Anglophiles—a point of view with which Roosevelt disagreed bitterly. Despite his love and respect for his Uncle Jimmy Bulloch, whose tombstone, as we have noted, read "American by birth, Englishman by choice," Roosevelt was impatient with the many Americans of his class who thought their native civilization somehow second-best to that of the British. He objected strenuously when his friend Admiral Alfred Thayer Mahan referred to Great Britain as "the mother country." He often criticized the popular practice of wealthy Americans marrying into the British nobility. And he once even advocated war with England, in defense of the Monroe Doctrine, during the Venezuela crisis of 1895. Americans, he told his son Kermit, had only one mother country—the country of the Founders.

The most important ally and friend with whom TR initially disagreed was Senator Henry Cabot Lodge of Massachusetts, minority leader of the powerful Senate Foreign Relations Committee. This was the same Lodge who, as a young man, had joined Theodore Sr. in the Republican reform movement of 1876 and who, in London at the start of European hostilities that August, categorically denounced Woodrow Wilson's neutrality policy as being too favorable to Germany.

The 64-year-old Lodge came from a family that was to Boston what the Roosevelts were to New York. Like Roosevelt, Lodge was a patrician of the highest order: a descendant of Cabots and Higginsons as well as Lodges—a scion of the highest rank of the Boston financial and intellectual aristocracy. His childhood was spent on Beacon Hill, in a cosmopolitan family, amid affluence and learning.

Lodge graduated from Harvard in 1871, married, fathered several children, and settled down to a life of scholarly leisure on Beacon Hill. He served as editor of the *North American Review* (1873–1876), and received his Ph.D. in 1876 after study in political science under Henry Adams. During the years 1876–1878, he lectured at Harvard (where TR was one of his students), and he wrote a number of historical works (including *A Short History of the English Colonies in America* [1881], and *Alexander Hamilton* [1882]).

Lodge, wrote Henry Adams, was "a creature of teaching" as opposed to Roosevelt. ("Roosevelts," wrote Adams, "are born and never can be taught. . . .") Of Roosevelt and Lodge, Adams believed Lodge the more interesting. Lodge was "Boston incarnate,—the child of his local parentage . . . He betrayed the consciousness that he and his people had a past, if they dared but avow it, and might have a future, if they could but divine it." An excellent talker, a voracious reader, a ready wit, and an accomplished orator with a clear mind and a powerful memory, Lodge was sometimes bitter, often genial, always intelligent. Like most other Boston Brahmins, Lodge was also, wrote Adams, "English to the last fibre of his thought,—saturated with English literature, English tradition, English taste . . ."[4]

In Theodore Roosevelt and Henry Cabot Lodge, we see the consolidation of what became a vigorous tradition of Brahmin public service in the spirit of George William Curtis, whom both men had known in their youths. TR and Lodge were the first generation of an eastern upper-class network of individuals educated at the Big Three colleges and law schools and entrenched in the Wall Street law firms and major banks. Strategically located at the heart of the economy and endowed with the advantages of genteel birth, this elite constituted— and still in many ways constitutes—the most highly developed and powerful sector of the American public. Trained for public service, Republican by tradition, cosmopolitan in outlook, this elite regarded itself—and, to some extent, still regards itself—as uniquely qualified for leadership, especially in foreign affairs.[5]

Like so many of their class, Lodge and Roosevelt viewed the Democratic Party as singularly inept when it came to foreign relations. This point of view was perhaps best articulated by Alfred Thayer Mahan.[6] Seventy-four years of age in 1914, a retired Admiral of the Navy, Mahan was author of the classic *Influence of Sea Power Upon History, 1660– 1783*. Mahan called the Democratic Party "a terrible party of insularity and ignorance." Believing the Democratic Party to be provincial and isolationist, Mahan likewise believed the Democrats were out of step with the course of world events. This overriding lack of global-strategic insight was, said Mahan, "no mere temporary aberration" occurring within the contemporary ranks of the Democratic Party, "but fundamental; or, as we say of an individual, constitutional. The taint is in the blood. . . ."[7] According to Mahan, the party had never escaped from the isolationist instinct of its embargo-loving founder. The party still dwelled "in Jefferson's tomb."[8] This traditional insularity and provincialism was, Mahan insisted, the reason why the party was "strongest in the least rich and least educated—narrowest minded—part of the country. . . ."[9]

That the Democrats were now in power, with war in Europe exploding, was a danger. History, said Mahan, proved that "insular democracies are lax and inefficient in preparation for war, and in natural consequence their wars have been long and expensive."[10] To TR the old admiral wrote despairingly that he felt as though the country was "in the hands of the Philistines—or worse."[11]

ᘓᘓ

The British ambassador to the United States, Cecil Arthur Spring-
Rice, was one of Theodore Roosevelt's oldest and closest friends. He
was one of the few people on the planet who dared call Roosevelt
"Teddy" to his face. Spring-Rice—on whom Roosevelt took revenge
by variously referring to him as either "Springy" or "Sprice"—had
stood as Roosevelt's best man when he married Edith in London in
1886. In the 1890s, when Sprice was in Washington serving as secretary
to the British legation and Roosevelt was there first as Civil Service
commissioner and later as assistant secretary of the navy, they were both
members of a salon that gathered regularly in the Washington home of
Henry Adams. Along with Theodore Roosevelt and Spring-Rice, Adams's group included the writer and diplomat John Hay, geologist Clarence King, stained-glass artist John LaFarge, sculptor Augustus Saint-
Gaudens, and of course Cabot Lodge.

After reading Theodore Roosevelt's articles in *The Outlook*, Spring-
Rice sent a few good-natured notes to his old friend, more to tweak
his nose than to influence his thought. Did Roosevelt really believe all
that stuff he was spewing about Germany's innocence, or could Sprice
cancel the psychiatrist he'd arranged to have drop by at Sagamore Hill?
To his government, Spring-Rice sent words of reassurance. He told
Prime Minister Lloyd George—who knew that Roosevelt's opinion
mattered and was therefore gravely concerned about his cold-blooded
political pragmatism as expressed in *The Outlook*—to not be so naïve
as to take everything Teddy said and wrote at face value. Neither should
one think the ex-president's thinking would not evolve in positive ways
over time.

As Theodore Roosevelt's good friend understood better than anyone, amorality came no more naturally to the old colonel than did
inactivity. Spring-Rice once wrote of Roosevelt that "Teddy is con-
sumed with energy as long as he is doing something and fighting somebody . . . he always finds something to do and somebody to fight . . .
[he] is happiest when he conquers but quite happy if he only fights."[12]

In other words, passivity was not Theodore Roosevelt's native state, and Spring-Rice knew it. As private correspondence from Roosevelt to Spring-Rice was soon to confirm, his reticence about the war was not likely to last long.

Other Englishmen did not know Roosevelt well enough to guess that what he said in public might not be the sum of what he genuinely believed. So they set out to change his mind. Roosevelt's friendly acquaintance Rudyard Kipling, whose only son was to die in September of 1915 at the Battle of Loos, suddenly became one of Roosevelt's most prolific correspondents. "My grief," he wrote, "is that the head of [your] country is a man unconnected by knowledge or experience with the facts of the world in which we live. All of which must be paid for in the lives of good men."[13] In another note Kipling insisted the Allies were "shedding their blood . . . for every ideal that the United States stands for."[14] At the same time, Sir Edward Grey, the British Foreign Minister, told Roosevelt that in the event of a German victory over Great Britain, Prussian militarism would dominate the whole of Europe. The prospect of such an occurrence, said Grey, ought to be "chilling" for those Americans with "any geopolitical sense whatsoever."[15]

As Grey understood—and as Roosevelt knew he understood—Theodore Roosevelt certainly had his share of geopolitical sense. Nevertheless, in his public statements, Roosevelt gave his British friends no immediate sign of sympathy with their position. In private, however, he was with them heart and soul. Speaking for publication in late August, Roosevelt said he shared Woodrow Wilson's view that an overwhelming victory for either side in the European war would prove detrimental to American interests. Privately, however, Roosevelt suggested to Progressive and Republican colleagues that he was not much concerned about the possible rise of Russia and Japan in the event of an Allied victory. Far more frightening to contemplate was the bracing thought of a victorious Germany dominating Europe and the high seas. In the latter instance, he said, "it would only be a matter of a very few years before we should have to fight her."[16] As late as 11 October, he publicly defended Germany's invasion of Belgium and northern

France as nothing more than a shrewd and necessary attempt at self-preservation. Yet as early as the first week of September he privately confided to Felix Frankfurter his belief that Germany had acted incorrectly in invading Belgium. In doing so, she had "wantonly and maliciously" struck a match "to the fuse of Europe."[17]

If Roosevelt restrained himself on neutrality, the geopolitical implications of the war, and the question of war guilt, it was for several reasons. First of all, as has already been mentioned, he was pledged to do nothing to hurt his Progressive comrades in the autumn election. Many Progressives were running in Midwestern districts heavy with German-American voters; others were running in urban districts where the Irish vote (almost as pro-German as the German vote) predominated. Any Rooseveltian pronouncement against Germany would have destroyed these candidates' already slim hopes of success. Then there was also Roosevelt's political baggage to contend with—his militaristic reputation that could easily work against the Party in pro-German districts and in those regions of the country where Christian pacifism was a strong force.

In mid-September, a Progressive Party leader from Chicago, Henry E. Coonley, wrote Theodore Roosevelt to say there was much "negative feeling" in the Midwest. People believed were he president instead of Wilson, the country would at that very moment be in war on two fronts: Mexico and Europe. Accordingly, Coonley pleaded with Roosevelt to stay away from any "extreme belligerency" in his public remarks. Other Progressive leaders, among them Albert Beveridge and Stewart Edward White, wanted him to keep quiet as well.[18] This, Roosevelt promised to do—at least until after the election.

Above and beyond protecting the Progressive Party, Roosevelt remained silent on abstract questions of neutrality and war guilt in order to tackle what he saw as a more pressing issue: national defense.

In public statements of September and October, Roosevelt adopted an outwardly neutral approach in his arguments for immediate and substantial defense increases. Looking for the most politically expedient way to advance the idea of military preparedness, Roosevelt chose to position it as an isolationist tool. American neutrality was all well and good, he said, but it desperately needed some teeth. Whatever the outcome of the war in Europe, the postwar world was sure to be an unstable and unsafe place. The defeat of Britain promised an energized, imperial Germany. Hungry for markets and colonies to recoup her war losses, she would most assuredly turn toward Latin America should the United States appear unable or unwilling to defend its sovereignty there. Balancing his rhetoric, Roosevelt also contemplated the prospect of a triumphant, newly militarized Britain, intoxicated with victory on the Continent, allied to a famished and militant Japan, embarking upon yet another of her challenges to the Monroe Doctrine. In either eventuality, the United States would have to be ready to take care of itself.

Current American military policy was, quite simply, to have no policy at all. In fact, in his initial announcement of American neutrality, Woodrow Wilson specifically stated that the United States would make no attempt to prepare for a war the country would much rather mediate than fight. In this stance the president was joined and fervently supported by Secretary of State William Jennings Bryan, a Christian pacifist who hailed from the rural progressive wing of the Democrat Party and whom Taft, with Roosevelt's support, had roundly beaten in the presidential race of 1908. Joined by rural Republican progressives such as Robert LaFollette and George W. Norris, Bryan condemned German militarism vehemently and in the same breath condemned the prospect of similar, counterbalancing, American militarism.

Bryan's fear was that the very act of preparing for the possibility of war would be seen by the Central Powers as a provocative move: a gesture toward the Allied camp and a first step toward hostilities, which would become inevitable the moment the United States started arming itself. Bryan and other pacifists suggested that it was the European arms race of the previous decade that led to the war in the first place. The United States, they said, should not fall into the same trap. For his part, Roosevelt said Bryan and other "peace-at-any-price people" were, through their failure to arm, actually inviting the war they sought to avoid.[19]

In holding that the United States should expand and strengthen its military capability, Roosevelt was in the minority, but he was not alone in the minority. Writing in the September 1914 issue of the *North American Review*, a former political adviser to Woodrow Wilson took issue with his old boss's nonpreparedness policy. George Harvey wrote that America should "neglect nothing for the sure maintenance of her position in a quaking world."[20] And Roosevelt's Rough Rider protégé Leonard Wood, now a major general in command of the Eastern Military District, stormed the countryside making speeches about preparedness.[21] Wood was joined in raising his alarm by Rear Admiral Bradley A. Fiske, who argued that the navy should be expanded in order to give clout to American diplomacy, and Lieutenant Commander Thomas A. Kearney, who said the United States was in danger of "dismemberment" so long as its navy was too weak to defend outlying possessions. Wood was also supported by the Navy League and the Foreign Trade Council, the latter being an organization of influential businessmen who wanted to expand the merchant service.

ॐ ॐ

In a letter to the *New York Times*, Alfred Thayer Mahan said lack of military preparedness was historically more often a cause of war than a harbinger of peace. Elsewhere, in an essay that the administration banned the retired rear admiral from publishing, Mahan suggested armament was not only a necessary endeavor, but a noble one. It was, he wrote, "the organization and consecration of force as a factor in the maintenance of justice, order, and peace. It is the highest expression of that element in civilization—force—that was created and now upholds society, giving efficacy to the pronouncements of law, whether by the legislature or in the courts. Organized force, alone, enables the quiet and the weak to go about their business, and to sleep securely in their beds, safe from the violent without or within."[22]

Mahan was barred from publishing this piece under a general order issued the first week of August 1914, which said no naval officer, on either the active or the retired list, could make any public comment on the war. Although the order officially silenced all officers equally, many thought it was aimed in particular at Mahan, who was one of the few widely published and widely quoted officers on the retired list. And it was probably so.

William Jennings Bryan believed, with reason, that Mahan was in part responsible for the prewar European arms buildup. After all, the First Lord of the British Admiralty said frankly that Mahan's books and theories were influential in the shaping of British naval policy. Much to Mahan's chagrin, the Kaiser was another fan. "I have heard several times of the Emperor's references to Captain Mahan's doctrines," wrote Elmer Roberts of the Associated Press's Berlin office. "The Emperor is familiar with all that Mahan has written, and his ready mind has woven the material supplied by Mahan with other studies, prepared chiefly in the general staff of the army, on the correlation of land and sea power."[23]

Woodrow Wilson's general order telling military officers to keep silent was, to say the least, mysteriously timed. It came the first week of August, almost immediately after Mahan had given an interview to the New York *Evening Post* that ran on the front page. The headline had been provocative: "Britain Must Fight, Declares Mahan—Salvation of Empire Is at Stake—Admiral Says the War Is One of Calculated Aggressiveness on the Part of Germany." In the adjacent column, headlined in exactly the same type, was an interview with Wilson: "President Wilson Appeals to People—Calmness Urged During War in Europe."[24] Roosevelt thought it interesting that Wilson's gag order came so quickly on the heels of those "battling headlines."[25] Mahan's son, Lyle Evans Mahan, recalled that his father considered the order of silence "a direct slap," since he was the only officer who had written or said anything publicly on the war in Europe up to the promulgation of the order.[26]

"I have received from the Navy Department," Mahan wrote the publisher Ralph Pulitzer, "a '[Special Order]' the gist of which is simply the transmission of the President's letter of August 6 to the Secretaries. Although the President's letter simply '*suggests*' to the Secretaries that they '*advise* and *request*' officers to abstain from public comment, etc., the Secretary of the Navy, beside the above heading, speaks of the letter as an 'order.' Neither "suggest,' 'request,' nor 'advise,' can bear that construction of meaning; yet the word 'order' binds me, till otherwise instructed."[27]

Mahan appealed directly to Secretary of the Navy Josephus Daniels for relief from the gag order on 15 August. "Personally," wrote Mahan, "at age of seventy-four, I find myself silenced at a moment when the particular pursuits of nearly thirty-five years, the results of which have had the approval of the naval authorities in almost all countries, might be utilized for the public. I admit a strong feeling of personal disappointment. . . . I believe that the terms of the Order exceed in stringencies the rules of any of the great naval states notably those of Great Britain. The Office of Naval Intelligence can probably inform the Department on this point. On my own behalf, I request the withdrawal of the Order as far as applicable to retired officers."[28]

"The President realizes," wrote Daniels in a response marked *Personal and Confidential*, "as much as you, that his order cuts off from the American people, for a time, information from some of the most competent sources. But the more I think of it, the more I am convinced the order is a wise one . . . the sensitiveness of so many of our people is such that these publications might be deemed to tread upon the line of American neutrality. . . . The President, as wise a man as we have had in America, feels deeply the necessity of not only for being careful, not only of standing straight in this emergency, but in case of doubt of bending backward rather than permit any officer of the government doing anything that might provoke the criticism of any belligerent."[29]

Mahan's editors and publishers labored along with him to have the ban lifted, but Daniels remained unrelenting. "We have worked very hard to persuade the authorities in Washington to make an exception in your case," wrote the managing editor of *The World* to Mahan. "Certainly it seems absurd to us that such a restriction should be enforced. The enclosed letter which I have just received from Secretary Daniels will acquaint you with the Navy Department's present attitude.

I shall continue my efforts to bring about a change in the attitude, although I confess it does not look very hopeful just at present. If you can suggest any efforts that I can make I shall be very much obliged to you."[30]

Roosevelt's friend Mahan was never to publish again. When he died in December of 1914, Roosevelt would say he had been "treated despicably" by the administration, just like so many other "patriots."[31]

ৼ ৼ

Unlike Mahan, Roosevelt was not under military discipline, and was not easily silenced.

From late September through late November, the colonel spoke out on preparedness in a series of articles published in the *New York Times* and syndicated nationwide. In his *Times* series, Roosevelt reiterated his support for neutrality, but nevertheless argued passionately for expansion of the army and navy, adoption of universal military service, and fortification of the Panama Canal. In the same series of articles, Roosevelt also recommended independence for the Philippines on the grounds that the archipelago constituted a hard-to-defend Achilles' heel. Through the autumn, Roosevelt's opinion was picked up and endorsed by a number of influential politicians and pundits, among them Grenville Clark, Charles J. Bonaparte, Major General W. W. Wotherspoon, Charles A. Munn (publisher of *Scientific American*), and Herbert Croly, editor of the *New Republic*, launched that November.

Suddenly, Roosevelt was not so much a political exile as he had been just months before. Those who knew him best thought they detected a happiness and purposefulness in him they had not seen for some time. Roosevelt appeared ready to trade the lost cause of the Progressive Party for a more winnable fight once the autumn elections were done with and his obligations to the Progressives fulfilled.

ৼ ৼ

While the national debate continued in the autumn of 1914, Roosevelt's alma mater, Harvard, and other influential Eastern colleges quickly became hotbeds of preparedness. At Harvard, troops of march-ing, khaki-clad students frequently disturbed the ambience of the peaceful campus with their workouts. The uniforms they wore were decrepit surplus from the Spanish-American War. Their archaic rifles—old Krief-Jorgensens—dated from the same era. The college trainees took target practice in the Belmont woods, set up bivouacs in the mid-dle of Harvard Yard, dug trenches around the Fresh Pond reservoir, and held drill practice in the recesses under the Harvard football sta-dium.[32]

At Harvard and other Eastern schools, preparedness did not have the neutral veneer with which it was coated in the early rhetoric of Theodore Roosevelt and other advocates. As bastions of European cul-ture, Harvard and other top colleges were bound to be intellectually and emotionally closer to the fighting in Europe than the rest of Amer-ica was. "At the western university where I was teaching when the war broke out in Europe, it seemed as unreal as the Wars of the Roses," remembered historian Samuel Eliot Morison, "returning to Harvard early in 1915, one was on the outskirts of battle." Malcolm Cowley remembered that during the academic year of 1914–1915, "our pro-fessors stopped talking about the international republic of letters and began preaching patriotism."[33]

For the average young Harvard student, the eloquently articulated war fought by the French and English to drive the easily demonized Hun out of northeastern France and Belgium had an attractive, story-book aspect. The London *Times* and other British journals read by undergrads were filled with inspirational war poems and essays written by the likes of Robert Bridges, Rudyard Kipling, Edmund Gosse, John Masefield, and Thomas Hardy. Soon Henry James appeared in print chronicling the exploits of the Norton-Harjes Ambulance Service founded by Richard Norton (Harvard, '92), director of the American School of Classical Studies in Rome and son of Charles Eliot Norton, President Emeritus of Harvard. (One interested fan of the Norton-Harjes Service was Guy Lowell, brother of Harvard President A. Lawrence Lowell, who would—much to his brother's annoyance—

launch a division of the American Volunteer Ambulance Corps in Italy in December 1917.) The poet Alan Seeger (Harvard '10), an infantry-man with the French, appeared in the *New Republic* and other publications with vivid, elegantly crafted essays and poems from the front. More books and articles chronicled the exploits of the Lafayette Escadrille, a privately financed unit comprised of wealthy American Brahmins serving under French commanders and integrated into the French military.

There was a rich Ivy League tradition of idealizing war as a source of cultural renewal. Only in war, said Civil War veteran Oliver Wendell Holmes Jr., in a speech to the Harvard graduating class of 1895, could men pursue "the divine folly of honor." It was from war that "the ideals of the past for men have been drawn—I doubt if we are ready to give up our inheritance."[34] In the same spirit, Princeton's president John Brier Hibben rhapsodized about the chastening and purifying effect of armed conflict. Novelist Robert Herrick praised war's capacity to resurrect nobility and restore meaning to cultures that would otherwise sink into triviality.[35]

Unlike President Emeritus Norton, Harvard's president A. Lawrence Lowell was neither in sympathy with Harvard's tradition of moral renewal through war nor was he a preparedness advocate. Lowell was a whole-hearted supporter of Wilsonian neutrality. To the astonishment of a sophomore who was instrumental in starting the Harvard military training program, Lowell wrote a letter to the young man's father, a Harvard overseer, informing him that the program was proving disruptive to campus life, so much so that those responsible would probably have to be punished. "President Lowell and certain others—took an extremely dim view of our activities," remembered Archie Roosevelt. "My father let me know that [Lowell] was seriously thinking of suspending me from the college on account of these activities."[36]

One of John Dos Passos's abiding memories of Harvard in 1914 was Archie Roosevelt "whooping it up for preparedness."[37] Yet Archie was an unlikely organizer. He had few friends. He was not well liked. He was, in fact, one of the least popular men in his class. And with good reason. There was, for example, the time when two of Archie's fellow students smuggled "a loose woman" (as Archie called her) into their campus rooms, and Archie turned them in to campus authorities. The same thing occurred whenever Archie got wind of liquor in the dorms.

Devout puritanism did not make for a great social life. Archie was not invited to join the staff of the Harvard *Crimson*, and no desirable campus club would have him. His father, his brother Ted, and Nick Longworth were all Porecellian men, but even their lobbying could not wrangle Arch an invitation to membership. "Archie's virtues," wrote his father, "and to some extent his excess of virtue, tend to keep him out. He won't yield in the smallest degree to anyone from any feeling for his own interests. . . . He is hardly politic enough, but it is a fault on the right side, and I am very proud of him."[38]

Even as a youth, Archie had a reputation for being inapproachable. Schoolmates and teachers often found him hard to get along with. Devoted to his parents, brothers, and sisters, he nevertheless had a forbidding demeanor that discouraged intimacy with anyone outside the family circle. Edith wrote that he was the one of her sons who possessed "the most contrary and autocratic nature."[39]

Nevertheless, Archie surprised everyone, family members and classmates alike, by making Harvard preparedness a success. For starters, Archie was instrumental in arranging for his father's old Rough Riders friend General Leonard Wood to help the Harvard program in significant ways. With the stroke of a pen—and in flagrant violation of the anti-preparedness plank in President Wilson's neutrality statement—Wood gave formal authorization for the Harvard program on behalf of the U.S. military. Wood also assigned several army officers and non-coms to Harvard to supervise training. (Later, after the United States entered the war, a number of French officers would also come to Harvard to teach strategy and tactics.) And he supplied the program with rifles and side arms from the U.S. supply depot at Boston.

ॐ ॐ

Along with supplies, the Harvard program also needed cash. Not surprisingly, one of Archie's chief contributors was his eldest brother, Theodore Roosevelt Jr. At 27, Ted was a partner in the Philadelphia investment banking firm of Montgomery, Clothier and Tyler—the Tylers being cousins of his mother. Ted's annual income from the firm was never less than $150,000. Although highly successful, Ted was somewhat bored by the life of a businessman and was thinking of going into politics, the military, or both.

Ted had long harbored ambitions to be an army officer. It was something he'd fantasized about ever since, as a boy, he would walk to work with his father, then assistant secretary of the navy. As they walked, the boy's father would describe famous military campaigns, and the great generals and admirals who had waged them. While a student at Groton during the early years of his father's presidency, Ted wrote a poem about his military ambitions and submitted it—unsuccessfully—under an assumed name to *Harper's Magazine*:

> Would God I might die with my sword in my hand
> My gilded spur on my heel
> With my crested helmet on my head
> And my body closed in steel . . .
> Would God when the morning broke
> I might by my friends be found
> Stiff in my war worn harness
> Ringed by dead foes all around.[40]

But when it came time for Ted to pursue a military career, his father did not allow him to do so. When Ted was ready to start college—during his father's presidency in 1904—Theodore Roosevelt refused to let Ted go to either Annapolis or West Point. Roosevelt's rationale for forcing his son into Harvard was based on his long-standing prejudice against career soldiers. "In the Army and the Navy," he wrote the boy, explaining his decision, "the chance for a man to show great ability and rise above his fellows does not occur on the average more than once in a generation. When I was down at Santiago it was melancholy for me to see how fossilized and lacking in ambition, and generally useless, were most of the men my age and over who had served their lives in the Army . . ."[41]

Now, with war a prospect, Ted realized he might finally have his chance to fulfill his childhood ambition. He knew his father would not object to military service in time of war; quite the contrary, he would insist on it. For his part, Ted was robust and ready for action. His childhood asthma, the same sickness with which his father had been afflicted as a boy, was far behind him. So too were the severe headaches and nervous prostration with which he'd been harassed at age 10. The cure had been entirely nontherapeutic. Convinced Ted's father was driving him too hard to excel in all things, the family doctor suggested the boy be sent to visit an aunt. Ted's recovery was miraculous. His sickness promptly disappeared. When the sensitive, slightly cross-eyed boy with the mild speech defect returned home, his father resolved not to pressure him so much in the future. "The fact is," wrote TR at the time, "that the little fellow, who is peculiarly dear to me, has bidden fair to be all the things I would like to have been and wasn't, and it has been a great temptation to push him."[42]

Now that Ted was grown, he did not need his father to pressure him. He pressured himself. And he looked forward to the prospect of war. He only hoped the thing wouldn't end before he could get into it. He wanted desperately to show his stuff, earn his stripes, and prove himself heir to something more than just a famous name. For the moment, however, he was happy simply to support preparedness training at Harvard, in this way helping his brother and other like-minded young men get ready to show their stuff as well.

He was, it must be emphasized, acutely aware of the resonances of his name, and had been ever since he was young. When still a boy he'd become quite good friends with an old Oyster Bay blacksmith. One day, as the blacksmith duly reported to TR, Ted asked him, "Don't you think it handicaps a boy to be the son of a man like father, and especially to have the same name? . . . There can never be another Theodore Roosevelt. I will always be honest and upright, and I hope

some day to be a great soldier, but I will always be spoken of as Theodore Roosevelt's son." Sister was sensitive to the problem. "Poor TR
Jr.," she told a friend. "Every time he crosses the street, someone has
something to say because he doesn't do it as his father would. And if
he navigates nicely, they say it was just as TR would have done it."[43]

It would always be so.

ৡ ৡ

In the end, even the admiring Roosevelt boys would wind up sick
and tired of Leonard Wood. "I agree with you about General Wood.
Confidentially he gives me a pain," Ted wrote Archie not long after
the war.[44]

Two years younger than Roosevelt, the lean, athletic Wood was,
like Roosevelt, a graduate of Harvard. Promoted to major general by
President Theodore Roosevelt in 1904, Wood served as chief of staff
between 1910 and 1914 (two years under Taft and two years under
Wilson) before being demoted to commander of the Eastern Military
District, in part because of his outspoken disagreement with many of
Wilson's foreign and military policies.

Opinionated, abrupt, self-confident, and theatrical, Wood was also
pompous and contemptuous of rank. He was likewise skeptical of politicians while at the same time respectful of Roosevelt and not without
certain political aspirations of his own. Few of his colleagues liked him.
Throughout his military career, Wood was noted both for insubordination *and* for bold and reckless tactical moves in combat, containing
within them more of Wood's personal need for glory than any calculated military logic. This professional skepticism of Wood, combined
with Woodrow Wilson's annoyance over Wood's public criticisms of
the administration, would ultimately cost Wood the cherished spot of
commanding the American Expeditionary Force when war was declared in 1917.

ৡ ৡ

Preparedness programs similar to the one at Harvard sprang up on other campuses, among them Dartmouth, Princeton, and Yale. There was also activity at the leading preparatory schools, including Andover, Exeter, Choate, St. Paul's, and Groton (where 17-year-old Quentin Roosevelt participated). Prep schools such as Groton were based upon the best elements of the English public school model as exemplified by Rugby. Here favored sons of first-class households were taught not just the fundamentals of mathematics and the stultifying syntax of Latin, but also a sense of honor and an attitude of patriotism and civic duty. It was not presumed that the students found at Groton and its sister schools in the United States came from ordinary homes or would turn out to be ordinary men. Quite the contrary. Groton and schools like it were viewed, completely and simply, as training grounds where one developed the character necessary for leadership. All four sons of Theodore Roosevelt absorbed the lessons of Groton under the tutoring of the legendary "Rector," the Rev. Endicott Peabody, founder of the school and cousin of Theodore Roosevelt's first wife, Alice Lee. (Only three of Theodore Roosevelt's sons graduated from Groton, although all four attended. Archie was expelled from the school after he sent a postcard to a Groton classmate from out West in which he inquired, "How's the old Christ factory?" He wound up finishing at Andover.[45])

Military preparedness was approached with an oddly carefree exuberance at both the colleges and the prep schools. "None of the young men my age knew anything about war," remembered Archie Roosevelt. "Our last great war was the Civil War, then 50 years away, and the Spanish-American War [was nothing more than] a rather enlarged football game."[46]

Of course, Archie was correct in his candid assessment of the Spanish-American War. In that fracas, which Roosevelt's friend John Hay called "the splendid little war," American forces never quite had time to lose the impetuous edge and element of play with which they first went into battle. Roosevelt's Rough Riders were a case in point. Seeing their first action in June of 1898, the Rough Riders were on a boat home by early August. The war had barely gotten started before the Spanish were forced to sue for peace.

In 1914, many on the Allied side thought the war in Europe would be brief. Confident British soldiers, many of whom would return home crippled and shell-shocked if they were lucky enough to return at all, were marching off in 1914 with an air of impetuous frivolity. As late as the Battle of the Somme (1916), some British soldiers actually went over the top from their trenches dribbling soccer balls. The Allies seemed so sure of themselves. American volunteer trainees guessed they'd never see any action at all—or that if they did, the moment would be brief. The Germans were bound to be defeated as quickly as the Spanish back in '98.

According to Archie Roosevelt's account of those early days of Harvard preparedness, the ups and downs of the war were followed with the same interest and excitement as was football. Talk at breakfast each morning was of the latest news from France: which side had scored, which hadn't. Throughout the autumn, the major interest was the continued fighting on the fifty-yard line of the Marne, the scrimmage at the first battle of the Aisne (fought along the chalk hills of Champagne), and the disappointing Race to the Sea that ended with the Germans scoring again and again, gaining control of every major Belgian port city, leaving the Allies defending just a few precious miles above French Dunkirk. Archie and his friends were all relieved when the Allies rallied, staging a minor comeback to seize the Belgian railhead at Ypres in November. Go team.

Chapter 6

ALL THE KINDS OF BOYS THERE ARE

*E*ach of Theodore Roosevelt's children except for Sister attended public schools during the early years of their educations, before being bundled off to private secondary schools—the boys to Groton and Ethel to the prestigious Cathedral School for Girls in Washington, D.C. During Theodore Roosevelt's presidency, while the older boys, Ted and Kermit, were at Groton and then Harvard, Archie and Quentin attended the Force Public School on Massachusetts Avenue in Washington. At Oyster Bay in the early 1890s, Ted and Kermit rode their bikes to the Cove Neck Public School, where they attended class with the sons and daughters of laborers and shopkeepers, many of whom remained their friends for life. Ethel enjoyed a similar public grammar school education in Albany during her father's governorship at the turn of the century.

In a day when security for the First Family was neither as overwhelming nor as stifling as it is today, Archie and Quentin were instructed to get to Washington's Force Public School under their own steam. Sometimes they walked, sometimes they roller-skated. Sometimes they rode their ponies. On their way home they invariably stopped at a firehouse not far from the White House where they were permitted to slide down the pole. During their first year at the Force School, a European visitor expressed amazement that "the children of the President of the United States sit side by side with the children of working men in a public school." Theodore Roosevelt replied he did not see what there was to be amazed about. Not much later, he told Owen Wister he was "dee-lighted!" with Quentin's response to an "impertinent" question from a haughty society matron. "How do you get along with those common boys?" the woman asked Quentin. The child shook his head. "I don't know what you mean," he answered. "My father says there are only four kinds of boys: good boys and bad boys and tall boys and short boys; that's all the kinds of boys there are."

"Common" children were always welcome at the Roosevelt White House, just as they'd always been welcome at the Governor's Mansion in Albany and at Sagamore Hill. Boys from the Force School—sons of ditchdiggers and policemen and groundskeepers—were frequent guests at the home of the president. They came and went, as did Archie and Quentin, riding their bicycles, or their ponies, in and out of the large gates.

Occasionally Roosevelt would take Quentin, Archie, and their assorted young colleagues for a ride on the presidential sloop. Out on the Potomac, as the sloop passed the home and grave of George Washington at Mount Vernon, he would always make the boys stop playing and stand at attention while the ship's bell sounded. Then he would explain to the boys—knowing they'd heard the speech before but also knowing it was worth hearing again—that the bell was tolling for the soul of a great man. "We're now passing his house, and the things he loved; his body, too, which he had to leave behind him. Wouldn't it be fine if you and I grew up to be thus respected? Of course, you may not be able to get thousands to respect you, as Washington did; but you can begin by getting two or three—maybe six or a dozen—and that's fine too."[1]

Theodore Roosevelt believed the essential, practical democracy he wished to promote among his children could best be taught the way he'd learned it: through camping, hiking, trapping, and hunting, and sharing the rigors of camp life with other men and women from all economic and ethnic backgrounds. Thus he was insistent that all his children, most especially his boys, experience life in the rough just as he had. Ted, as an adolescent, was dispatched to the cabin of John Burroughs in upstate New York, there to spend a week hiking and fishing and bird-watching with the grizzled old naturalist. All the boys were, in their turn, shipped off to the West for extended hunting expeditions. As Kermit recalled, "By the time we were twelve or thirteen we were encouraged to plan hunting trips in the West. Father never had time to go with us, but we would be sent out to some friend of his, like Captain Seth Bullock, to spend two or three weeks in the Black Hills, or perhaps we would go after duck and prairie-chicken with Marvin Hewitt. Father would enter into all the plans and go down with us to the range to practice with rifle or shotgun, and when we came back we would go over every detail of the trip with him, revelling in his praise when he felt that we had acquitted ourselves well."[2]

There were times, however, when Theodore Roosevelt suspected that even the unforgiving landscape of the Western wilderness was not challenging enough to instill in his sons the raw, democratic masculinity he thought indispensable. "[Archie] is off in the Black Hills with Captain Seth," he wrote to Ted in the summer of 1910, when Archie was 16, "but I think the Black Hills have changed a good deal since your day, and even since Kermit's, and that he is merely having a bunny time with a Groton playmate."[3]

Both the boys and the girls were taught to shoot at an early age. Ted was nine when he received his first rifle, a Flaubert. Years later, he still remembered the day his father brought the rifle home to Oyster Bay from the city. "At once, I made for his room where I found him just preparing for his bath," remembered Ted. "He was as much excited as I was. I wanted to see it fired to make sure it was a real rifle. That presented a difficulty. It would be too dark to shoot after supper and Father was not dressed to go out at the moment. He took it, slipped a cartridge into the chamber and, making me promise not to tell Mother,

fired it into the ceiling. The report was slight, the smoke hardly no-
ticeable, and the hole made in the ceiling so small that our sin was not
detected."[4]

Eventually each child received his or her own gun, always a .22. In
time, Theodore Roosevelt roamed the woods of Oyster Bay and the
Washington, D.C. hinterlands with all four of the boys in search of
various game. The boys were invariably proud of their kills and inces-
santly competed with each other to see who could bring Father the
biggest buck, the largest grouse, the finest duck. The two girls, however, did not care to shoot at anything but targets.

જી જી

In October of 1914, Representative Augustus P. Gardner, a Massachusetts Republican who was the son-in-law of Henry Cabot Lodge,
proposed a Congressional inquiry into the condition of the country's
military. In announcing his proposal, Gardner said U.S. defenses needed
to be beefed up specifically because of the looming German threat to
American interests and "the principles of democracy."[5] Gardner's was
not the first Congressional proposal related to expanding the military
to be discussed after the start of the European war. A month earlier,
the Virginia Democrat James Hay, chairman of the House Military
Affairs Committee, suggested that the president be empowered (funded) to strengthen the army and navy substantially. The recommendation
was withdrawn when James Mann, Republican minority leader who
represented a heavily German district in the Midwest, objected on the
grounds a buildup would convey a dangerous impression to the Kaiser
and his advisers.

Gardner's call for hearings was greeted favorably by the press. The
New York Times, which was already publishing Theodore Roosevelt's
prolix series on preparedness but had previously been on record editorially as against defense increases, now endorsed Gardner's statement
and declared bluntly there was "an urgent need to strengthen American
defenses on land and sea."[6] It is worth noting that the *Times* was generally considered a Democratic newspaper. Despite this, the paper did

not hesitate after October of 1914 to disagree with Wilson's nonpreparedness policy, sometimes stridently. Other major newspapers came out in favor of Gardner's remarks as well—the *Wall Street Journal*, the *Boston Transcript*, the *Washington Post*, the *Louisville Times*, the *Chicago Tribune*, and the *Richmond News-Leader* among them. Dissenting were William Jennings Bryan's *Commoner*, Robert LaFollette's *Weekly*, the *New York Journal of Commerce*, and the *Louisville Courier-Journal*.

Initially, Theodore Roosevelt himself said nothing publicly about Gardner's measure. The proposal smacked of just the sort of interventionist sentiment Roosevelt wanted to stay clear of until after the elections. Even if Roosevelt thought of speaking up for Gardner, his Progressive comrades would have urged him not to. "I told my friends," he wrote Lodge, explaining why he had not immediately endorsed Gardner's proposal, "that as I was doing what I could for them this Fall I should not make an attack which they thought would hurt them but after the election I should smite the administration with a heavy hand."[7]

His reticence did not help the Progressives, who as a party did not meet with any more success in 1914 than they had in 1912. Even after the elections, however, TR was still initially hesitant to associate himself with any pronounced anti-German sentiment or directly to confront the popular president. At the end of November he published a piece in the *New York Times* in which he criticized the administration for failing to protest the German invasion of Belgium. Yet he stopped well short of calling for an end to American neutrality and appeared to consider the formal protest little more than a diplomatic nicety that had been overlooked. Roosevelt seemed to be criticizing Wilson's style rather than his substance.

When Roosevelt eventually spoke out in support of Gardner's call for hearings, he pointedly distanced himself from Gardner's most aggressive anti-German rhetoric. Roosevelt instead indicated his concurrence with some of Gardner's more moderate rationales for building up American defenses. He agreed wholeheartedly, for example, with Gardner's statement that "since the beginning of time victorious nations have proved headstrong and high-handed," and that the Monroe Doctrine could not be enforced "by moral suasion and financial might alone."[8] Indeed, Roosevelt spoke a great deal about the Monroe Doctrine in the autumn of 1918, always emphasizing the need for an adequate army and navy to enforce it. He reminded audiences that several roots of the European war could be traced to colonial conflicts in Africa. Without the Monroe Doctrine, there would have been similar conflicts in South America, conflicts that would inevitably have drawn the United States into "the present deadly struggle."[9]

In early December, Gardner's father-in-law Lodge announced that he intended to sponsor a Senate investigation into the state of naval preparedness. The discreet Lodge indicated he thought the United States should maintain "a strict and honest neutrality" while at the same time preparing itself for "any eventuality." Lodge called for hearings despite President Wilson's pronounced opposition to "unlimited publicity" on the question of national defense.[10] Lodge said he could not credit Wilson's concern that un-named foreign powers would misconstrue such discussions and take offense. Lodge insisted that what the senators and representatives of the people of the United States discussed in the halls of the Capitol was a matter for the American people and their leaders to decide, and no one else—certainly not the Kaiser. Lodge said he hoped the president of the United States was not suggesting otherwise.

Under strong pressure from William Jennings Bryan, President Wilson remained unyielding in the face of growing calls for military preparedness, even though some of his own advisers tried to change his mind. As early as the first week of November, Wilson's chief military aide, Colonel Edward M. House, urged the president to establish a reserve army. After a meeting with General Wood, House came away convinced Germany was poised to win the war and, further, that it had ambitions in South America. Wilson, however, rejected House's arguments on grounds that a victorious Germany would be "too exhausted" to launch a serious offensive thousands of miles from home.[11]

In his annual message to Congress, delivered at the end of the first week of December, Wilson made no significant concession to Republican preparationists. Wilson tentatively endorsed a voluntary reserve system instead of the draft proposed by Roosevelt. He also suggested that state militias could be strengthened a bit, and concluded the navy might be due for "a few more ships." However, he flatly denied that American territorial integrity was threatened from any quarter. Wilson went on to make what to Roosevelt was an astounding assertion: Simply because the world had changed, said Wilson, was no reason for U.S. policy to do the same. For the United States to expand her military merely because of events in Europe would mean "that we had lost our self-possession, that we had been thrown off our balance by a war with which we have nothing to do, whose causes can not touch us, whose very existence affords us opportunities of friendship and disinterested service which should make us ashamed of any thought of hostility or fearful preparation for trouble." The United States, he concluded, should "embody and exemplify the counsels of peace and amity."[12]

Wilson's statements with regard to preparedness and foreign policy received enthusiastic applause from the Democratic majority, but next to none from members of the Republican minority.[13]

The following morning at breakfast, Theodore Roosevelt, while reading the text of Wilson's remarks, was both enraged and horrified. He concluded the president, "blinded by his naïveté," was incapable of perceiving the dangerous complexities of the current situation. The subtext of Wilson's remarks seemed to be that the outcome of the European war, whatever it might be, was bound to be of no consequence to the vital interests of the United States. The president, said Roosevelt, did not grasp the "common-sense thesis" that a total victory by either side in the war would inevitably lead to an unpredictable postwar world, a world in which an armed United States would be an essential counterpoise to a Europe out-of-balance.[14] Wilson, Roosevelt observed, seemed to be banking on the increasingly unlikely prospect of a mediated settlement that would leave no warring party in a position of dominance.

In his Naval War College speech of 1897, Roosevelt warned the nation away from leaders afflicted by a "timid lack of patriotism . . .

doctrinaires whose eyes are so firmly fixed on the golden vision of universal peace that they can not see the grim facts of real life until they stumble over them, to their own hurt, and, what is much worse, to the possible undoing of their fellows."[15] Now a world crisis loomed, and so far as Roosevelt was concerned the very doctrinaires of whom he'd warned held the reins of American diplomacy and defense. It was his worst nightmare.

გუ გუ

The Roosevelt clan gathered at Sagamore Hill on Christmas. The house, so often silent and lonesome now with the children grown and gone, once again reverberated with the enthusiastic, hyperactive, fast-paced chatter of multiple Rooseveltian voices.

Alice and Nick Longworth came. Nick had just recaptured his old seat in Congress which, Alice told her father, meant nothing so much as it meant her escape from Ohio. She did not mention to Roosevelt her hope that the change of scenery—the return from Ohio to Washington—would mean a change in Nick, who'd been unfaithful to her again and again in the two years he'd been out of Congress. She did not dare mention Nick's indiscretions to her father, who was sternly forbidding when it came to all such matters and could, quite possibly, resort to violence over the issue. Neither did she mention the situation to any of the three brothers she saw at Sagamore that Christmas, each of whom was quite capable of a similar reaction.

There was incessant and excited conversation around the Christmas dinner table. Archie was full of news about Harvard military training. Ted—in attendance with his wife, Eleanor, and their two children, little Gracie and the infant Theodore Roosevelt III—was eager for details. As Ted well knew, General Wood was planning a summer training camp at Plattsburg, New York, for college trainees as well as interested men of business. Many of the Harvard preparationists would be there, along with contingents from Yale, Dartmouth, Princeton, and other schools. Ted planned to attend. Even young Quentin would be going, along with some of his cronies from Groton.

Kermit was the only son absent from Sagamore that Christmas. He and Belle Willard had been married that June, shortly after Kermit and Theodore Roosevelt's ordeal on the River of Doubt. Belle was the daughter of the U.S. ambassador to Spain. The couple were married at the American embassy in Madrid. Kermit's cousin, Philip Roosevelt, served as best man. Kermit's father was also in attendance. Queen Maria Christiana made a point to be out of the city throughout Roosevelt's visit, so that she would not have to meet and be polite to the Rough Riding colonel who'd humiliated her troops in Cuba in 1898. King Alfonso, on the other hand, was friendly. After the wedding, on a steamship carrying the newlyweds to Kermit's new job in the Buenos Aires branch of the First City Bank, the honeymooners heard news of the murder of Archduke Franz Ferdinand at Sarajevo.

Quentin—home from Groton and just going on 18 years of age—spent much of Christmas Eve in the barn tinkering with a used motorcycle he'd purchased locally for five dollars. Once Quent was done resurrecting the broken machine—oiling up the gears and tuning the old engine so that it started promptly and ran smoothly—he intended to give it to a friend, the son of an Oyster Bay clam-digger, as a Christmas present.

Quentin occasionally had to take a break from leaning over the engine. He had problems with his back, resulting from an accident two summers before, when he was hunting in New Mexico with his father and Archie. A packhorse rolled over on him, an incident that nearly broke his back. It left him with recurring pain. The pain, he said stoically, was better than the alternative. He might never have walked again. In addition to his bad back, Quentin also had very poor eyesight (inherited from his father).

He looked like the colonel. He had the same chunky, muscular body. His face, though not as jowlly as his father's, nevertheless tended toward the same roundness. Old friends of the family commented on Quentin's resemblance to Roosevelt at the same age. Quent was also like his father in his quick wit, urgent sense of principle, and great mastery of the English language. Unlike his father—and unlike everyone else in his immediate family—he absolutely loved baseball. He was fanatical about it, so enamored of the sport that he went out of his way to cultivate the great old Chicago White Sox player Ping Bodie and often went to games with him. When he was a boy in the White House, Quentin became notorious with a groundskeeper who'd been there since the days of Lincoln when he carved a diamond into the White House lawn.

Although not at the top of his Groton class, neither was Quentin anywhere near the bottom. Like his father and all his siblings save Ethel and Archie, he was a gifted prose stylist. He served as both editor and typesetter for the school literary magazine. Nevertheless, his taste in literature was lowbrow: mostly detective stories along with the adventure tales of his favorite novelist, Jack London.

When Quentin tried his hand at writing, he tended to churn out macabre tales of madness, desperation, and suicide that he did not dare show his parents. Every authority figure in Quentin's stories was a disguised version of Jack London's dark superman from *The Sea Wolf*, Wolf Larsen. And every hero was a tragic, thoughtful, existential intellectual: brave but doomed, and usually alone not just in a practical sense but a cosmic sense as well.

Quentin's literary output was at sharp contrast with his apparently happy life, filled with friends. It seemed to most observers that he did not have a care in the world. It seemed he was the epitome of optimism, confidence, and contentment. He was perhaps not always content. He once almost drowned after being dared by his older brothers to jump from a high rock into a deep-water cove near Oyster Bay. The brothers were constantly challenging him, the youngest, to brave each and every right of passage they had braved. They sensed that as the baby, he had it somewhat easier than they; they sensed he was a bit more pampered—if indeed any Roosevelt was ever pampered. Thus the others were always on him to jump long, ride fast, run far, dive deep. They pushed him again and again; and again and again he responded with good-natured perseverance.

No Roosevelt boy ever had so many Roosevelt men to come up to the mark for.

৵ ৵

Dick Derby, then aged 31, and his wife, Ethel Roosevelt Derby, 23, spent Christmas of 1914 in a modest room in the staff's quarters of a makeshift hospital at Neuilly-sur-Seine, near Paris. Dick lit two candles and put them on the wooden fruit box that served as a table at the foot of their cots. Lying in the little glow of the candles, huddling for warmth that was at once a practicality and a luxury, the couple recalled their wedding at Christ Church, Oyster Bay, one year before. The guest list had included Henry Cabot Lodge, Owen Wister, and Winthrop Astor Chanler, whose daughter Hester was one of the bridesmaids. On their wedding night, Dick gave Ethel an unexpected present: a precious and exorbitantly expensive emerald pendant to match her engagement ring.

They had first met many years before, when Ethel was a child. Tall, lanky Dick was then a Harvard undergraduate, one of a select group invited to Sagamore Hill by the then Vice President Theodore Roosevelt, for a seminar on government. When Dick walked around a corner of the house, Ethel—an energetic nine-year-old—came charging into him from the other direction. They met again, occasionally, when Dick visited the White House. In 1910, after finishing medical school at Harvard, Dick chanced to encounter Colonel and Mrs. Roosevelt in Berlin during the colonel's postpresidential world tour. Ethel—now 19—was traveling with her parents. A courtship soon began that was wholeheartedly encouraged by Roosevelt, who thought Dick one of the finest young men he knew. The admiration was mutual, and sincere. Ethel wrote her father a few days after her wedding to assure him she was still his little girl, and that they were all still one big family. "Dick feels just the way we all do about you and mother. It is just the same thing with him."[16] While Ethel became a Derby in name, Dick became a Roosevelt in practice.

In 1913, Dick and Ethel had spent most of their four-month honeymoon in Paris, where their son was conceived. But now, only a year later, they were two much more serious people inhabiting a very different France.

Their connection—Dick as a surgeon and Ethel as a nurse—was with a five- to six-hundred-bed hospital in the Lycée Pasteur, a school the French government had put at the disposal of a group of Americans in Paris. Financed through voluntary subscriptions, the Ambulance Américaine Hospital asked various American universities to supply, for rotating periods of three months, sufficient professional personnel to staff key wards of the hospital. Dick and Ethel not only signed on with the group of six surgeons, seven house officers, and four nurses from Harvard, but Dick—the son of an old and wealthy Boston family—also helped underwrite the costs of the venture.

A major driving force behind the Ambulance Américaine, and a close associate of Dick and Ethel's during their time there, was 54-year-old Robert Bacon. Like Dick, Bacon came from an old Boston family. He attended Harvard with Theodore Roosevelt. There he had been a football hero and for four years president of his class. His subsequent career took him into banking, where he proved his mettle in negotiating complicated affairs at home and abroad for both the Morgan Bank and Philadelphia's Drexel & Co. In 1906, President Theodore Roosevelt named him First Assistant under Secretary of State Elihu Root. When Root resigned in 1909 to become senator from New York, Roosevelt appointed Bacon to Root's cabinet post. A year later, President Taft appointed Bacon as ambassador to France, a position he held until 1912 when Harvard offered him the post of Fellow. Bacon returned to Paris in 1914 to head up the Ambulance Américaine while his wife remained behind in the States to spearhead funding drives for the project.[17]

The majority of Dick and Ethel's other associates in and around Paris were members of the colony of Americans—mostly from elite backgrounds—who had been coming to France since 1870 to study art and architecture and engage in international banking ventures. Dick

and Ethel were on good terms with 42-year old Richard Norton, son
of the celebrated Harvard professor Charles Eliot Norton, who with
the backing of his father's literary friends Henry James and Edith Wharton, had organized an Anglo-American unit of the St. John's Ambulance. The latter had a long tradition of service going back to the
Knights of Jerusalem and was an active arm of the British Red Cross.
Norton called his new service the American Volunteer Motor Ambulance Corps and appealed to his alma mater, Harvard, for volunteers.

Henry Herman (H. Herman) Harjes, then aged 39, was another
friend. Harjes founded a division of American Red Cross ambulances
that would later merge with the Norton corps. (Harjes is best remembered today, however, for his later role as president of the American
Relief Clearing House.) Harjes's father, John, came to Paris in 1864 to
establish the Paris subsidiary of Philadelphia's Drexel Bank, the Drexel-
Harjes. This became the Morgan-Harjes bank in 1895. Both Henry and
his father were directors of Morgan-Harjes. Harjes senior and junior
were members of the Episcopalian communion based at Paris's fashionable Holy Trinity Church (which Ethel and Dick attended during
their time in France). They were also founders of the American Hospital
established at Neuilly-sur-Seine before the war (and still in operation)
to serve the American expatriate community.

Others of note associated with the Ambulance Américaine were
Samuel Newell Watson (53-year-old dean of Holy Trinity and doctor
of medicine), Laurence V. Benét (co-inventor of the Hotchkiss machine gun and former president of the American Chamber of Commerce in Paris), and his wife, Margaret Cox Benét, who played an
important role in the nursing corps. Ethel's superior, who handled the
day-to-day management of the nurses at the hospital, was Anne Harriman Vanderbilt, daughter of Edward Harriman and wife of W. K.
Vanderbilt. (In addition to Mrs. Vanderbilt's personal services, the W.
K. Vanderbilts also contributed considerable amounts of cash to this
and other Allied ventures. They purchased the first ten automobiles for
the Ambulance Américaine, and also paid for the first Nieuport airplanes used by the Lafayette Escadrille, formed in April of 1916.) Mrs.

Vanderbilt's cousin by marriage, the sculptress Gertrude Vanderbilt Whitney, made further sizable contributions to the Ambulance.

Dick's colleague Harvey Cushing, a 47-year-old surgeon and instructor from the Harvard Medical School, was by far the most prominent participant in the project. Originally from Cleveland, Cushing was educated at Yale and the Harvard Medical School before the turn of the century. In addition to being a renowned surgeon, he enjoyed great fame as a painter. In Boston he was a member of the Saturday Club, that venerable institution founded in 1857 by James Russell Lowell, Oliver Wendell Holmes, Ralph Waldo Emerson, John Lothrop Motley, Richard Henry Dana Jr., Louis Agassiz, Henry Wadsworth Longfellow, and Nathaniel Hawthorne. Along with Cushing, other contemporary members included A. Lawrence Lowell, M. A. DeWolfe Howe (then editor of the *Atlantic*, which the first generation of the Saturday Club had founded), and Bliss Perry (venerable professor of English at Harvard). Cushing was a close friend of both Leonard Wood and Theodore Roosevelt.

Dick spent most of his days in surgery, dealing with the removal of bullets and the occasional removal of limbs, while Ethel ministered to those in the recovery unit, chatting away in French as she gave sponge baths and administered pills, assuring all the prone and amazed inquirers that yes, she was indeed the daughter of "the great Roosevelt."[18]

"There are so many vivid pictures to paint," Dick wrote his father-in-law. "I am struck by the stoic patience of the men, many of them gravely wounded, many of them realizing (how could they not?) that they are doomed to live with dreadful deformities for the rest of their lives."[19] In addition to battle wounds, cases of influenza were numerous.

Ethel wrote her father of visiting the medical distributing station at La Chapelle, a 250-foot-long railroad freight shed made of corrugated steel and, in winter, terribly cold. Here the wounded were divided into three classes: those who could walk, those in wheelchairs, and the badly wounded on stretchers. "The thing that haunts you is the silence," Ethel wrote her father. "People talk in whispers. All the time whispers.

And then there is the calm—the calm after the storm? Or before? There is no rush. Only relief. The war is over for them. They are exhausted, grimy, muddy, stolid, bloody and completely uncomplaining. It would make you weep. They emerge from behind the curtain that covers the doorway, doing a poor job of keeping out the wind. Then they cast a tired look around—see where they are to go—and resignedly walk or push or pull themselves in the appropriate direction." Ethel also wrote her father of the victims of German gas attacks, in particular describing one patient who was "so busy fighting for air" he failed to note "a newly missing arm." It was, wrote Ethel, "a most terrible way to die."[20]

Driving through abandoned battlefields after the fighting had moved on, Ethel and Dick considered the many "stories told" by the "barren afterlandscape" of war. "A month has passed since the battle on these French fields rolling toward Ypres in Belgium," Dick wrote Roosevelt not long before Christmas. "But it could have been yesterday. The wounds on the land heal slow and the scars endure." Derby described fields and roadsides dotted with crosses, and hillsides cratered from artillery blasts. Here and there, a rifle or a dagger or cartridge belt lay scattered in the weeds or mud. One was hesitant to look too closely, "for fear of finding a hand or a foot or a head in the mix." Each haymow showed, by the grim evidence of the graves surrounding it, how its futile protection had been sought "against the scythe of another kind of reaper."[21]

ॐ ॐ

When Theodore Roosevelt did not have letters from Dick and Ethel, he would often find news of them in French dispatches published in the *New York Times* and other papers. It seemed the daughter of Theodore Roosevelt was news. The public was just as interested in her now as they'd been when she was a wild tomboy climbing trees on the White House lawn.

She'd been a notoriously pugnacious child. Stocky, muscular, and athletic, she had legs her father described as the size of bedposts. He called her "Elephant Johnny" and told a friend she was "a jolly naughty whacky baby too attractive for anything, and thoroughly able to hold her own in the world." Swinging from trees with her brothers, running relay races, rowing on Oyster Bay, and riding a succession of favorite horses, she became as robust as any of Theodore Roosevelt's children. Edith once commented that Ethel was so "strong and rough that I am almost afraid when she comes near me."[22] Ethel routinely wrestled with her next-eldest brother Kermit, the one of her siblings to whom she was closest in age. At age 12, however, she suddenly stopped wanting to climb trees and wrestle. She transformed, quite suddenly and mysteriously, into a lady.

Roosevelt once said that while Sister was the "liability child," Ethel was the "asset child."[23] Ethel had none of Sister's annoying peculiarities. While Sister was sharp-tongued, irreverent, and would go to her grave an avowed atheist, Ethel was from the start a model of Christian virtue, piety, and good works. Sister was flamboyant, impulsive, and provocative; Ethel was chaste, reserved, and conservative. Sister courted the superrich and endeavored to socialize with the poshest society of New York and Newport; Ethel contemplated volunteering at Jane Addams's Hull House. During the White House years, Ethel dutifully joined her mother on receiving lines for state affairs (something Sister, busy smoking in the pantry, absolutely refused to do), and taught Sunday School to underprivileged youths.

In Paris with Dick for those few months of late 1914 and early 1915, Ethel stayed true to form. When she was not nursing the wounded, she worked at a halfway house for homeless refugee children. On Sundays she sang in a choir. And she prayed. She told Dick she prayed for all the people she loved, but most earnestly for her father and brothers, to whom she guessed God would be sending many trials in the days to come.

Chapter 7

THE KALEIDOSCOPE SHAKEN

"*T*he [political] kaleidoscope has been shaken," Roosevelt wrote early in the spring of 1915. "All the combinations are new and I am out of sympathy with what seems to me to be the predominant political thought in this country."[1]

Going into 1915, the Republican Party was in a shambles, particularly with respect to the issue of preparedness. While Democrats were largely unified in their stance against building up the military infrastructure, the G.O.P. was fragmented. Only a minority of the party, the eastern wing—as represented by such conservatives as Lodge and Gardner—was solidly for expansion of the military. The large western wing of the G.O.P.—dominated by German-Americans and rural progressives such as Robert LaFollette—tended to side with Wilson on the topic of national defense. The Republicans were fractured further by the continued, labored existence of the mortally wounded Progressive Party. It seemed so long as the Bull Moose lingered, so too would animosities from the split of 1912.

Despite the animosities, Roosevelt was hopeful that preparedness could serve as an issue to reunite the Progressive Party with the G.O.P.

Indeed, national defense seemed to be the one topic upon which urban progressives (who dominated the Progressive Party) and conservative Republicans (who controlled the eastern wing of the G.O.P.) could agree. Roosevelt's friend and fellow preparationist, Charles J. Bonaparte, probably confirmed this premise for Roosevelt when he forwarded a letter from the prominent Progressive William Dudley Foulke in which Foulke said, "The only thing which would ever induce me to unite with the scoundrels who stole the nomination two years ago would be the consciousness that they comprised the only part who insisted upon an adequate navy and army for defense."[2]

As Roosevelt well knew, if what remained of the Progressive Party allied itself with the eastern wing of the G.O.P., the two groups would instantly emerge from the fringe to form a majority block within the Republican camp. The midwestern German and rural-progressive Republicans, who now dominated, would instantly become a powerless minority. Republicans would then be able to position theirs as the party of preparedness, strong defense, and national pride. This was Roosevelt's ambition. At the same time, Roosevelt realized no party could afford to offend or alienate the large German-American population in the Midwest and still hope to be viable nationally. Thus his rhetoric of defense—and that of his comrades—remained staunchly neutral.

ॐ ॐ

There were a few notable exceptions to Democratic unity against preparedness. Secretary of War Lindley M. Garrison advocated major army increases in his annual report of 1914 and then repeated this recommendation when interviewed by *The Outlook*, a publication sympathetic to preparedness.[3] Four Democratic senators likewise broke ranks: Benjamin F. Shively of Indiana, Thomas S. Martin of Virginia, Furnifold M. Simmons of North Carolina, and George E. Chamberlain of Oregon. Chamberlain went so far as to introduce a bill to establish a Council of National Defense, which, of course, went nowhere in the Democratic-controlled Senate.

Through late 1914 and early 1915, Theodore Roosevelt's young cousin, Franklin Delano Roosevelt, was having a rough and unhappy time serving as Assistant Secretary of the Navy under Josephus Daniels. Daniels, a white-supremacist newspaper editor (and Christian pacifist) from North Carolina, was not Franklin's cup of tea. (Ted Jr., who met Daniels after the war, characterized him as "a queer character, a combination of ignorance, kindheartedness, and shifty opportunism."[4]) FDR alarmed his cousin Theodore with clandestine reports of Daniels's inefficiency and utter ignorance of naval affairs. Both Roosevelts found frighteningly accurate a cartoon portraying Daniels dressed like Little Lord Fauntleroy, sitting in a chair too big for him, struggling to master an enormous book entitled *How to Tell Ships from Automobiles*. FDR further alarmed Theodore with news that thirteen second-line battleships were out of commission because the navy was short eighteen thousand men to crew them, and nothing was being done to fill the gap.

Unlike his boss, Franklin was all for preparedness and, more quietly, for intervention as well. He had long been influenced by Alfred Thayer Mahan's theories of maritime warfare and geopolitical strategy. Even as a boy, he read and reread Mahan's seminal *Influence of Sea Power Upon History, 1660–1783* until, as his mother recalled, he'd "practically memorized the book."[5] FDR was sympathetic to Mahan's arguments for a strategic Anglo-American imperium—an Atlantic alliance— through which the United States would abandon forever the policy in isolation and accept the fact that to take her share in the travail of Europe was to assume an inevitable task, an appointed lot in the work of upholding the common interests of civilization. England, said Mahan, was the natural partner with which the United States should join to dominate the seas. FDR concurred completely.

In addition to his infatuation with Mahan, Franklin was as well infatuated with his cousin Theodore, whom he idolized and whose favorite niece, Eleanor, he had married. Despite his displeasure in finding himself working for Wilson and Daniels, Franklin was delighted to be in a job Theodore once held. He was also pleased to be living in a house intimately associated with Theodore's presidency.

As soon as Franklin got his appointment as assistant secretary, he and

Eleanor rented the Washington home of Theodore Roosevelt's sister and close political confidante, Anna Roosevelt Cowles. During Theodore Roosevelt's White House years, the Cowles home on N Street was a frequent refuge for the president—so much so that journalists dubbed it "the little White House." There was no structure in the city quite so much associated with Franklin's famous cousin, and the younger Roosevelt was proud to be calling the place home. Anna Cowles and her husband were now living at their country house in Farmington, Connecticut. Amid an environment hostile to all interventionist sentiment, FDR worked furtively at the Navy Department to do all he could to advance the country's military and emotional preparedness for war.[6] Early on, as war threatened through the spring and early summer of 1914, FDR corresponded with the disenfranchised Alfred Thayer Mahan, asking advice and at the same time suggesting themes and funneling information meant to be of use in Mahan's editorializing for preparedness. "Personally, I do not think it would be wise to have it appear that a regular campaign is being started," wrote Franklin not long before Mahan was officially silenced by government edict. "This would almost inevitably lead to opposition, and my own feeling is that the opinion of yourself and the ex-President [Theodore Roosevelt] would, if given a very wide range of circulation, carry the greatest possible amount of weight . . ."[7]

Once Mahan was silenced, FDR was forced to break off contact with him. He was under direct orders to have absolutely no communications with his guru, and he followed those orders, even when Mahan tried to get an appointment to see him personally. After Mahan died in a Washington hospital in December of 1914, FDR sent a florid note of condolence to his widow. Mrs. Mahan's response was terse: "Shortly after his arrival in Washington my husband went to the Department to pay his respects to you. He told me that he had not seen you and that his card had been returned to him. I mention this as I would like you to know that he tried to see you and was disappointed."[8]

There is evidence FDR always felt guilty about the way he had treated his great hero—and his cousin Theodore's great friend—at the end. Many years later, as president, he sought to make amends. He encouraged his Director of Naval Intelligence, Captain W. D. Puleston, to write an adoring biography of Mahan. And he arranged for the navy to take loud notice of the admiral's centennial. As reported in the Washington *Evening Star* of 27 September 1940: "President Roosevelt today joined the navy in paying tribute to the late Rear Admiral Alfred Thayer Mahan with a statement that the Nation owed a lasting debt of gratitude to the 'great strategist and statesman.' In a letter to the Secretary of the Navy on the 100th anniversary of Admiral Mahan's birth, Mr. Roosevelt declared that the 'threats of aggression can best be met at a distance from our shores rather than on the seacoast itself.' "[9]

ॐ ॐ

Three major pro-preparedness organizations—each of them endorsed by Theodore Roosevelt—were formed in late 1914: the American Defense Society, the National Security League, and the Army League. Like the Navy League, these organizations were officially nonpartisan and were also officially neutral. The charter of each claimed opposition to "militarism" and stated a desire to promulgate an army and navy only so large as was necessary for defensive purposes.

In fact, however, the organizations were founded and dominated by the eastern Republican establishment and included extreme pro-Allied voices in their leadership. When men such as Major General Francis V. Greene (Ret.), Colonel William C. Church (editor of the *Army and Navy Journal*), and former Secretary of War Henry L. Stimson met to adopt the moderate, ostensibly pro-neutrality charter of the National Security League, they first listened to publisher George Haven Putnam give an address in which he suggested preventive war would most likely be required in order to foil a likely German invasion of Canada after the defeat of Britain.

Of all the organizers of the National Security League, Stimson was most representative. Born to a wealthy New York family in 1867, he spent summers visiting an autocratic southern grandmother who entertained him with her recollections of childhood friendship with the elderly George Washington. Educated at Andover, Yale, and the Harvard Law School, Stimson ran unsuccessfully in 1910 as Theodore Roosevelt's handpicked Republican candidate for the governorship of New York. Then he served as Secretary of War under Taft (as he would again under FDR during World War II).

As propaganda tools, the new organizations, together with the Navy League, were indispensable. For example, on the eve of Woodrow Wilson's December address to Congress, the Army League issued a press release announcing the alarming results of a recent defense study. The sad fact, said the Army League, was that all cities on the largely undefended Pacific coast were likely to be overrun very quickly in the event of a war on that front. On the same day, the Navy League issued another release postulating the theory that it was Belgium's lack of armaments—rather than the preponderance of the same in the hands of other countries—that made inevitable the August invasion by Germany.[10] Shortly thereafter, the American Defense Society announced the urgent necessity for military training of all fighting-age men.[11] And in the first week of 1915, President John Grier Hibben of Princeton University, a member of the National Security League, publicly called for the military training of all college men and specifically cited the Harvard program as a model. When the *New York Times* shortly afterward looked further into the topic of campus military training, no fewer than eighteen presidents of top-ranked colleges across the country indicated they favored military training for their students.[12]

Business leaders, as well, began to notice and become concerned about the preparedness issue. The Merchants Association of New York and the U.S. Chamber of Commerce were among the commercial organizations to come out for military increases and universal military service in January of 1915. Later that same month, Henry B. Joy, president of the Packard Motor Company, printed copies of a preparedness speech by Theodore Roosevelt and distributed it to all 11,000 of his employees.[13]

Like other preparedness advocates, most leading businesspeople were outwardly neutral. However, it is interesting to notice where the big money was going. In the autumn of 1914, after the United States reversed its briefly held policy of forbidding commercial loans to combatants, the National City Bank immediately made a $10 million loan to the French. One year later, a consortium of northeastern banks provided a loan to the combined allies of $500 million. Before American entry into the war in 1917, U.S. banks were to invest well over $2 billion in Allied bonds as compared to less than $20,000 in German bonds.

It obviously helped that preparedness advocates had wealth on their side. It also helped that the press was largely sympathetic to the cause of preparedness propagandists. A poll conducted in January indicated that American newspaper editors nationwide were two to one in favor of increasing military defenses generally, and almost three to one in favor of expanding the navy.[14]

Adding to the pro-preparedness media environment were works by leading authors of the day who, unlike their political allies, did not feel restrained when it came to identifying Germany as villain in the world's drama. In the spring of 1915, Theodore Roosevelt's friend Owen Wister was busy cobbling together a short, 148-page book entitled *The Pentecost of Calamity*. The book details a purported Prussian indoctrination program that since 1870 had proclaimed the creed of a superrace and superstate, silencing all dissenters, and preparing Germany for her "wild spring at the throat of Europe." Now, wrote Wister, Germany presented "a hospital case, a case for the alienist; the mania of grandeur, complemented by the mania of persecution."[15]

Another Harvard man, John Jay Chapman, was equally strident, publishing numerous essays and editorials condemning Germany and her cause. In early 1915 Chapman's son Victor, an architectural student in Paris, enlisted in the Lafayette Escadrille and began training as a flier. Victor was shot down over Verdun a year later, becoming the first American aviator to die in the war and, more important, a symbol of Anglo-French-American unity for many of his class.

With rich business executives, journalists, best-selling writers, and even a fair number of academics convinced preparedness was necessary, it only remained to convince the people. But laborers and farmers, unlike the intelligentsia, were not so easily persuaded. In fact, an enormous grassroots, anti-preparedness movement sprouted at the same time as preparedness forces gained strength. The anti-preparedness majority drew its leadership from the hierarchies of the independent progressives, the Christian pacifists, the rural progressive followers of William Jennings Bryan, and some rural Republicans as well.

Throughout early 1915, anti-preparedness activists focused on three key ideas: that the very act of arming was the most immediate cause of the European war, that the United States was in no danger of invasion, and that any defense buildup would at once threaten to draw the United States into the war. At the same time, they argued, a defense buildup would jeopardize the appearance of absolute neutrality that the United States needed in order to offer itself as a viable mediator toward a negotiated "peace without victory." This negotiated peace, anti-preparedness ideology held, would most assuredly be the ultimate outcome of the war so long as the United States held true to neutrality in thought as well as deed and refrained from the temptation to arm.

While the minority preparedness alliance of businessmen, journalists, and academics possessed great prestige and enormous financial resources, the anti-preparedness majority made up for the lack of these with sheer numbers of subscribers to the cause. Quite simply, the country was against arming. The electorate believed what pacifist organizations and the Wilson administration said: that to arm was not only to invite disaster for the United States, but also to forswear an obligation to help Europe emerge from her moment of carnage with a just and lasting peace.

જી જી

Theodore Roosevelt expected trouble to come. And he expected it to come in the North Atlantic. That, he wrote his son Ted in early 1915, "is where neutrality will not count for anything in the end, no matter how many white flags a coward might care to fly."[16]

As part of neutrality in thought as well as deed, the Wilson administration attempted to maintain trade relations with all combatants. As a practical matter, such a course was impossible to implement. The situation on the high seas quickly grew ominous for American shipping as the war on land continued its bloody stalemate and the Allies and Germany endeavored to starve each other out through economic blockades.

Merchant shipping was always fair game in time of war. Americans had relied heavily on an ancient form of wartime piracy—pivateering—during the Revolution, the War of 1812, and the Civil War. The exploits of Confederate privateers (among them James and Irvine Bulloch) were etched in Roosevelt's mind. During the 1860s, the business of controlling the high seas was a gentlemanly pursuit devoid of the insidious weapons for anonymous attack, and devoid of serious threats to civilians. The Civil War saw only one prototype submarine. This submersible "torpedo-boat," the *C.S.S. Hunley,* sank three times in trials, drowning three crews in the process. After its third resurrection in 1864, the *Hunley* managed to attack and sink one Union blockade ship near Charleston just moments before going down herself for a fourth and final time. Theodore Roosevelt—the first American president to travel in a submarine—knew that by 1915 the technology of high-seas terrorism had advanced significantly. Furthermore, Roosevelt did not for a moment doubt the Kaiser's willingness to use his U-boats to control the flow of goods between the United States and Britain.

The Declaration of the London Maritime Conference of 1908–1909, which specified free passage for neutral vessels during time of war, was hardly even noticed by any of the warring parties, let alone adhered to. In October and December of 1914, British Orders in Council imposed a series of restrictions on neutral vessels. In October, British warships blockaded German ports, and British minefields effectively closed the North Sea. In December, the British announced that all neutral shipping bound for Germany had to be cleared through British ports, there to be searched for contraband. In February of 1915, the British expanded the list of contraband articles to embrace virtually every and any goods imaginable, including food. And on 2 March, they took the redundant step of imposing a total blockade on the entire German coast.

After the February announcement by the British, the Germans responded by declaring the waters around Great Britain and Ireland, including the English Channel, a war region in which German U-boats would have a free hand. British ships in the zone would be destroyed. Neutral ships would also be targeted, said the Germans, because of the chronic "misuse" of neutral flags.

Shortly, a paid announcement appeared in a New York newspaper signed by Count Bernstorff, Germany's ambassador to Washington, warning American citizens not to take passage on Cunard's *Lusitania*— the very ship on which Dick and Ethel had made their Atlantic crossing in the autumn of 1914. Theodore Roosevelt was outraged when the Wilson administration declined to protest this threat. Roosevelt insisted privately that were he president, he would have the Department of State to prepare Bernstorff's passports. "I would have handed them to him and said, 'You will sail on the *Lusitania* yourself next Friday; an American guard will see you on board, and prevent your coming ashore.' "[17]

But Theodore Roosevelt was not president. Wilson was.

ॐ ॐ

Generally, throughout the first months of 1915, the preparationists were civil in their criticisms of Woodrow Wilson's nonexistent strategy for national defense. Occasionally, however, Roosevelt would slip up in the passion of one of his speeches and raise eyebrows by condemning what he called William Jennings Bryan and Woodrow Wilson's "cult of cowardice."[18] When he did so, he was simply giving a public face to the deep personal enmity expressed routinely by many eastern Republicans behind closed doors.

Elihu Root, who like Taft had served under Roosevelt as Secretary of War, told associates he believed Wilson's anti-preparedness policy was worse than foolish, it was criminal.[19] John Jay Chapman wrote a friend that Wilson was a "mendacious coward," a "putty-faced, un-truthful person," who "rowed with one oar and backed water with the other."[20] Lodge, meanwhile, convinced himself Wilson actually had a pro-German bias. "He has remained silent in regard to the violations of Belgium's neutrality by Germany, as to the Hague conventions, which have been shot to pieces," wrote Lodge to Roosevelt, "and then he suddenly finds his voice to protest to England, one of the Allies, about interference with our trade."[21]

Through well-placed British associates as well as friends within the administration (most notably FDR), Roosevelt's circle knew that though Wilson touted the United States' "divine mission" to mediate the European conflict, in fact his mediation efforts were hardly viable and verged upon being diplomatic embarrassments. When Colonel Ed-ward House went to England in January of 1915 armed with an offer from the United States to help broker a peace, the Allies—confident in their military position—announced they were not interested. The German drive toward Paris was stalled. Italy seemed about ready to throw her weight behind the Allies. And the Germans were being outgunned for control of the high seas. Given these circumstances, the French and British governments believed they could force the Germans to terms within a relatively short period of time, thus achieving peace *with* victory and *without* diplomatic meddling by the United States.

A number of weeks after arriving on the Continent, House made his way to Berlin where he found the Germans equally confident and equally obstinate. At least they were confident enough to say they would not pull out of France or Belgium without payment of war reparations—in other words, a ransom.[22] It seemed the only thing the belligerents agreed on was their fundamental disinterest in Wilson's idea of peace without victory. Thus Roosevelt wrote Kermit in late April to say the whole prospect of mediation was simply "vaporous."[23]

Nevertheless, despite what the preparationists knew to be the facts of the case, Wilson continued to speak forcefully to the American peo-ple about how it was the mission of the United States to be the voice of reason for Europe. Roosevelt and the other preparationists could not dispute Wilson in public, because they were not at liberty to discuss their privileged knowledge of House's confidential meetings. But in private they called Wilson a liar and worse—just as they called the Kaiser a buccaneer and an expansionist. And they agreed among themselves that the days for reticence were growing short.

Chapter 8

TOO PROUD TO FIGHT

*I*n the spring of 1915, some of Theodore Roosevelt's strident rhetoric of the 1914 Progressive Congressional campaign was coming back to haunt him. The ex-president found himself on trial for libel. The complaint, lodged by G.O.P. power broker and Albany Republican boss William J. Barnes Jr. (chairman of the New York State G.O.P.), alleged that Roosevelt had slandered Barnes in a campaign speech during which he urged Albany County voters, in the absence of viable Progressive candidates, to support anti-Tammany Democrats. It was better to do so, said Roosevelt, than to reelect "cogs" of the corrupt Republican machine run by Barnes. "The interests of Mr. Barnes Jr. and Mr. Murphy [a Tammany boss] are fundamentally identical," he said, "and when the issue between popular rights and corrupt and machine-ruled government is clearly drawn, the two bosses will always be found on the same side, openly or covertly. . . ."[1]

Barnes's suit asked for $50,000 in damages—money Roosevelt could ill afford to part with. He might well have had to part with it, too, if he had not succeeded in having the venue for the case moved from Albany—where Barnes ruled and no jury would ever find against him—to Syracuse. One of the witnesses Roosevelt produced to testify in his favor was young FDR, who was active in the Democratic Party in the mid-Hudson Valley. Identifying himself in relation to the defendant as a "fifth cousin by blood and a nephew by law," FDR gave evidence that Barnes had refused repeated requests to help support independent Democrats running against the Tammany machine—the implication being that Barnes was indeed in league with Murphy. Largely owing to Franklin's testimony, Roosevelt was vindicated and Barnes's suit failed.[2]

On 7 May, in the midst of the trial proceedings, a messenger came into the courtroom and handed Roosevelt a telegram. The news was grim. The *Lusitania* had been sunk off the Irish coast by a U-boat. Twelve hundred people—including 128 Americans—were dead. The American casualties included several celebrities, among them Arthur Gwynne Vanderbilt, Elbert Hubbard, and New York County Progessive Party Chairman Lindon Bates.

The devastating news of the *Lusitania* was not the first such interruption in the trial. Shortly before the start of the proceedings, the British ship *Falaba* was sunk (28 March), with the loss of 104 passengers and crew, one of these an American. Then, on 1 May, the American tanker *Gulflight* was torpedoed off the Scillies—becoming the first American ship to fall victim to German fire. The *Gulflight* did not sink, but three people died. In the midst of all this, reports came daily of the carnage going on in France: the Germans holding fast to the heights between the Swiss border and the Ardennes Forest, both sides dug in, neither moving, each becoming increasingly efficient in the ruthless science of mass extinction. While the trial followed its methodical course in the Syracuse courtroom, the second battle of Ypres resulted in more than 100,000 casualties; and in the Artois fight that followed, the French lost 100,000 men, the Germans 75,000: all for the sake of just a few miles of inconsequential real estate.

After reading the telegraphed news of the *Lusitania*, Roosevelt's lawyer leaned over to him and implored him to say nothing to the press. The lawyer reminded Roosevelt there were two German-Americans on the jury. Later, in the crowded foyer outside the courtroom, Roosevelt, with typical self-dramatizing flair, reiterated his lawyer's request to the gathered journalists and explained he could not accede to it. The time had come to stop shadowboxing, to throw off the robe of neutrality, and to come out swinging. The barbaric act of Germany, he announced to the reporters who crowded around him, represented outright murder on the vastest scale. "It seems inconceivable that we can refrain from taking action in this matter, for we owe it not only to humanity but to our own national self-respect."[3]

For a few days, as emotions ran high, it appeared as though the country agreed wholeheartedly with Roosevelt's militant way of thinking as stated in Syracuse. The morning after the sinking, the *New York Herald* echoed the sentiment of many (though by no means all) in a banner headline: WHAT A PITY THEODORE ROOSEVELT IS NOT PRESIDENT! "From our Department of State," editorialized the *New York Times*, "there must go to the Imperial Government at Berlin a demand that the Germans shall no longer make war like savages drunk with blood."[4] The *Tribune* announced "The nation which remembered the sailors of the *Maine* will not forget the civilians of the *Lusitania*."[5] In fact, only two English-language newspapers in the United States—one in St. Louis and the other in Milwaukee—defended the sinking. "Condemnation of the act," wrote the editor of the *Literary Digest*, "seems to be limited only by the restrictions of the English language."

An enormous crowd gathered in Times Square, demanding that the United States declare war. Three former attorneys general of the United States—John Griggs of New Jersey, George Wickersham of New York, and Charles J. Bonaparte of Maryland—put out a public letter in which they declared the time for "watchful waiting" had come to an end.[6] And a large group of fighting-age men from the upper classes—Theodore Roosevelt Jr. among them—sent Wilson a petition stating that the outrage of the *Lusitania* could not go without a military answer. Ted wrote his brother Kermit in South America to say the sinking of the *Lusitania*, "combined with other attacks, has caused a serious crisis here. I believe war is thoroughly possible. . . . Should war be declared of course we all will go." A few weeks later it fell to Archie to pass to Kermit the sad news of peace. "For a short time up here things looked like war," he wrote, "but as usual the dear old administration has managed to back out of it and fool everyone into the fact that we have acted in a magnificent manner."[7]

The administration's response to the sinking of the *Lusitania* was at first so meek that it honestly surprised Roosevelt before it enraged him. Secretary of State Bryan announced that Germany had a right to prevent contraband going to the Allies "and that a ship carrying contraband should not rely upon passengers to protect her from attack."[8] Three days after the sinking, in a speech to a gathering of newly naturalized citizens at Philadelphia's Independence Hall, Woodrow Wilson made no reference whatsoever to the *Lusitania*. Instead he simply reiterated his already familiar message of American passivity. "There is such a thing as a man being too proud to fight," said Wilson. "There is such a thing as a nation being so right that it does not need to convince others by force that it is right."[9]

Roosevelt was annoyed to note that public reaction had cooled considerably less than a week after the sinking. Voices that a few days before had called for war now called for moderation. (Indeed, a Progressive leader from Kansas wrote Roosevelt that the Midwest's sense of outrage had "died down as suddenly as it had risen," and had virtually exhausted itself within forty-eight hours of the sinking.[10])

Now a delicate, eminently polite note of protest went to the German ambassador over the signature of William Jennings Bryan, who thought the reasoned missive too stern but nevertheless put his name to it. The United States, said the letter, "confidently expects . . . that the Imperial German Government will disavow the acts of which the United States complains, that they will make reparation so far as reparation is possible for injuries which are without measure, and that they will take immediate steps to prevent the recurrence of anything so obviously subversive of the principles of warfare for which the Imperial German Government have in the past so firmly contended."[11]

The note was generally regarded as a masterful diplomatic stroke.

Most who commented said it set just the right tone—neither so firm and uncompromising as to seem to invite further hostilities, nor so plaintive and soft as to suggest American weakness. The country as a whole—in a rapid shift of gears that suggests how conflicted the electorate really was, and how emotionally charged were the issues being debated—rallied in support of the restrained, even-tempered response that came to be called the first *Lusitania* note. The note was endorsed by even such moderate preparationists as William Howard Taft and Charles W. Eliot, who at this point still sought to avoid war.

The only camp critical of the first *Lusitania* note was that of Roosevelt, Lodge, and other radical preparationists. In the face of vast public support for the course Wilson had taken, however, they kept their comments to themselves and did their best not to demonstrate publicly the extent to which they were spoiling for battle. Confidentially, to his friend William Roscoe Thayer, Roosevelt let out some of his anger by expressing amusement that Wilson, by profession a historian, had spent so much time in his note lauding Germany's long history of being constantly engaged in the business of justice and humanity. Roosevelt reminded Thayer that Germany under Frederick the Great had "stolen Silesia" and "dismembered Poland" and, in more recent decades, "garroted" Denmark, forced a "wicked" war on Austria, "trapped France by lies into another war," and only recently "wiped its hands, dripping with blood, from the Chinese."[12]

In his private rhetoric, Roosevelt was beginning to demonize not only the Germans but also Wilson and Bryan. He told his son Archie that the president and the secretary of state were simply looking after their own political interests by catering to the majority "flubdub and pacifist vote." The president and secretary of state knew better, said Roosevelt, but were nevertheless kowtowing to "the large constituency of insularity and ignorance," saying and doing whatever was necessary to win popularity among a provincial people not yet astute enough to accept their place in the world. The people, said Roosevelt, thought very little about foreign affairs generally and "don't realize that the murder of the thousand men, women and children on the *Lusitania* is due, solely to Wilson's abject cowardice and weakness in failing to take energetic action when the *Gulflight* was sunk." (The *Gulflight*, of course, was not sunk.)

Wilson and Bryan, wrote Roosevelt, were "abject creatures" who wouldn't go to war unless they were "kicked into it." Still, he added hopefully, "there is a chance that Germany may behave in such fashion that they will have to go to war."[13] To his sister Anna, Roosevelt wrote "I am sick at heart over the way Wilson and Bryan have acted toward Germany, and above all, over the way that the country, as a whole, evidently approves of them and backs them up."[14]

Roosevelt must have said a prayer of thanksgiving after he read the German response to Wilson's first note, received on 31 May. The Germans were not contrite, conceded nothing, and gave none of the assurances upon which Wilson insisted. The German missive triggered a second, stronger note from Wilson in which the president told the Germans he would hold them strictly accountable for the safety of American shipping and American citizens on the high seas. This second *Lusitania* note, which Bryan refused to sign, was dispatched on 7 June. On the same day, the White House announced Bryan's resignation. Shortly, Roosevelt released a statement endorsing Wilson's message to the Kaiser.[15] Likewise the Republican press affirmed their support of the second *Lusitania* note, as of course did the leading Democratic journals.

As for Bryan, Roosevelt was of course glad to see him go. Yet he realized the country was not much closer to intervention than it had been previously—nor was it any closer to an aggressive national-preparedness program. Issues of neutral rights and freedom of the seas aside, the public remained dramatically opposed to the idea of American intervention and to any military buildup that might be seen as a prelude to intervention.

As Roosevelt also realized, the antiwar elements had just gained a new, vibrant, and resourceful leader. Immediately after his resignation, Bryan found himself ridiculed and lampooned in the Eastern press. Nev-

ertheless his prestige among his traditional followers—the rural progressives and Christian pacifists—increased. He also picked up significant support among isolationists and German-Americans. Within a
week of resigning, Bryan was stumping the country, charging Eastern
aristocrats with fomenting a war in which Midwestern farmers and
machinists would do most of the dying.

ॐ ॐ

Kermit was one of his father's closest confidantes and sounding
boards during this period. Through almost daily letters, Roosevelt
voiced opinions and concerns that shortly turned up in his public rhetoric.

Kermit was in some ways the son most similar to his father. Like
Roosevelt, he loved hunting, exploration, history, and languages. In
addition to Spanish and French, he taught himself Greek and Romany
(Gypsy), and could read Sanskrit. Growing up at Sagamore, Kermit—
like his brother Ted—often availed himself of the thousands of volumes
of history and natural history in the Roosevelts' library. Like his father,
Kermit read at least one book a day. In the coming years, Kermit would
actively follow the same muses once stalked by his father, writing a
score of books about explorations and hunting excursions into strange
and exotic lands. (Ted, it should be noted, wrote several excellent books
as well, two of them in collaboration with Kermit.)

Like his father, Kermit had many literary friendships—a few of
which he'd maintained since youth. He claimed acquaintance not only
with Rudyard Kipling but also the poet Edwin Arlington Robinson,
whose work he'd first encountered as a student at Groton. When 15
years old he sent his father, then president, a copy of Robinson's *The
Children of the Night* and asked him if he could not find a job for the
struggling young poet. "I hunted him up," remembered Roosevelt,
"found he was having a very hard time, and put him in the Treasury
Department. I think he will do his work all right, but I am free to say
that he was put in less with a view of the good of the government

service than with a view to helping American letters." To his son, TR reported "Robinson, your poet, has been appointed and is at work in New York."[16]

All the brothers frankly admired Kermit, who shared a very special bond with their father. Kermit had been the lucky son perfectly positioned to serve as their father's playmate when Roosevelt left the White House in 1909. Finished with school but not yet enmeshed in a career and family, it was Kermit who went hunting with their father in British East Africa in 1909 and then went again, exploring the River of Doubt, in 1914. Roosevelt and Kermit often addressed letters to each other using the names their African guides had given them during the 1909 safari. Roosevelt was *Bwana Makuba*, the Great Master. Kermit was *Bwana Merodadi*, the Dandy Master. Theirs was a very small and exclusive club comprised of just two members.

Unlike Roosevelt, however, Kermit was easily depressed and afflicted with a deep, brooding pessimism. His father once wrote that "Black care rarely catches up to a rider whose pace is fast enough." Yet the ceaseless, restless activity that kept Roosevelt enthusiastic and optimistic did nothing to help Kermit outrun the unnamed ghosts haunting him. The only blond among all the Roosevelt children, his mother once described him as "the one with the white head and the black heart."[17] And Roosevelt anxiously noticed Kermit's pronounced tendency to drink too much too often.

Roosevelt lived with a dire, nagging premonition about Kermit, grounded in family history. Roosevelt's brother Elliott (the father of Eleanor, Franklin Roosevelt's wife) was both an alcoholic and a morphine addict by the time he was 30. The family tried everything to help Elliott escape the demons plaguing him, including several "cures" at a variety of European spas, followed by commitment to an asylum on a writ of lunacy. But it was no use. In 1894, ostracized from his family and living under an assumed name with his mistress in New York City, Elliott died at age 35 from complications of his various addictions. Ever afterward, family members called drink the "curse of the Roosevelts," and Theodore Roosevelt feared that this curse was something one or more of his sons might fall heir to. Adding to his concern about his children—most particularly Kermit—was the fact that Edith's father had also been an alcoholic.

Kermit was the moodiest of the boys. His letters to his parents were always respectful, informative, literate, and entertaining—but they were never jovial like the less-artful letters of Ted or Quentin, nor even gleefully malicious like the bitter black humor sometimes doled out by Archie. Sober, Kermit seemed incapable of happiness, although after a few drinks he usually could display the esprit his brothers came by more naturally.

His participation in family games and activities was always good-natured, but never joyous. As boys, while his brothers would happily trudge behind Roosevelt on his famous point-to-point hikes (in the course of which one might go over, under, through, but never around obstacles), Kermit would follow doggedly and somberly while the others shouted and laughed. What was a game to the others was a gauntlet to Kermit. The boy was just as capable as any of his brothers, Roosevelt told one of Kermit's teachers. Where they succeeded, he likewise succeeded. But it was a question of attitude and motivation; that was where the "fatal" difference lay, said Roosevelt.[18]

క్ర క్ర

In the stifling summer heat of August 1915, Theodore Roosevelt spent at least one day looking—and feeling, as he said later—quite presidential. Standing in the back of a large open convertible, Roosevelt tipped his hat to more than a thousand khaki-clad men who stood at rigid attention in the morning sun, awaiting his inspection. In the distance behind the men, Roosevelt could see hundreds of tents laid out one after another in long, straight rows. On the perimeter of the tent city, he could see an obstacle course, a drill field, a rifle range, and even a practice area for firing mortar. The whole enterprise encompassed some thirty acres of army land left over from decades earlier, when regiments had been posted here—at Plattsburg, New York, in the Adirondacks—in case of British incursions from Canada.

The car came to a halt. Roosevelt stepped out. A number of officers came forward to present themselves and shake hands, among them Roosevelt's old friend Leonard Wood, commandant of the completely unofficial, ad hoc encampment. Once the greetings were over, Roosevelt turned and paced so quickly up and down the ranks that even spry General Wood, walking beside him, would have had trouble keeping up save for Roosevelt's frequent pauses to greet his many friends of all ages.

One of the first to be pulled from the line and slapped on the back by Roosevelt was Robert Bacon, the former secretary of state and U.S. ambassador to France, who was closely associated with the Ambulance Américaine. Next, Roosevelt came to the all-American Harvard athlete Hamilton Fish, grandson of the secretary of state of the same name and cousin of Roosevelt's colleague of Rough Rider days (also of the same name).[19]

Down the line, Roosevelt encountered Henry L. Stimson, Mayor John Purroy Mitchell of New York City, George Wharton Pepper (later senator from Pennsylvania), Arthur Woods (New York City police commissioner), Dudley Field Malone (Collector of Customs for the Port of New York), Bishop Perry of Rhode Island, and a host of other leading professors, lawyers, bankers, journalists, and businessmen whom Roosevelt knew well. Roosevelt also, in turn, came upon Ted Jr., Archie, and Quentin—along with no small number of their Harvard and Groton classmates. (Kermit would have been here too, but for the fact that he was still in South America.)

These were volunteers all. In fact, more than just volunteers, they were men and boys who had come to Plattsburg for a month's training in military rudiments, for which they paid a fee to support the otherwise unfunded camp. Here, as at Harvard, General Wood was the prime moving force. "As General Wood knew a lot of Harvard men, both young and old, it was natural that Harvard took the greatest interest in it and supplied a very large percentage of the students as well as giving it a great deal of publicity," remembered Archie Roosevelt. "In this [Wood] was helped enormously by a group of very intelligent graduates who had already established themselves in the business world. My brother Ted, already a partner in a very prosperous . . . firm, was among the leaders of this group, if not *the* leader."

Princeton, Dartmouth, Yale, and Columbia were amply represented as well, as were all the leading preparatory schools. The volunteers were trained by officers assigned by Wood, all of whom had seen, as Archie phrased it, "active service of a sort." Some of them had been on the border of Mexico. Others had been in the Filipino insurrection. Some had seen action in the Boxer Rebellion.[20]

Roosevelt spoke to the trainees for more than an hour. During his speech, he criticized the assertion—made by William Jennings Bryan and others—that if war came, the working class would fight while sons of hawkish eastern aristocrats would be kept out of harm's way. If Bryan really believed that, demanded Roosevelt, then why was he opposed to universal military service?

Roosevelt congratulated the men and boys standing before him. They, he said, were the best answer that could be framed to Bryan's unjust and ungentlemanly accusation. Roosevelt also criticized the journalist Richard Harding Davis, who'd said the Plattsburg experiment was nothing more than a summer camp for fox-hunting squires and dilettantes from the Ivy League.

Returning home after the visit to Plattsburg, Roosevelt wrote that the camp was "a glimmer of hope" and represented "the best of our race and our class."[21]

Chapter 9

EQUAL BILLING
WITH WOODROW

*T*heodore Roosevelt thought he understood the logic behind the unrestricted submarine warfare waged by the Germans. In a grudging way, he respected their approach. Why should the Kaiser pay attention to righteous complaints from the United States about abstract notions such as neutrality and freedom of the seas? The United States had no active navy with which to back up its rhetoric. From a strategic point of view, the German priority simply had to be to starve out Britain. This was the best way for the Kaiser to win the otherwise stalemated war. An embargo of the British was bound to succeed long before a distant and dormant United States finally began to slouch toward battle.

Roosevelt likewise understood that time was something the Kaiser feared more than he feared the United States. Germany had to have victory soon, or not at all. After all, Britain's reciprocal blockade of Germany was driving the inflation of reichsmarks ever higher, threatening an economic crisis. And then the Kaiser had his own peace wing to contend with—his own Bryans and LaFollettes. Antiwar sentiment was beginning to rise in the Reichstag among Social Democrats. The longer the war and its devastating economic effects continued, the more discontented the German population was bound to be with the prospect of prolonged hostilities.

Roosevelt told his friend John Burroughs that in sinking the *Lusitania* and promising more of the same—quite possibly more of the same aimed at American shipping—the Germans were simply responding to a situation Woodrow Wilson was guilty of creating. Had Wilson embarked upon an aggressive program of preparedness a year earlier, at the start of the war, the United States would by now, in the summer of 1915, have a formidable defense. Then the Germans would quite likely behave better. They would have to, in order to not risk the United States suddenly coming into the war on the side of the Allies. As things stood now, even if the United States declared war immediately, it would be at least a year before a viable army could be fielded and the largely mothballed fleet activated.

The United States was nothing for the Germans to worry about, Roosevelt told Burroughs. England was the opponent for the Kaiser to beat, and the only way for him to beat England was to starve England. No matter what the Germans promised, there would be more U-boat warfare before there was less. There would be more martyred American civilians. And Woodrow Wilson would be more their murderer than was the Kaiser, "but for our purposes we will give Willy equal-billing with Woodrow."[1]

To his brother-in-law, retired Admiral William Sheffield Cowles, Roosevelt wrote that the day when the United States could have avoided war was long past. Perhaps, if the first calls for preparedness had been heeded, things would have been different. But now, given the obvious military weakness of the United States, not to mention its "lack of national pride and resolve," there would be no stopping the German outrages at sea. These were bound to continue and, in continuing, would eventually force "even Wilson" into a declaration of war. It was the classic scenario, said Roosevelt. Were the United States prepared for war, then war might be avoided. Now, with the country completely unprepared, it was just a matter of time. And the sooner preparations began, the better.[2]

What was needed was education, Roosevelt told another friend. That was the only way to sell the notion of preparedness and make the "war-feeling" that predominated on the Eastern seaboard spread to the "good people of the west and the south." These people were not cowards, and were "no less patriotic than anyone in Harvard Yard," but were at a "cultural disadvantage" when it came to understanding world events.[3] Ted Jr. was more blunt in a note to his brother Kermit. "The people we need to convince are people who have never seen an ocean, let alone a ship like the *Lusitania*, and have no idea of Europe. If the Germans were torpedoing haywagons filled with the wives and children of those farmers, we could convince them. If the Germans were raping and burning and plundering through Iowa and Alabama the way they have through Belgium, we could convince them."[4]

Both Theodore Roosevelt and his son were oversimplifying; both knew better than this. The West and the South were, of course, largely antiwar. But insular provincialism was only part of the reason why. The Midwest, as has already been mentioned, included a large German-American constituency, many of whom not only had an idea of Europe, but had been born there. They were not so much antiwar as they were against a pro-Allied intervention on the part of the United States. No amount of education was going to change their point of view, which was based less on naïveté than it was on calculated, cynical, fifth-column maneuvering in support of the Fatherland. Neither was education likely to change the minds of the Christian pacifists—whose aversion to war went beyond political rationales. These activists claimed all men had an obligation to their maker, and to the constraints laid down in the Ten Commandments, before they had an obligation to any nation-state. War was evil in the eyes of God.

There were, as well, minority constituencies in the eastern Brahmin community who were both anti-intervention and antiwar. Harvard had at least one peace organization. The anti-preparedness and anti-intervention organizations at such institutions were small but robustly and loudly mobilized. As their pamphlets pointed out, while they may have represented campus minorities, they were nevertheless allied with a huge national majority. At Harvard, notable antiwar alumni visited and made speeches against preparedness in the midst of the bivouacs set up in the Yard. These visitors included newspaper publisher Oswald Garrison Villard, the pacifist grandson of abolitionist William Lloyd Garrison. Campus disagreement about the war was echoed within prestigious eastern families. Oswald Villard's nephew Henry Serrano Villard dropped out of Harvard to drive an ambulance for the Allies in Italy.[5]

ও ও

On 19 August, while the men at Plattsburg went about their training, the British White Star Liner *Arabic* was sunk off the coast of Ireland. Two U.S. citizens went down with the ship. As at the time of the sinking of the *Lusitania*, the official American response was one of brief outrage followed by intimidated and powerless restraint. Within the administration, several key associates of Woodrow Wilson—among them Colonel House; the new Secretary of State Robert Lansing; Assistant Secretary of the Navy Franklin Roosevelt; and Secretary of War Lindley Garrison—took the sinking of the *Arabic* as proof of Theodore Roosevelt's oft-expressed opinion that no amount of note-writing or diplomatic maneuvering could ever protect American lives in the North Atlantic. The four men were also convinced that prospects for mediation were dim, that the best American interest lay in a total Allied victory, and that the best path toward that victory was outright intervention by the United States.[6]

Their boss did not agree. While Woodrow Wilson's advisers were coming around to a Rooseveltian worldview, Wilson himself hung back. Wilson repeated his belief that the American people were counting on him to keep the country out of the war. And he reiterated his analysis that the most likely way for the United States to avoid war was to broker a mediated peace that awarded total victory to no side. Toward this increasingly unlikely end, he desperately sought to maintain the appearance of American neutrality. Thus, in responding to the attack on the *Arabic*, Wilson reiterated his call for strict German accountability while at the same time protesting British infringements of neutral rights. It was the Germans, however, who were actually attacking and sinking neutral vessels.

Roosevelt sharpened his rhetoric as well. Roosevelt was now calling confidently and loudly for intervention on the side of the Allies—a position he had maintained publicly ever since the sinking of the *Lusitania*. The president, Roosevelt said, was using "elocution as a substitute for action." The time for words, he insisted, was long past. "It is inconceivable . . . that our government representatives shall not see that the time for deeds has come."[7] American national pride had been insulted. America's neutral rights on the high seas had been violated. Now more than ever the United States needed to prepare—but no longer for mere defense.

It seemed Roosevelt was out of pace in early September, when the Germans agreed to modify their policy of submarine warfare in a manner designed to help protect the lives of American neutrals on the Atlantic. Many hailed this development as a diplomatic coup for Wilson and proof of the power of moral suasion over bellicose warmongering; but Roosevelt indicated he was not mollified and the Germans should not be congratulated for finally ending their "policy of assassination."[8] He said further that he would be surprised if the Germans and other Central Powers kept their word for very long. In this he was proved correct when an Austrian sub sunk the Italian liner *Ancona* in the Mediterranean on 7 November, occasioning the loss of twenty American lives, and then again when the British armed liner *Persia* was sunk off Crete, causing the death of hundreds of civilians, among them an American consul. Wilson responded to both incidents with notes of protest that steadily escalated in the forcefulness of their language.

༜ ༜

In December of 1915, Roosevelt published a book-length collection of his pro-preparedness and pro-intervention editorials and speeches.

Theodore Roosevelt Sr. Theodore Roosevelt Collection, Harvard College Library.

A Sagamore Hill obstacle race, ca. 1895. Theodore Roosevelt Collection, Harvard College Library.

Below left: Ted's first buck, 1902 or 1903. Theodore Roosevelt Collection, Harvard College Library.

Below right: Kermit Roosevelt and his dog Jack at the White House in 1902. Theodore Roosevelt Collection, Harvard College Library.

Clockwise from top:
Quentin Roosevelt atop the Sagamore Hill
ice house, ca. 1903. Theodore Roosevelt
Collection, Harvard College Library.

Archie Roosevelt photographed in 1904 by
Edward S. Curtis. Theodore Roosevelt
Collection, Harvard College Library.

Alice Roosevelt—a.k.a. Sister—photographed
at Sagamore Hill in 1897. Theodore Roosevelt
Collection, Harvard College Library.

Ethel Roosevelt ca. 1901. Theodore Roosevelt
Collection, Harvard College Library.

Theodore Roosevelt and his Rough Riders immediately after the "crowded hour" in 1898. Theodore Roosevelt Collection, Harvard College Library.

Ethel, Ted, Kermit and cousin Lorraine Roosevelt with Theodore Roosevelt and some Rough Riders at Camp Wikoff, Montauk, Long Island in August of 1898. Theodore Roosevelt Collection, Harvard College Library.

Sagamore Hill ca. 1914. Theodore Roosevelt Collection, Harvard College Library.

Theodore Roosevelt in 1914. Theodore Roosevelt Collection, Harvard College Library.

*Kermit Roosevelt and Belle
Willard on their wedding day in
June of 1914. Theodore Roosevelt
Collection, Harvard College Library.*

*Kermit and Belle in 1915. Theodore
Roosevelt Collection, Harvard College
Library.*

Theodore Roosevelt with his grandson, Richard Derby Jr., in 1914. Theodore Roosevelt Collection, Harvard College Library.

Above left: Kermit as sketched in his British uniform by John Singer Sargent on 8 July 1917. Theodore Roosevelt Collection, Harvard College Library.

Above: Ted as sketched in Paris in 1918. Theodore Roosevelt Collection, Harvard College Library.

Left: Sister as she looked in 1919. Theodore Roosevelt Collection, Harvard College Library.

Right: Eleanor Alexander Roosevelt in her YMCA uniform, Paris, 1918. Theodore Roosevelt Collection, Harvard College Library.

Below left: Flora Payne Whitney photographed in 1917. Theodore Roosevelt Collection, Harvard College Library.

Below right: Flora and Quentin photographed by Ethel in the spring of 1917. Theodore Roosevelt Collection, Harvard College Library. Publication by permission of the Houghton Library, Harvard University.

Ted (center) and Eleanor (right) with Brigadier General Frank A. Parker at Romagne, 1918. Theodore Roosevelt Collection, Harvard College Library.

Kermit in the Middle East, 1917. Theodore Roosevelt Collection, Harvard College Library.

Ethel Roosevelt Derby pins a medal on Dick, ca. 1917. Theodore Roosevelt Collection, Harvard College Library.

Archie with one of his nurses, 1918. Theodore Roosevelt Collection, Harvard College Library.

Archie in his bed at Blake's Hospital, Paris, July 1918. Theodore Roosevelt Collection, Harvard College Library.

Quentin and friends at Mineola in the spring of 1917. Quentin stands in the far left of the second row. He is resting his hand on the shoulder of Rod Tower, who eventually married Flora. Theodore Roosevelt Collection, Harvard College Library.

Quentin and Ham Coolidge enjoying Sunday breakfast at the home of the Norant family in May of 1918. Theodore Roosevelt Collection, Harvard College Library. Publication by permission of the Houghton Library, Harvard University.

Quentin in his "Doc Yaak" plane. Notice Doc Yaak painted on the side. Theodore Roosevelt Collection, Harvard College Library.

One of many newspaper stories contrasting the sons of Theodore Roosevelt with the sons of the Kaiser, and in so doing contrasting two forms of governance. Theodore Roosevelt Collection, Harvard College Library.

Quentin's grave, photographed in 1919. His propeller blade, which served as his original grave marker, was sent back to Sagamore Hill. The makeshift wooden cross placed at the grave by Bill Preston, Col. McCoy, and Father Duffy in August of 1918 can be seen leaning against the grave fence, at right. Theodore Roosevelt Collection, Harvard College Library.

Theodore Roosevelt photographed in August of 1918, about a month after Quentin's death, holding infant Archibald Roosevelt Jr. as the baby's mother, Grace Lockwood Roosevelt looks on. Edith Roosevelt, center, holds Richard Derby Jr. Ethel Roosevelt Derby, at far right, holds infant Edith Derby. Richard Jr. holds the Roosevelt family service flag. Just above the fold and out of sight is the gold star recently sewn in to represent Quentin. Theodore Roosevelt Collection, Harvard College Library.

Above left: Ted and Quentin II in 1941, shortly before Ted's promotion to Brigadier General. Theodore Roosevelt Collection, Harvard College Library.

Above right: Archie Roosevelt as a lieutenant colonel in the South Pacific during World War II. Theodore Roosevelt Collection, Harvard College Library.

Brigadier General Ted in his jeep "Rough Rider" during World War II. He holds his cane in his right hand. Note the bullet hole in the windshield. Theodore Roosevelt Collection, Harvard College Library.

Theodore Roosevelt in one of his last photographs: late 1918. Theodore Roosevelt Collection, Harvard College Library.

Entitled *Fear God and Take Your Own Part*, the book was somewhat ironically dedicated to Julia Ward Howe (five years' dead) who—though author of "The Battle Hymn of the Republic" and a supporter of the renegade abolitionist John Brown—was a dedicated and vocal pacifist throughout her later years. Nevertheless, Roosevelt praised Howe—whom he'd met on several occasions—for living a life that epitomized "stern and lofty courage" shrinking "neither from war nor from any other form of suffering and hardship and danger."[9] While a few of Howe's children and grandchildren were horrified by what they considered the misuse of her name, others were honored.

Explaining his title, Roosevelt said that to fear God meant to love God, respect God, and honor God. And the only way one could relate to God in this manner was to love one's neighbor, "treating him justly and mercifully, and in all ways attempting to protect him from injustice and cruelty." For nations this sometimes meant using force—"a mighty arm of righteousness"—to help one's neighbor, as well as one's self, to escape injustice and aggression. And the mighty arm, he said, should be a powerful army and navy ready at all times to spring, instantly, to the defense of humanity.

In the same book, Roosevelt argued for an intense spirit of parochial Americanism and contrasted this with what he saw around him every day: a flabby cosmopolitanism that led in turn to flabby patriotism. Roosevelt said there was no room in the United States for "hyphenated Americanism." There was room for only one national allegiance among the citizens of the United States—not two or three. As for himself, he insisted he was not a Dutch-American, but rather simply an American. He noted that the leaders of the hyphenated-American movement (by which he meant activist German-Americans and Austro-Americans) were also leaders in the movement against preparedness. In this, said Roosevelt, they played the part of traitors, pure and simple. "Once it was true that this country could not endure half free and half slave," he wrote. "Today it is true that it cannot endure half American and half foreign. The hyphen is incompatible with patriotism."[10]

Following through on the militant rhetoric in his book, Roosevelt endorsed the formation of the American Rights Committee, founded that December. Unlike the various defense societies founded a year before, the American Rights Committee paid no lip service to neutrality and in fact put forth a blatant anti-German interventionist message. The American Rights Committee argued that human rights worldwide would be threatened by a "Teutonic triumph" in Europe.[11] In this spirit, the organization called for severance of diplomatic relations with Germany and "direct cooperation" with the Allies.[12] Although ostensibly national in scope and nonpartisan, the organization was top-heavy with northeastern Republicans and held its meetings at Boston's Tremont Temple, where the fiery abolitionist Theodore Parker once preached. "It is a wonderful group," wrote Roosevelt to Archie, who attended some of the meetings, "but my fear is that it is no more representative of the country than Boston is representative of Detroit."[13]

Roosevelt was correct in his pessimism. While more and more members of the Eastern intelligentsia (including influential members of the Wilson administration as well as the leadership of both the Progressive and the Republican Party) migrated to a prowar stance throughout 1915 and early 1916, the country as a whole did not. Lodge told Roosevelt he believed many Midwestern Republicans were engaged in "keeping as neutral as Wilson, and as silent about international duties." He was also upset that many Midwestern Republicans did not support preparedness. "We can hardly count on them for anything."[14] Likewise, Roosevelt reminded Lodge, the ranks of the Progressive Party were pervaded with antiwar sentiment owing to the high incidence of German-American and pacifist members outside the cities. And of course, said Roosevelt, the Southern and Western wings of the Democratic Party always had been and always would be "a lost cause."[15]

Occasionally, politics made for strange bedfellows. During the winter, Lodge, Gardner, and other preparationists on Capitol Hill found themselves on the same side as Wilson when radical isolationists sought to ban Americans from embarking on merchantmen armed for defense. The measure, of course, contained an inherent repudiation of Wilson's insistence on neutral rights and on German responsibility for the safety of Americans and other neutrals on the high seas. With the support—though not the unified support—of Senate and House Republicans marshaled by Lodge and Gardner, the measure was tabled though not defeated. Lodge's support of Wilson's position in this was categorical, as was Theodore Roosevelt's. "The President takes the precise position that I have taken, and have been urging him in public speeches for the last eighteen months. Of course I shall stand by him," said Roosevelt.[16] Lodge also helped Wilson defeat Democratic measures to call for a world peace conference and nationalize the armaments industry.

Like Lodge, Roosevelt was heartened that Wilson stood firm—and in so doing stood up against strong elements within his own party as well as the majority of the electorate—on the issue of neutral rights. Both Roosevelt and Lodge recognized that while Wilson would never be induced to declare war for the sake of supporting the Allies alone, he might well wind up declaring war in the defense of neutral rights. Indeed, they could not fail to notice that this was the rhetorical corner into which Wilson, urged on by his increasingly militant advisers, was painting himself with his escalating denunciations of each succeeding outrage at sea.

න් න්

On 13 May 1916, while the battle of Verdun raged, Theodore Roosevelt stood with other pro-preparedness dignitaries on a Fifth Avenue reviewing stand and, by his own calculation, tipped his top hat 627 times. An enormous parade of preparedness organizations passed before him. It was, he said later, "a bully time."[17] Roosevelt occasionally spotted a familiar face amid the thousands parading before him. Ted, Archie, and Quentin marched in their reserve uniforms, as did many other Plattsburg men. Even the dignified Edith Kermit Roosevelt—who despised public appearances—marched inconspicuously in a group of twelve hundred society women organized by her daughter-in-law, Ted's wife, Eleanor.[18]

Eleanor Alexander Roosevelt was the daughter of an affluent New

York family. Her father and uncles were all Wall Streeters who considered Theodore Roosevelt a class traitor. Nevertheless, Eleanor fit snugly into the Roosevelt family once she got used to the hyperactivity that characterized the clan. Of her first stay at Sagamore Hill, before her marriage to Ted, she recalled: "Every night they stayed downstairs until nearly midnight, then, talking at the top of their voices, they trooped . . . upstairs. For a brief moment all was still, but just as I was dozing off to sleep . . . they remembered something they had forgotten to tell one another and ran shouting through the halls." The next day, at the crack of dawn, the prim young society girl was dragged along on a two-hour row to a sandbar where the Roosevelts enjoyed a picnic lunch of "rubbery clams" followed by a four-hour row home against both the wind and the tide. Despite such rough initiations, Eleanor Alexander was nevertheless very much in tune with her in-laws. As Sister wrote, Eleanor Alexander was "the type of mother and Ethel rather than the ecstatic and brilliant me."[19]

Given her prominent family, Eleanor had all the right connections to assemble an impressive array of distinguished friends and associates marching under the banner "Independent Patriotic Women of America." In addition to her mother-in-law, Eleanor recruited the likes of Mrs. Robert Bacon, Mrs. J. Borden ("Daisy") Harriman, and Mrs. Hamilton Fish. Eleanor walked at front wearing a broad blue ribbon reading "Marshal" in gold letters. Behind her walked Daisy Harriman carrying the organization's banner. And behind Daisy came the Independent Patriotic Women, twelve hundred strong.

"We passed the reviewing stand and kept on up Fifth Avenue," remembered Eleanor. "I have never seen so many people. They jammed the sidewalks, hung out of windows, looked down from roofs. We reached the Public Library, where people were crowded on the wide steps. . . . Directly opposite was the Union League Club, which had its own private grandstand filled with men we knew. I felt rather self-conscious at this point and was going along with my chin up, looking neither to the right nor to the left as the band played . . . when suddenly Ted [who had marched earlier in the day] ran out from the sidewalk and grabbed me by the arm. 'For heaven's sake, stop!' he shouted. 'You've lost your battalion!' "

The police had halted the parade at Thirty-fourth Street to let some crosstown traffic go through. From there Daisy Harriman and Eleanor had marched alone behind the band under the banner "Independent Patriotic Women of America." Just the two of them. "I looked back over what seemed miles and miles of empty asphalt with little white figures in the distance," remembered Eleanor. "Men in the Union League Club stand were doubled up with laughter."[20]

༄ ༄

The Preparedness Parade was a brief moment of pleasant optimism for Roosevelt, who realized the country as a whole remained in a stupor of indifference. "I despise Wilson," he wrote, "but I despise still more our foolish, foolish people who, partly from ignorance and partly from sheer timidity, and partly from lack of imagination and of sensitive national feeling, support him."[21]

His psychic isolation from the electorate was so severe in the spring of 1916 that when Owen Wister and thirty-five other writers briefly formed a "Draft Roosevelt" committee, he categorically rejected the prospect. Though he hated Wilson, and though some believed only Roosevelt could defeat him, he felt they were probably wrong. "I most earnestly hope the Republicans will *not* nominate me," he wrote his sister Anna, looking ahead to the convention, "for my belief is that the country is not in heroic mood; and unless it *is* in heroic mood, and willing to put honor and duty ahead of safety, I would be beaten if nominated. . . ."[22]

"The country is not waked up," he wrote in another letter discounting his 1916 presidential prospects. "The farmers and labor people think only of their immediate interests . . . the public men, business men and publicists who should be the leaders are but little influenced by the consideration of great and vital national needs, and do not look ahead. They are absorbed either in paying off private grudges or in securing, as they believe, conditions which will be to their advantage for a year or two. They cannot look beyond. Under these conditions there is in my judgement hardly a chance that the Republican convention will turn to me; and no one else of prominence, except Leonard Wood, realizes in vital fashion the gravity of the problem, and has a solution. Mere outside preaching and prophecy tend after a while to degenerate into a scream. After that point has been reached the preacher can do no good, and had better keep quiet; and I am within [close] distance of that point."[23]

But he was not actually anywhere near striking distance of that point. He thought of himself—perhaps correctly—as the one man in the country uniquely positioned to educate and change public opinion on the vital topics of preparedness and intervention. Given that, were he to remain silent, he would have been shirking his duty as a citizen. And Roosevelt was never one to shirk what he saw as his duty.

خ خ

In February of 1916, John Jay Chapman circulated a petition signed by leading writers demanding an end to American neutrality. Among the signers were Theodore Roosevelt, Owen Wister, William Dean Howells, Jack London, and Henry James. Shortly thereafter, Wister supplemented his signature with a poem: "To Woodrow Wilson, Feb. 22, 1916."

> Not even if I possessed your twist of speech,
> Could I make any words (fit for use) fit you
> You've wormed yourself beyond description's reach;
> Truth, if she touched you, would become untrue.
>
> Satire has seared a host of evil fames,
> Has withered emperors by her fierce lampoons;
> History has lashes that have flayed the names
> Of public cowards, hypocrites, poltroons.
>
> You go immune. Cased in your self-esteem,
> The next world cannot scathe you, nor can this;
> No fact can stab through your complacent dream,
> Nor present laughter, nor the future's hiss.

But if its fathers did this land control,
Dead Washington would wake and blast your soul.

Roosevelt told Wister he "entirely approved" of the poem, which
met with wide criticism. "Do not mind at all what the mushy brotherhood say of it; it's going to last. The people will in the end be glad that
the foremost man of letters speaks of the Buchanan of our day as it is
right to speak."[24] The next time Roosevelt saw Wister he exclaimed,
"The only trouble with that sonnet was that it wasn't half severe
enough." Roosevelt was to make the same comment literally every
time he saw Wister thereafter.[25]

སྤྲ་སྤྲ་

Cecil Spring-Rice was advised by his government to avoid Roosevelt at all costs for fear of alienating Woodrow Wilson, with whom
he had to do business. Spring-Rice was candid about this with his friend
Roosevelt, who understood completely. "If ever you think it safe,"
wrote Roosevelt, "do come out and visit us . . . and if you don't think
it advisable, let us know when you are passing through New York and
we will come in and lunch or dine unobtrusively with you."[26] For his
part, Spring-Rice was frustrated. "I propose to have a real long talk as
soon as I can get the chance," he wrote. "It is sufficiently tantalizing.
Damn it all . . . Oh, TR, how I wish I could see you."[27]

Although they would not see much of each other, Spring-Rice and
Roosevelt wrote voluminously in a clandestine correspondence. Roosevelt seems to have used Spring-Rice as a sounding board for utterances that, shortly after they appeared in the correspondence and were
approved or amplified by Spring-Rice, were heard in the regular public
statements Roosevelt made in speeches across the country during the
spring and summer of 1916. In speech after speech, Roosevelt turned
up the heat on Wilson, fervently attacking American neutrality while
at the same time attacking the government for failing to prepare for
even the possibility of war.

Wilson, said Roosevelt, was the chief spokesperson for the "flub-dubs," "mollycoddles," and "flap-doodle pacifists" who were too yellow to fight. Roosevelt declared that if *he* had been president in 1914, he would have lived up to the "charter of destiny" that demanded that the United States play a role in "so vital a fight."[28] Bombastically and unrealistically, Roosevelt insisted that had he been president, he would have stepped in and saved Belgium from being overrun by the Germans. (This he would not have done, for he could not have. The German invasion of Belgium was complete within days of its commencement. The United States could not possibly have mobilized in time to do anything to defend Belgium. Roosevelt's misstatement was calculated to arouse war sentiment while at the same time castigating Wilson.)

Roosevelt's speeches rang with the repeated indictment of Wilson as too "cowardly" and "ladylike" to declare war in the face of German atrocities at sea. Wilson, said Roosevelt, was too "damnably frightened" to use the great naval power at his command. At the same time, he insisted that if Germany appeared—in between occasional outbursts of murder—to be living up to its promise to restrict submarine warfare, it was only because the Germans did not have enough U-boats at their disposal to stage the massive naval Armageddon they hoped and planned for. Even now, said Roosevelt, the Kiel machine shops were busy day and night forging the next generation of German subs with which, in a few short months, the Kaiser would dominate the seas even more ruthlessly than before.

In a speech delivered at New York's Cooper Union in the summer of 1916, while the Battle of the Somme raged, Roosevelt made scathing reference to the posh F. W. Woolworth estate of Shadow Lawn (now Monmouth College) in New Jersey, where Wilson was spending the summer. "There should be shadows enough at Shadow Lawn," Roosevelt said. "The shadows of men, women, and children who have risen from the ooze of the ocean. . . . The shadows of the helpless whom Mr. Wilson did not dare protect lest he might have to face danger; the shadows of babies gasping pitifully as they sank beneath the waves. . . . Those are the shadows proper for Shadow Lawn. . . ."[29]

Chapter 10

DUST IN A
WINDY STREET

*T*he midterm elections of 1914 had demonstrated quite clearly that the Progressive Party was disintegrating. In early 1916, as a presidential race loomed, the question many were asking was the obvious one: Should the Progressive Party try to revive its strength, or should it acquiesce to the inevitable? Perhaps the most sensible thing for Progressives to do was to join with Republicans, choose a satisfactory candidate, and do the utmost to defeat Wilson. Roosevelt believed the latter scenario was the wisest, but nevertheless he did not want to abandon the Bull Moosers outright.

The Progressives and Republicans held their conventions on the same day, 5 June, in the same city, Chicago. The Progressives nominated Theodore Roosevelt. The Republicans nominated Supreme Court Justice Charles Evans Hughes, a former governor of New York whom Roosevelt sometimes called "the bearded lady" or "Wilson with whiskers." There was, in fact, an acre of thin ice between Roosevelt and Hughes, and had been for some time. They were once close political allies, but Roosevelt said Hughes had abandoned Progressive politics after ascending to the bench in 1910. The breach between the two men opened wider when Hughes refused to testify on Roosevelt's behalf in the Barnes trial.

Despite his dislike for Hughes, Roosevelt soon realized that the only other real alternative was Wilson. As we've already seen, Roosevelt had been pessimistic since February about his own chances for election. He had no illusions. He did not want, he told one of his sons, to repeat the "grave" mistake of 1912. He would not allow himself to be made to look like a spoiler intent on handing the election to the Democrats. Thus, a few days after giving the Progressives his "conditional acceptance" of their nomination, he switched gears, announced publicly that he was not a candidate for the presidency, and asked the Progressive National Committee to endorse Hughes.

Wilson included a preparedness plank in the Democratic platform while at the same time running on the slogan *He kept us out of war!* Several months before the autumn elections, Wilson got Congress to approve the National Defense Act, which called for doubling the size of the army over a five-year period. The program was scheduled to culminate in 11,450 officers and 223,580 enlisted men in 1921. The act also established a Reserve Officers' Training Corps (ROTC) in colleges. It likewise endorsed the Plattsburg summer camp, which would henceforth be run as a duly authorized program of the army. Perhaps more important, the act allowed the expansion of the militia (National Guard) to a strength of 17,000 officers and 440,000 enlisted men nationally while also requiring, for the first time, that militia personnel take a double oath of loyalty to the federal as well as state governments. Finally, the act gave the president power to commandeer factories vital for national defense and establish a government-owned and operated nitrate plant.

True to his word to support Hughes, Roosevelt gave a number of powerful speeches on the candidate's behalf. Hughes, however, proved an undynamic candidate: so soft-spoken and gentlemanly that his own solid adherence to the Republican Party's platform pledge of strict neutrality was easily overshadowed by Roosevelt's energized rhetoric of

preparedness and intervention. In the end, Roosevelt's strident interventionist speeches may well have hurt Hughes more than they helped
him in the face of Wilson's brilliant campaign strategy of running on
"preparedness and peace."

As Wilson shrewdly understood, the country was not yet in a war
mood. On election day, 5 November, Wilson defeated Hughes by a
narrow margin, holding 277 electoral votes to 254 for Hughes. In the
popular vote, Wilson got 9,128,000 *v.* Hughes's 8,536,000.

From here on in, the argument Theodore Roosevelt and other preparationists would have with Woodrow Wilson was not whether to
build up national defense, but rather how this should be done, at what
rate of speed, and at what level of efficiency. As Roosevelt and other
preparationists were quick to point out, even the meager buildup called
for by the National Defense Act immediately fell behind schedule under
the inept and unenthusiastic leadership of pacifist Newton D. Baker,
the Ohio lawyer whom Wilson appointed to replace Lindley Garrison
(a militant interventionist) as Secretary of War. (When, shortly after
being installed in his post, Baker made the mistake of mentioning to a
reporter that he enjoyed flowers, his detractors immediately assigned
him the nickname "Pansy.")

At the same time that he failed to prepare in an efficient manner,
Wilson was pulled steadfastly toward war not so much by Roosevelt
and other interventionists as by German actions. On 3 February, 1917,
confronted with the Germans' announced intention to return to unrestricted submarine warfare, Wilson felt forced to sever diplomatic
relations.

In the weeks that followed, as one American vessel after another
slipped beneath the waves, Roosevelt wondered out loud why the president did not immediately declare war. "Seven weeks have passed since
Germany renewed with the utmost ruthlessness her never wholly abandoned submarine war against neutrals and noncombatants," he wrote
on 20 March. "She then notified our Government of her intention.
This notification was itself a declaration of war and should have been
treated as such. During the seven weeks that have since elapsed she has

steadily waged war upon us. It has been a war of murder upon us; she has killed American women and children as well as American men upon the high seas. She has sunk our ships, our ports have been put under blockade . . . If these are not overt acts of war then Lexington and Bunker Hill were not overt acts of war. It is well to remember that during the last two years the Germans have killed as many, or almost as many, Americans as were slain at Lexington and Bunker Hill; and whereas the British in open conflict slew armed American fighting men, the Americans whom the Germans have slain were women and children and unarmed men going peacefully about their lawful business."

Breaking relations with Germany, he said, was "eminently proper" but "amounted to nothing." It was an empty gesture if it was not followed by vigorous and efficient action. Yet during seven weeks (which, he pointed out, was a time as long as the entire duration of the war between Prussia and Austria in 1866), the United States had done nothing. "We have not even prepared." Armed neutrality, he said, was only another name for "timid war." And Germany despised timidity as it despised all other forms of feebleness. "She does not wage timid war herself and she neither respects nor understands it in others."

Roosevelt noted with some relief that the German strategy of submarine warfare seemed to be failing, and was less menacing in late March than it had been in early February. But this change of affairs was "due solely to the efficiency of the British navy. We have done nothing to help ourselves. We have done nothing to secure our own safety, or to vindicate our own honor. We have been content to shelter ourselves behind the fleet of a foreign power."

Such a position, Roosevelt insisted, was intolerable. "Let us dare to look the truth in the face," he wrote. "Let us dare to use our own strength in our own defense and strike hard for our national interest and honor. There is no question about 'going to war'. Germany is already at war with us. The only question for us to decide is whether we shall make war nobly or ignobly. Let us face the accomplished fact, admit that Germany is at war with us, and in our turn wage war on

Germany with all our energy and courage, and regain the right to look the whole world in the eyes without flinching."[1]

ﺟﺮ ﺟﺮ

Finally, on 2 April, responding to the anger of the country over revelations of proposed German military alliances with Mexico and Japan against the United States, Wilson's hand was forced. The president at last demanded a declaration of war on Germany. "The ostrich riseth," wrote Quentin to his father from Harvard.

Only the ignorant assumed the United States would be able to lend instant military aid to her new partners. As Wilson's address to Congress concerning the Declaration of War made clear, this was not to be. Wilson spoke of cooperation "in council and action," of loans, and of mobilization. Deployment of the army and navy, however, was another matter entirely. A significant percentage of the fleet was simply not ready to sail. And the army consisted of only 5,791 officers and 121,797 enlisted men, most of these busy on the Mexican border.

How fast could the United States raise, train, and field a meaningful army? That was the question on Roosevelt's mind, just as it was on the minds of many in the British, French, and German governments.

ﺟﺮ ﺟﺮ

On 14 April, 1917—twelve days after the American Declaration of War—Archie married his fiancée, Grace Lockwood, in a hastily arranged service at Emmanuel Church, Boston. Quentin Roosevelt was best man. During Archie's brief time with Grace before leaving for France, he sired a child who would be born while Arch was overseas: a son, Archie Jr.

Theodore Roosevelt wrote to Woodrow Wilson immediately after the Declaration of War requesting permission to raise a company similar to his Rough Riders of 1898. "I doubt whether the President lets me go," Roosevelt wrote to his sister Anna, "and [I am] sure he will try his best to cause me to fail if he does let me go. We all have our troubles!

Quentin has grave difficulty with his back; the other three boys, [in officers' training] at Plattsburg, have no idea what they will be sent to do. It is exactly as if we were fighting the Civil War under Buchanan— and Wilson is morally a much worse man, and much less patriotic, than Buchanan. At present they have made absolutely no provision to utilize the young men between 18 and 21—those who did more, relatively, than those of any other age in the Civil War."[2]

In mid-April Roosevelt made a trip to Washington to try to convince Wilson personally to allow him to go to France. During his time in the capital, he stayed with the Longworths. One evening shortly after his arrival, he visited Franklin Delano Roosevelt's home on N Street—the "little White House" from his days as president. After dinner, Roosevelt played in the fourth-floor nursery with FDR's sons Franklin Jr. and John (ages three and one, respectively). "I'm taking two little pigs to market!" Roosevelt shouted, grabbing them and holding them, one under each arm, while he lumbered down and then back up the long flights of stairs. Franklin Jr. remembered that he was terrified—not because he thought Roosevelt might actually be taking them to the butcher shop, but because he was afraid the old man would fall and they would all go crashing down the stairs.[3]

After the children were in bed, Roosevelt settled down into a chair in the front parlor and, to his niece Eleanor's annoyance, spoke for more than an hour about how Franklin should resign as assistant secretary of the navy and get into uniform at once, just as Roosevelt himself had done in 1898 and hoped to do again very soon. Then Roosevelt asked if Franklin would try to arrange for him to have an interview with Wilson. Franklin spoke with Secretary of War Newton D. Baker the next day and asked him to act on Roosevelt's request for an interview with the president. Baker went to the Longworth home that evening for a visit with Roosevelt, and wound up inviting the former president to the White House the next day to meet with Wilson.

Wilson, by all accounts, was surprisingly cordial to the man who had been vilifying him in editorials and speeches for nearly three years. The president sat with a slight smile on his face as he allowed Roosevelt to ramble uncomfortably, attempting to make peace with Wilson in order that he might be allowed to personally make war on Germany. Roosevelt discounted his criticisms of the administration. "Mr. President," he insisted, "what I have said and thought and what others have said and thought is all dust in a windy street." Trying to eliminate the bitter taste of his earlier criticisms, Roosevelt resorted to sugar-coated compliments. He told Wilson he believed his recent war message to Congress would rank with the great state addresses of Washington and Lincoln. He begged the president to allow him to help inspire the country to act through his example, "and so to justify and live up to [your] speech."[4]

At the end of Roosevelt's remarks, Wilson said he would consider the matter but made no promises and, indeed, conveyed the distinct impression that he viewed Roosevelt's proposal with profound skepticism. Wilson reminded Roosevelt that the days of "The Charge of the Light Brigade" were over. Modern warfare called for professional soldiers rather than dashing amateurs. "I don't believe he will let me go to France," Roosevelt said to Colonel House shortly after the meeting. "I don't understand. After all, I'm only asking to be allowed to die." House, it is reported, then answered, "Oh? Did you make that point quite clear to the President?"[5]

There was already legislation pending on Capitol Hill that would empower the president to raise a draft army. Now friends of Roosevelt's—including Lodge in the Senate and Gardner (along with Nick Longworth) in the House—introduced additional legislation allowing the president to authorize up to four divisions of special volunteers, Roosevelt's to be one of them. Wilson, however, was not to be pushed.

After Wilson's decision to disallow Roosevelt's service it would be charged by Republicans that Wilson banned Roosevelt from the battlefields of Europe for the basest political reasons. There was, to be fair, more to the story. First, there were issues of personnel. Roosevelt's list of officers he would need for his unit included the very best the army had to offer: Henry T. Allen, Robert L. Howze, and James G. Harbord, each of whom was eventually to lead a division of his own. And Roosevelt's choice for division chief of staff was George Van Horn Moseley, who was destined to become an invaluable staff officer and a brigadier general in the American Expeditionary Force (A.E.F). These men, Wilson concluded, simply could not be spared to serve in a limited capacity under a military amateur noted for risky maneuvers and insubordination.

Further, reasoned Wilson and Baker, Roosevelt's proposition of a high-profile volunteer unit jeopardized the prospect of raising a draft army, which they hoped to be doing in short order. Wilson believed that if he allowed Roosevelt and a few other headline-prone dilettantes to raise their own units of volunteers, these would cast draft units immediately into the role of "second-class soldiers" as compared to the volunteer divisions.

In addition to all of these reasons for denying Roosevelt's petition, there was also the simple fact of the ex-president's dismal physical condition. Roosevelt was half-blind, overweight, and ravaged by infection and rheumatism. He was in no condition for active service in any capacity. As we now know, he was to be dead of natural causes within two years.

Still, the necessary denial of Roosevelt's request could have been handled more gracefully. About a month after Roosevelt's visit to the White House, Wilson dashed his hopes with a condescending press release from the White House: "It would be very agreeable to me to pay Mr. Roosevelt this compliment, and the Allies the compliment, of sending an ex-President," wrote Wilson, "but this is not the time for compliments or for any action not calculated to contribute to the immediate success of the war. The business now at hand is undramatic, practical and of scientific definiteness and precision." In remarks leaked to the press, Wilson went further, saying Roosevelt "and many of the men with him are too old to render effective service" and also that Roosevelt "as well as others have shown intolerance of discipline."[6]

Roosevelt was crushed. "I shall never cease bitterly regretting that I was not allowed to go to the other side," he wrote John Burroughs. "I would not have expected to come home alive."[7] Georges Clemen-

ceau also lamented the decision. Roosevelt should be brought over to
France, he argued, because Roosevelt's was the "one name which sum-
mons up the beauty of American intervention." The war-weary French
needed more than just arms and men, they needed miraculous vitality
of the type only certain rare and wonderful personalities could provide.
"Send Roosevelt!" demanded Clemenceau.[8]

ॐ ॐ

When General John J. "Black Jack" Pershing was assigned to command the A.E.F., he was chosen over five generals who were senior to
him. Of these, Hugh Scott, Tasker Bliss, Thomas Barry, and J. Franklin
Bell were in their sixties and very close to retirement. The fifth general
who was senior to Pershing, though several years younger, was Leonard
Wood. Given Wood's numerous criticisms of Wilson, no one was really
surprised when Newton Baker announced Wood would not be commander of the A.E.F. In private, Wilson said he knew from experience
that Pershing would follow presidential orders while Wood would not.
In public, Wood's disqualification was ascribed to his minor limp.

After Pershing's appointment, Roosevelt wrote him a note combining frank and honest admiration with an earnest request. "I very
heartily congratulate you," wrote Roosevelt in May, "and especially
the people of the United States, upon your selection to lead the expeditionary force to the front . . . I write you now to request that my
two sons, Theodore Roosevelt Jr., aged 27, and Archibald B. Roosevelt, aged 23, both of Harvard, be allowed to enlist as privates under
you. . . . The former is a Major and the latter is a Captain in the Officers' Reserve Corps. . . . PS: If I were physically fit, instead of old and
heavy and stiff, I should myself ask to go under you in any capacity
down to and including a sergeant; but at my age, and condition, I
suppose that I could not do work you would consider worth while in
the fighting line (my only line) in a lower grade than a brigade commander."[9]

Pershing could not lightly say "no" to Roosevelt, to whom he owed
much and shared a common bond. They'd been together in Cuba.

Then, in 1906, President Roosevelt promoted Pershing from captain to brigadier general, jumping him over 257 captains, 364 majors, 131 lieutenant colonels, and 110 colonels—in all, 862 officers senior to him. There was no man in the country to whom Pershing was more indebted than Roosevelt. Despite this, Pershing was at first not sure he'd be able to grant Roosevelt's modest request of 1917. The Wilson administration had already denied Roosevelt himself a chance to muster; and Roosevelt remained a loud, discordant critic of Wilson and his Cabinet. He outright despised them, and they him. That Wilson and his men might deny their enemy's sons the chance to distinguish themselves was a distinct possibility.

A few days before departing for France at the end of May, Pershing had a brief farewell meeting with Secretary of War Newton D. Baker. Near the end of the meeting, Pershing addressed the question of Theodore Jr. and Archie directly. "If I cable requesting that the two Roosevelt boys be sent to France, will you grant the request?" asked Pershing. "Certainly," responded Baker without hesitation.[10] There would be no need, however, for them to serve as privates. With their training at the Plattsburg camp under their belts, they would be officers—Ted a major and Archie a first lieutenant.

Getting one's orders for Europe was one thing; making sure of a place on one of the first, crowded transport ships was quite another. As it happened, General J. Franklin Bell—the commandant at Governor's Island who was also in charge of embarkation—was an old acquaintance of Ted's wife, Eleanor. Through the good offices of General Bell, Ted and Archie were assured a spot on the very first transport to leave after their orders came through.

They sailed from New York for France on 20 June, 1917. The whole family was there to see them off, including their wives, Alice Longworth, Quentin, the Derbys, and of course Theodore and Edith. Roosevelt's mood was one of grim delight. He made some of the party uncomfortable when he was heard to anticipate, with apparent elation, that at least one of his sons might be wounded, or possibly even killed, on the glorious field of battle.[11]

Although named the *Chicago*, Ted and Archie's vessel was a French ship launched in 1908. She was a coal-burning, twin-screw, steel-hulled steamer with a spare deck stem to stern for ocean-watching, and three decks below. For her day, she was fast with a cruising speed of seventeen knots. She was also middling-large at 10,501 gross tons, wireless-equipped—and a tempting prize for German U-boats. One year later, in May, the young ambulance driver Ernest Hemingway would take the same ship from New York to Bordeaux. On both voyages, a French destroyer served as the *Chicago*'s convoy.

ᴣᴏ ᴣᴏ

Unlike Ted, Archie, and Quent, Kermit had not spent much time at Wood's Plattsburg camp. He had only a few weeks of officer training in the spring of 1917. He possessed no real military expertise to speak of but nevertheless left Plattsburg with a recommendation that he be awarded a captaincy in the U.S. army. Kermit, however, doubted the Americans would actually get into combat quickly and, like many other young men, sought to enroll in the Canadian or British ranks as a faster route to action. His father helped expedite things. Roosevelt asked his friends Arthur Lee and Cecil Spring-Rice to help Kermit obtain a position in the British armed service. "It is, of course, asking a favor," he explained to Spring-Rice, "but the favor is that the boy shall have the chance to serve, and if necessary be killed in serving."[12]

Kermit was the Roosevelt brother who was least enthusiastic about the profound, unending competition that defined the relationship of the four, yet he engaged in the competition rather than be left behind. (In other words, he did not disdain the game so much as want to forfeit.) He was the same when it came to war. He might not be partial to it personally, but being a Roosevelt he'd dive right in as expected. "I don't like the war at all because of Belle and Kim [his new son]," he wrote his father, "but as long as it's going on I want to be the first in it."

In another letter written about this time, Kermit gave further voice to his ambivalence about the war while summoning memories of the many adventures he and his father had shared. "The only way I would have been really enthusiastic about going would have been with you," he wrote Roosevelt. "After Africa and South America . . . I wish you were in this war so that I could go off with you again and try for the malevolent hyenas with the courage of simba. . . ."[13]

⤳ ⤳

Ted and Archie touched the shores of France at the end of June. Pulling into the broad, tranquil estuary of the Garonne, they disembarked in Bordeaux, where all the citizens were greatly excited about the arrival of *les Américains*. "To the average Frenchman who had always been accustomed to a sound scheme of preparedness and trained men who could go to the colors for immediate service, we were taken to be simply the first contingent of an enormous army which would follow without interruption," wrote Ted. "The poor people were bitterly disappointed when they found that the handful of untrained men alluded to by our papers in this country as 'the splendid regular army' represented all that we had available in the United States and that ten months would pass before a really appreciable number of troops would arrive."[14]

From Bordeaux Ted and Arch went by rail to Paris. On the train, the same interest in the arrival of the Americans continued. Archie and Ted's compartment was full of French soldiers who asked them all about their plans, the number of their troops, and when more Americans would be arriving. The Frenchmen were unhappy with the answers, as were Ted and Archie.

Upon arrival in Paris, Ted and Arch reported to General Pershing. Pershing assigned Archie to the 16th Infantry and ordered Ted to go with an advance billeting detail to the Gondecourt area, where American troops were to train. Ted was accompanied in his assignment by Colonel (later General) McAlexander, Major (later General) Leslie McNair, and one Colonel Porter of the medical corps. "We knew nothing about billeting," Ted remembered. "The sum total of my knowledge was a hazy idea that it meant putting the men in spare beds in a town and that it was prohibited by the Constitution of the United States."[15]

Major Ted joined the 26th Infantry of the 1st Division, billeted in a town called Demange-aux-Eaux, in mid-July. He was given command of a battalion. His father was delighted. "I am surprised and immensely pleased at Ted's having been assigned to duty as a major in the line," Roosevelt wrote to Archie. "I shall not be a bit disappointed if he ultimately has to serve as a captain or first lieutenant . . . I wish I were over myself; not that I could do very much in the training; but I would have had at least a hundred thousand volunteers, of just the type of those in my [Rough Rider] regiment, in France now if I had been allowed to act six months ago; and as many more ready to follow."[16]

Lieutenant Archie, initially assigned to the 16th infantry of the 1st Division, was stationed not far away from Ted. The posting summoned nostalgia in the old colonel. "I was not only greatly pleased but also greatly interested at your being assigned to the 16th," wrote Roosevelt to Archie that August. "At the San Juan fight the 6th & 16th, under Hawkins, were to the immediate left of our dismounted cavalry. We took Kettle Hill and I found myself in command at the top; and I ordered our men to fire at the San Juan blockhouse and trenches which the 6th & 16th were assailing; we fired until they got so near the top that we were afraid of hitting them. Well, *that* skirmish seems about as far off as Bunker Hill, compared to this war!"[17]

Archie shortly arranged for a transfer to the 26th, where he was to serve directly under Ted. Roosevelt let both his sons know he thought this a bad arrangement, but they insisted on staying together.

The 26th, not to mention the entire 1st Division, was a ragtag gathering of men. As the first hastily assembled combat division sent to France, the 1st Division was put together with what soldiers could be spared from other regular-army units. Of course, the men who could best be spared from the other units were of the bottom of the barrel, and in many cases from the guardhouse. As the optimist Ted was fast to point out, however, guardhouse graduates often made the very best combat troops. But first they had to be taught to follow orders. Ted worked diligently to make the 26th combat-ready, turning what was simply a tough outfit into an excellent fighting machine—albeit one he would sometimes squander in unnecessary and occasionally suicidal heroics.

At the same time that Ted, and under him Archie, worked to bring the 26th into line, they also worked to gain the respect of their fellow officers, all of whom were regular army and therefore inclined to be contemptuous of Ted and Arch's reserve status. The division included a number of majors several years Ted's senior who not only sized him and Arch up for amateurs, but also had them figured for cowboys and adventurers. In this, it was whispered, they resembled their father, without whose famous name they would not have received their stripes in the first place. Given this dynamic, it was imperative that Ted, in particular, prove himself quickly as the master of his men.

In doing so, he was occasionally severe. Once, on maneuvers, he noticed some men marching along rather too quickly under the weight of what were supposed to be full packs. When the packs were discovered to contain nothing but straw, Ted replaced the straw with rocks. On other occasions, he prescribed punishments in amounts of push-ups and pull-ups so extreme that one man, forty years later, recalled the workouts as torture.

But there was more to Ted than punishment. Much of the training he prescribed for his men rested on a foundation of competition. (In this it was not unlike the training for life Ted and his brothers had received from their father.) In one competition, the men were called empty-handed from their billets. Then, on command, they raced back to return ASAP with full equipment; the fastest platoon in each company was excused from reveille the next morning. The quickest in the battalion was given a more substantial reward. Training in combat skills was also competitively based—this much at variance with more mundane training techniques employed by Ted's fellow officers.

Along with gaining a reputation as a stern, uncompromising commander, Ted quickly acquired a reputation for being a "regular" fellow. Even soldiers who resented him as a harsh, demanding commander respected the fact that he did not place himself above the many dis-comforts he inflicted on his men. Some had assumed Ted and Arch would have their noses in the air, that they would think and act as if they were better than everyone else. But this prejudice was gradually dispelled as the brothers performed little acts that soon entered the folklore of the division.

In one instance, Ted and Arch decided the latest food ration was inadequate for the "boys" and, with three of them in tow, went to a nearby farm to buy fourteen chickens with their own money, chickens which they then helped slaughter and pluck. They recalled for the privates how they'd been taught to clean chickens by a cook at the White House who had been there since the days of Lincoln. On an-other occasion, an enlisted man—hesitating during a demonstration when it came time to dive under some barbed wire hung over a muddy bog—was instantly replaced by Major Ted who, even as he pushed through the slime, lectured the privates loudly on how the mud was their friend and how the more they looked like their friend, the mud, the less of a target they'd be. And there was the time when Archie brought out a box of books he had in his tent, telling the men to take whatever they'd like to help relieve the monotony of the camp. Each and every volume bore the bookplate of the voracious reader and ear-nest recycler of books whom Archie had not thought important to mention as the donor: Theodore Roosevelt.

Chapter 11
EVERYBODY WORKS BUT FATHER

*D*espite his poor eyesight and ongoing trouble with his back, 20-year-old Quentin was enrolled in flight training at the Mineola air-drome, on Long Island, not far from Sagamore Hill, in the spring and early summer of 1917. (Quentin and his cousin, Hall Roosevelt—brother of Eleanor Roosevelt—both of whom had poor vision, memorized the eye chart in order to pass their military physicals.) At this point, Quentin had completed two years at Harvard (where he had majored in mechanical engineering and actively participated in Archie's preparedness program) and two summers at Wood's Plattsburg camp. He was now, as his father boasted, "an enlisted man in the Aviation corps, with the rank and pay of Sergeant."[1] (He would be made an officer once he completed his training.)

The boy slept every night in his old room at Sagamore Hill and commuted down to Mineola every day for flight training. On many of his training flights, he would buzz Sagamore, flying low, tipping his wings and waving to his father, who stood on the porch in a white suit, shielding his eyes from the sun with one hand and waving back enthusiastically with the other.

When flying, Quentin usually wore a long, oil-splattered, leather coat and something rather odd to hold his hair in place. "He sometimes went bare-headed with just a pair of goggles," remembered Hamilton Coolidge, his fellow aviator and friend from Groton and Harvard, "but more often he wore a black silk stocking on his head. The stocking was full length and hung down his back like a pig-tail."[2]

In an adoring memoir, written after Quentin's death, Coolidge painted Quent as a master of the art of flying. He described Quentin as a skilled aviator who could easily take any tin can up into the heights and return to earth with touchdowns so smooth that, with eyes closed, one would not realize the flight was over. But in fact Quentin's take-offs were cockeyed, his landings brutish, and his daily routine short on practice of strategic moves that might help one survive a dogfight. Quentin just liked to fly. And he spent most of his time either staging mock attacks on Sagamore Hill or flying lazy circles around his girl-friend's house.

All of Quentin's instructors at Mineola said he was the most affable, down-to-earth, good-natured student they had. Yet he was also the least disciplined, the most whimsical about serious business, and the least likely to succeed. Still, he would pass his course and earn his commission. This, he knew, was a virtual certainty. After all, the country possessed only thirty-five qualified army pilots nationwide—and what was worse, Quentin's training plane at Mineola was one of only fifty-five such aircraft available in all of North America. The army was in no position to waste either the plane or the training. Everyone would pass.

It was sometime that spring that Quentin brought 20-year-old Flora Payne Whitney home to meet Theodore and Edith. Flora, who lived in nearby Westbury, was the eldest child of Harry Payne Whitney and Gertrude Vanderbilt Whitney, benefactors of the Ambulance Améri-caine, with which Anne Harriman Vanderbilt, Gertrude's cousin by marriage, was closely involved. Flora's maternal grandfather, Cornelius Vanderbilt II, was president of the New York Central Railroad. Her paternal grandfather, William C. Whitney, was a lawyer, businessman, and brother-in-law of Standard Oil's Oliver Hazard Payne. He also served as secretary of the navy under Grover Cleveland. Flora's uncle, Arthur Gwynne Vanderbilt, died in the sinking of the *Lusitania*. Her cousin, Whitney Warren, studied architecture at Paris École des Beaux-Arts and was a friend of Ethel's and Dick's.

Flora—along with her younger brother and sister, Cornelius Vanderbilt (Sonny) Whitney and Barbara Whitney—was raised mostly by governesses in her parents' various homes. These included a Fifth Avenue mansion, a seven-hundred-acre estate in Old Westbury, and additional residences in Newport, the Adirondacks, Aiken (South Carolina), and Saratoga. When she became old enough, Flora attended both the Brearley School and, later, the Foxcroft School for Girls.

Flora's father, Harry Whitney, was a great sportsman. Like Roosevelt, he loved hunting, shooting, and polo. Whitney and Roosevelt also shared a fascination with natural history and both strongly supported the American Museum of Natural History in New York City. There, however, all similarities between the two men stopped. Unlike Roosevelt, Harry Whitney's principal occupation was keeping himself entertained. Whitney owned some of the finest thoroughbreds and polo ponies in the world. His horses were a fixture of the British racing scene from 1909 onwards. In 1920 he invaded British polo as captain of the Meadowbrook Club's "Big Four," intent on bringing back the America Challenge Cup that had reposed in England since 1886. After Harry's team won, Flora joined her family in being received by the king and queen of England as well as by other members of the British aristocracy, including her cousin Consuelo Vanderbilt, the former duchess of Marlborough.

Flora's mother, Gertrude Vanderbilt Whitney, was an artist and great benefactor of American painters and sculptors. Gertrude maintained studios in Manhattan, Old Westbury, Newport, and Paris, and was eventually to found the Whitney Museum of American Art, featuring a core collection of seven hundred paintings by such artists as Thomas Hart Benton, George Bellows, Edward Hopper, Maurice B. Prendergast, and John Sloan. Gertrude's sister, Dorothy Whitney, was married to Willard

Straight, the Cornell-educated founder of *The New Republic*. Ethel was a close friend of Dorothy Straight, and both Dorothy and Willard Straight were important supporters of the Progressive Party.

Possessed of fabulous wealth as compared to the Roosevelts' upper-middle-class position, the Whitneys belonged to "the out-door sport wing of the smart set" that Roosevelt considered, on the whole, to be far too "self-absorbed" to be of much use to anyone.[3] Edith in particular disliked the champagne-drenched, polo-playing, horse-racing type of which Harry Whitney was the epitome. Although Flora seemed perfectly nice at table, the first assumption on the part of Theodore and Edith was that she must ultimately be as trivial as so many of her family and class. Over the course of several weeks, however, Flora won over Quentin's parents, completely conquering their prejudice.

Roosevelt began to warm to Flora when he learned her brother and cousin were defying the stereotype of their set. Flora's brother Sonny was training as an aviator. And her cousin Caspar Whitney was with the infantry. (Roosevelt would be delighted when, in January of 1918, Caspar—returning stateside on extended leave to recover from wounds sustained at the front—spoke out publicly about how short supplies and the poor training of American forces conspired to prolong the war. "Caspar Whitney has done a very great service by coming back from the front—especially to escape the censor and tell at least a portion of the truth," he wrote.[4])

Edith warmed to Flora once she realized the girl was entirely out of sympathy with, and alienated from, the flashy social round that defined her parents. Flora made it clear she preferred the understated work-and-duty ethic of the Roosevelts to the glamorous party life of her parents. In the early summer, Quentin wrote his mother a note to say he was glad she liked Flora, now that Edith had "got past the fact that she was one of the Whitneys and powders her nose."[5]

༄ ༄

The youngest Roosevelt, Quentin was the most outwardly light-hearted of them all. While at Harvard, he addressed scores of postcards to Flora on which were not notes, but rather glued-on cartoons clipped from newspapers. Telegrams, too, were used as a style of comedy that exuded carefree, delighted self-confidence:

> FLORA: AM IN IMMINENT DANGER OF RELAPSING INTO BAR-BARISM NAIL BRUSH TOOTH BRUSH SHAVING BRUSH RAZOR ALL LEFT AT WESTBURY DONT MIND THE FORMER BUT THE RAZOR IS FAMILY HEIRLOOM IN FACT IT HAS REMOVED A GREAT MANY HAIRS MY HANDSOME PROFILE BEGINS TO LOOK LIKE A TENTATIVE DESIGN FOR A GERMAN WIRE ENTANGLE-MENT OR A BADLY STIFFENED PILLOW HOWEVER I SHALL BE OUT OF HIDING BY WEDNESDAY TELL GORDON TO BE GOOD TO RAZOR ITS NAME IS MAGINITY[6]

The humorist was no saint. He was, rather, an impetuous young man in uniform. Active, headstrong, and enthusiastic, he often fell out-side the rules of decorum by which a gentleman of his class was meant to govern his life, only to return to them shamefully, full of remorse over his transgressions.

Drinking to excess was, of course, one transgression particularly frowned upon at Sagamore Hill, where the family lived every day with the outraged tribal memory of Quentin's tragic Uncle Elliott. Not long before he left for Europe, Quentin did his own brief joust if not with alcoholism, then with the shame, condemnation, and psychic isolation that are always payment, long or short term, for the sin of combining liquor with excess.

"Talk may be insincere," he wrote Flora contritely in the spring of 1917, "but a letter is not, which accounts for this. I am thoroughly ashamed of myself. Aside from all this, what a hypocrite you must think I am. I have preached disapproval, and said that you shouldn't get drunk with girls around, and then—it is true, tho,—for I have never before acted as I did last night. What is more, I meant what I said, when I talked of such things, and my opinion of myself is pretty low. Last night . . . was absolutely unintentional. Father says that 'didn't mean to' is no excuse. I realize fully that I have no excuse, that there is no excuse. To show that I mean this, and am not going for effect, I agree to abstain entirely from now until—you can fill in the date yourself. Dear Fouf, please do not hold it up against me. I know I acted as no gentleman should, but I apologize from the bottom of my heart. . . ."[7] We are not sure what date Flora filled in, but three months later Quentin was still on the wagon and complaining bitterly about it to anyone who would listen.

"Quentin seems really to be making a success of his flying," wrote Roosevelt to Archie at the end of June.[8] A week later, there was more news of both Quentin and Kermit. "Quentin soon goes over with the first ten flyers to the French Aviation School. Kermit soon sails to report as a staff officer to the British General in Mesopotamia. Everybody works but father! All I can do is wade into the pacifists, pro-Germans and rioters here—which is a pretty poor substitute for work at the front." Roosevelt put an asterisk after the line "Everybody works but father!" At the bottom of the page he wrote: "This shall be my motto hereafter!"[9] Some letters to his sons he signed "The Slacker Malgré Lui"—*the slacker in spite of himself.*

Kermit shortly sailed for England, there to pick up his commission. Inexplicably, despite the grave risk from German U-boats, he brought Belle and little Kermit Jr. (known as Kim in the family) along with him. The plan was for wife and child to spend the war at the home of her parents: the American Embassy in Madrid. Alice Roosevelt saw the little family off on their way to the ship. Years later she remembered Kim's toilet-training seat falling out of the overpacked, half-closed taxi trunk as the car pulled away.

Quentin was to sail 23 July from New York. On his last night at Sagamore Hill, his mother went upstairs as usual to tuck him in. He was still, after all, the baby of the family. The following morning, after a large breakfast, Edith and Theodore accompanied their boy to his ship, which was docked at the 14th Street wharf on the West Side of Manhattan. Flora—now Quentin's fiancée—arrived on the Whitney yacht to say good-bye. She carried with her a small bottle of saltwater, which she sprinkled on his uniform for luck.

When it became clear the departure of Quentin's ship was to be delayed for several hours, his parents decided to cut short the agony of the long good-bye, and departed for Sagamore. Before leaving, Edith hid some homemade bread and chocolate in Quentin's luggage with a note saying it was from Margaret, the Sagamore Hill cook.[10]

After Quentin's parents had left them, he and Flora went for a bite of lunch and then returned to the ship. "Of course it didn't go at two, not till nearly three, so she and I sat on a bale of hides and waited until it was almost time for the boat to go. Then I packed her off for I don't think she could have stood watching the boat pull out. She was wonderfully brave, and kept herself in. I don't know how she did it." He confessed in a letter to his parents that he was pretty "down" after Flora left. He felt worse still later, as his ship pushed through the narrows and he watched the Statue of Liberty and the New York skyline drop below the horizon. "Still, I'll be back sometime within a year, I've a hunch, and anyway, I'm gone now, and there's no use objecting."[11]

To Flora he wrote ". . . if I am not killed, there will be a time when I shall draw into New York again, and you will be there on the pier, just as you were when I left, and there will be no parting for us for a long time to come."[12]

During the trip across the Atlantic, as Hamilton Coolidge recalled, Quentin "was thoroughly enthusiastic about the job ahead; his enthusiasm was fundamental, and seemed to me distinct from that of many of his comrades who apparently acquired theirs in the much talking and speculation that accompanied the after dinner smoke."

At times, however, Quentin's enthusiasm gave way to "black gloom." Taking walks at evening on the deck, which was unlighted so as not to become a beacon for U-boats, Quentin spoke in terms Coolidge would later call "fatalistic."[13] He would not be surprised at all if he did not return; a violent ending on foreign shores seemed, in a strange sense, to be what he'd been born to and groomed for. He did not know why he felt that way, but he did. Destiny beckoned, whether he liked it or not. (After Quentin's death, Ted Jr.'s wife would write to Edith Roosevelt: "Quentin had said to me that if one of the family

had to go, he hoped that he would be the one, on account of the wives
& children of the others."[14]) His favorite poem, prophetically, was Alan
Seeger's "I Have a Rendezvous with Death," with its lines:

> I have a rendezvous with Death
> At some disputed barricade,
> When Spring comes back with rustling shade
> And apple-blossoms fill the air—
> I have a rendezvous with Death
> When Spring brings back blue days and fair.

> It may be he shall take my hand
> And lead me into his dark land
> And close my eyes and quench my breath—
> It may be I shall pass him still.
> I have a rendezvous with Death
> On some scarred slope of battered hill,
> When Spring comes round again this year
> And the first meadow-flowers appear.

> God knows 'twere better to be deep
> Pillowed in silk and scented down,
> Where loves throbs out in blissful sleep,
> Pulse nigh to pulse, and breath to breath,
> Where hushed awakenings are dear . . .
> But I've a rendezvous with Death
> At midnight in some flaming town,
> When Spring trips north again this year,
> And I to my pledged word am true,
> I shall not fail this rendezvous.

Quentin carried a volume of Seeger's verses in his footlocker. Seeger, a Harvard man who died fighting with the French Foreign Legion
on 23 July 1916, only recently had been transformed from poet to
upper-class martyr. Some called him America's Rupert Brooke. Theodore Roosevelt—of whom Seeger had written, "I would go through
fire and shot and shell . . . if ROOSEVELT led"—eulogized him as
"gallant, gifted young Seeger." Seeger's verses, most of which had been

composed during two years spent huddled in billets near Champagne, were Byronic not only in their meter but also in their themes of heroism and noble sacrifice. In "Rendezvous" and other poems, Seeger extolled death for a higher cause as the best of all possible futures. Seeger expressed the same sentiment in letters to his family and essays published in the *New York Sun* and the *New Republic.* His volume of poems, published shortly after his death, became a best-seller. A year later his essays and letters sold just as well. Both books were required reading for sensitive, literate, often fatalistic young men on their way to war—especially young men such as Quentin who came from Seeger's alma mater, Harvard.

Quentin's black gloom must have been exacerbated not only by Seeger's poetry, but also by the relatively uncomfortable conditions on the ship that took him across: conditions created by the threat of the even greater discomfort promised by German U-boats. On this as on all troop-transport vessels, not only were decks unlighted at night, but portholes were plugged up and painted black, creating a great stuffiness throughout the vessel. The days were filled with a seemingly endless round of lifeboat drills. Men were made to keep their life vests on at all times—constant, compelling reminders of lurking potential for tragedy.[15]

Quentin had a private cabin. "It means," he wrote Flora, "that if we strike rough weather, and I am forced to show outward and visible signs of my inward and spiritual discomfort, I can seek the seclusion that my cabin grants without inflicting my woes upon an unlucky room-mate."

His chief occupation on the boat was bridge. He told Flora that either his game would improve or his spending money would be gone by the time Europe heaved into sight. Once one got past the interesting challenge of bridge, life onboard ship went on at "a uniform level of dullness." Quentin's daily round was one that he summarized as "breakfast, sit and read or write, a little boxing with Jim Miller, lunch, shuffleboard, reading, calisthenics, tea, reading, dinner, bridge, and last and best, bed and oblivion to war with its aeroplanes and Huns."

Bed and oblivion became less regular, however, once Quentin's ship had hopscotched up the shoreline of the Eastern seaboard and, on August 5, departed Greenland for Liverpool. After that, Quentin was officer in charge of the men who were watching for submarines. In this capacity he was up most of every night.[16]

Although things onboard were generally "dull and stupid," Quentin enjoyed getting to know his fellow airmen. They were really, he wrote, "a corking bunch." Quent, as the youngest of the group, was referred to as either "Babe" or "Kid." They told him he would be required to underwrite the bar tab for his own baptismal party once they reached Paris.

He missed home. After Flora, the girl he would be gladdest to see again was "that greenfaced old fright who sits on Bedloe's Island to greet those who return to their homes from across the seas": the Statue of Liberty.[17]

Chapter 12

RUE DE VILLEJUST

*D*espite premonitions of doom, there was a certain air of frivolity with which the work of the inevitable and, it was generally assumed, swift defeat of the Germans was carried out. At first, the war was perceived by many Americans, including American soldiers, as but a brief interruption of the usual social round. In a way, it was.

It is important to remember the very worst western land battles of World War I—the trench warfare that included the battles of Ypres, Verdun, and the Somme—were fought by the French and British during the years of American neutrality. The American losses in 1917–1918 were to be tiny compared to the vast slaughter of the previous years. The French absorbed one million casualties at Verdun; the French and English together suffered another million at Flanders. The British lost sixty-six thousand men on the *first day* of fighting at Passchendaele, Belgium; the Russians sustained a million fatalities in Brusilov's breakthrough on the Eastern front—all of these events in 1916 alone. Yet total American casualties at the end of World War I would be just 52,947 killed, 202,628 wounded.

Once the Americans met the Germans in combat, there would be little more than a year to go before the Armistice of November 1918. A year, of course, is quite long enough to be involved in any war. And it should not be assumed that the American soldier had an easy time of things. Nor was his contribution insignificant. The doughboy held the line when the Germans tried to advance in the second battle of the Marne, turned back Ludendorff's troops at Soissons, liberated the hotly contested Saint-Milhiel salient, opened the Saint-Quentin Canal complex of the main Hindenburg Line, captured the bastion of Blanc Mont near Rheims, crossed the near-flooding Scheldt to give Belgian troops bridgeheads to Brussels, and—most important—dove into the Meuse-Argonne front to forestall a German retreat to the Rhine. But still, compared with the war experienced by all other combatant nations, the war of the Americans was relatively brief and in many ways not unlike Theodore Roosevelt's "splendid little war" of 1898.

Levity was everywhere, as was a sense that soldiers would be home in the very near future. "Don't forget that you still owe the party that you promised . . . as soon as this little job of beating up the boche is over I will haunt you on your doorstep until you give that party . . . ," wrote Harry Cushing, a friend of Quentin Roosevelt's, from France to Flora Whitney. "We had a great time coming [across the Atlantic] and had all the thrills there were to have. It was much better than Coney Island on a hot June evening. Our steamer was chased by submarines for two days and the racket made by the firing was far superior to any Fourth of July celebration I have ever attended."

Cushing, a lieutenant, had an easy, noncombat job serving as assistant to the chief of the first section of the General Staff of the Second American Corps. "But war is war," he wrote, "even if I do have strawberries and cream for breakfast every day." He told Flora that, should she care to write him, she'd best not direct the letter through the regular army mails, which were slow, but rather through his financial men in the Paris office of the Morgan Bank.[1] (The Roosevelt boys received their mail via the Paris branch of the Farmers Loan & Trust Company, where a cousin, Oliver Roosevelt, was employed.)

Cushing—with his money, his Paris connections, and the many fine homes in which he was welcome—had ample luxurious options when it came time to take a day or a few days off from duty. So did most young men of Cushing's class, including the Roosevelts.

But the draft army was full of relatively unsophisticated privates from the working class, with limited resources. To provide recreation for them, the Y.M.C.A. set up programs fulfilling the same role the USO would play during World War II. As an institution, the Y in Europe paternalistically sought not only to entertain but also to educate and uplift the young enlisted men. That den of iniquity called Paris was forbidden to enlisted men on leave. In its place, the Y established a system of "Leave Areas" in other cities and provinces. The first of these, in Savoy, included the towns of Aix-les-Bains, Chaméry, and Challes-les-Eaux. Soon another area was established at Aix, the famous spa many of the elite women volunteers of the Y.M.C.A. knew well. Eventually ten such sites were developed. The Savoy area—typical of the others— was set up to host four thousand soldiers at a time, with about six hundred arriving and leaving every day.

Rolling libraries were a part of every Leave Area, and occasionally were sent to the front. Not a few of the books in the library vans were sent by Theodore Roosevelt, who usually sent at least ten used volumes per week to the rolling library program, if not to his sons, for their men. Back in Oyster Bay, Ethel Roosevelt Derby organized a drive to collect books. She spent a Saturday morning helping to erect a fifteen-foot-high doughboy outside the public library. The giant held two signal flags high in the air. The sign below him read: "He is signaling: SEND BOOKS!"

Among the young workers who volunteered for the Y in Europe was Ted Jr.'s wife, Eleanor. In 1917, she and Ted had been married for seven years and had three children: Gracie (five years old), Ted III (three years old), and Cornelius (one and a half). Eleanor knew Paris well. She had spent considerable time there as a child and loved the city. In the spring of 1917, shortly before Ted went overseas, Eleanor spoke to him about the possibility of following him to France and serving in some capacity. The children, she explained, could be left with her mother in New York for the duration of what both Ted and she believed would be a relatively short war.

While not opposed to his wife's coming over, Ted asked that she wait until he had a chance to look into the general situation in France and make sure she would be safe. Eleanor was still waiting to hear from Ted in mid-July when she received word of a new ruling, about to go into effect, that would prohibit the wives of soldiers from traveling to France. Anxious to get across before the ruling became active, Eleanor immediately applied to William Sloane, chairman of the National War Work Council of the Y.M.C.A., to be accepted as a full-time overseas volunteer. Sloane took her up on her offer, and she sailed aboard the *Espagne,* departing New York 24 July 1917—beating the regulation by three weeks and following just one day behind her brother-in-law Quentin.

Ted's father had announced emphatically that *no* women of the family were to go to France until after hostilities had ceased. When apprised of Eleanor's plan, however, Roosevelt was supportive, even enthusiastic. To his delight, her action soon afforded him a sharp jab at Woodrow Wilson. When informed by a reporter that President Wilson's son-in-law was going to France as a volunteer for the Y.M.C.A., Roosevelt grinned ferociously and loudly replied: "How very nice. Mrs. Roosevelt and I are sending our *daughter*-in-law to France in the Y.M.C.A.!" ("[The Y.M.C.A.] does capital work," Roosevelt wrote to Archie, "but it is always in danger of falling into just such sissy business as is implied in permitting young men to dodge out of real and dangerous duty by joining it; the President's son-in-law set a most unwholesome example . . . he should be heartily ashamed of himself. . . ."[2])

Roosevelt likened Wilson's son-in-law to the sons of the Kaiser, who were all posted to safe assignments well away from the line of battle while their father sent hundreds of thousands of other men's sons to death at the front. "The crux of the problem is that Wilson is just the type of man, and represents just the type of thinking, that we are *fighting against,*" wrote Roosevelt. "No wonder he is so uncomfortable with the war; no wonder he wants 'peace without victory.' He would rather avoid defeating his own kind. Our snobbish little boor of a president does not realize the difference between the terms aristocratic and autocratic. They are both, after all, new concepts for him."[3]

Eleanor, as luck would have it, was posted nowhere near the presidential son-in-law who now, thanks to repeated barbs from Roosevelt, found himself a prime embarrassment. The embarrassment was sent to a remote outpost on the Italian frontier, far away from reporters, while Eleanor headed for Paris, where she was shortly put in charge of all Y women volunteers in France. Her assistant was Edith Stedman, daughter of poet and Wall Street financier Edmund Clarence Stedman.

Eleanor's aunt, Alice Hoffman, owned a spacious townhouse backed by a beautiful garden on the corner of the avenue du Bois de Boulogne (now avenue Foch) and the rue de Villejust (now rue Paul Valéry). While Mrs. Hoffman remained in New York for the duration of the war, Eleanor was invited by her aunt to live in the house and make it home base for any and all Roosevelts who found themselves in Paris. (At various times within the next year and a half, the house would give shelter and comfort not only to Ted, but also to Archie, Quentin, Kermit, Dick Derby, his brother Lloyd, and also the Roosevelt cousins George, Philip, and Nicholas. Invariably, when Quentin or any of the boys turned up at the house on the rue de Villejust, the maid would bring a tray loaded with food and then inquire if there was anything that needed mending.)

Mrs. Hoffman usually ran the house with five maids and a laundress. Eleanor, in a concession to the economies required during war, made do with just one maid in addition to the caretaker. The latter was Augusta Girardin—Mrs. Hoffman's former head maid of seventeen years—who lived in the servants' quarters with her husband, a cab driver, and their young son. The woman hired to do the bulk of the cleaning was one Annaïs, a young girl who, according to Augusta, had worked several years for Mrs. Hoffman until, as Augusta put it, "she had a little accident and has a little child."

The great mansion was made somewhat less splendid by the devastating shortages of food, fuel, and other essentials with which Paris was afflicted. In summer it was comfortable, but not so during the unusually cold, snowy winter of 1917–1918. There was no coal to be had for the furnace. "A little stove in the front hall had a stovepipe going up through the curves of the spiral staircase which gave the illusion of warmth on the second floor," remembered Eleanor. During the winter, Eleanor slept in woolen pajamas with sewn feet, a hood, and mittens. There was fuel for a wood fire only occasionally, and hot running water just twice a week.

In spring and summer, Mrs. Hoffman's formerly beautiful garden was a scene that would have made the old woman faint. Rare bulbs had been removed to make way for lettuce and beans. Chickens, ducks, rabbits, and geese, which Augusta now bred in order to have meat and eggs for the table, nipped at rare and exotic flowers that had previously won numerous awards from the Greater Paris Garden Club. "If Mrs. Hoffman does not know, she will not mind," said Augusta philosophically.[4]

༈ ༈

"It seems to me that Sheffield ought to go to Plattsburg," Roosevelt had written his sister Anna concerning her son, William Sheffield Cowles Jr., then 18 and just finishing at Groton. "All of my boys except Kermit have finished their two years there, and Ted and Archie are now in the U.S. volunteer officers reserve corps, available for . . . use in event of war. . . . I regard it as every boy's duty to go at this time if he possibly can. . . ."[5] Roosevelt was delighted when Anna affirmed that Sheffield would indeed spend the summer of 1917 at the camp.

Sheffield's planned Plattsburg stint hit a snag, however. After the United States declared war, the civilian program at Plattsburg was shut down as was civilian training at all U.S. military installations. Plattsburg was henceforth devoted to crash courses for combat officers. Consequently, new camps for the college and school men were opened on properties not controlled by the army—at Plum Island, New York, and several other sites.

"Wilson dislikes courage and patriotism," Roosevelt wrote Anna, "and resents ardor and fervor. He is pursuing with much ingenuity the course best calculated to put a premium on tepid indifference and to discourage the qualities in our boys and young men which above all others ought to be encouraged. He is using his conscription proposal not, as it ought to be used, to make every one serve the country, but to prevent as many as possible from serving the country. 'Universal service' means that every body must serve. He is using it as a means to prevent the very men who can best render service from rendering it. Sheffield and his companions offer a case in point. Training camps should be provided for all such boys. As it is I would suggest that he *and a large body of his friends* arrange to go to the Plum Island or some similar camp."

Roosevelt's letter went on to send regards to Anna's husband, Admiral William Sheffield Cowles, now retired: "*He is doing his part!*"[6] Cowles's part included taking command of several cruising yachts owned by millionaire friends but now used by the Coastal Patrol Power Squadron. The squadron was charged with safeguarding the Connecticut River against incursions by German submarines. "Dear Uncle Will," wrote FDR in his capacity as assistant secretary of the navy, "I am delighted that you are having such interesting work with the River Patrol, and I have a theory that the only reason we have not had a lot more internal attacks, explosions, etc., is because of local patrols of just this kind."[7]

When war came and Sheffield volunteered to be a machine gunner for the marines, Roosevelt was more than satisfied that the young man was making good. "Really, I am more proud of Sheffield than I can say," he wrote to Anna.[8] Elsewhere he spoke admiringly of Sheffield's "rough work—the work of a man, and of a fighting man."[9] When Sheffield had the chance to take a desk job but instead opted to remain in the combat ranks, his uncle was ecstatic. "By George, Sheffield is as fine a fellow as ever wore the United States uniform! It made me thrill with pride to have him refuse to be an aide and stick by his machine gun; it is like him—and like my boys—to wish for a place in the fighting line."[10]

Chapter 13

ISSOUDUN

Quentin arrived in France on 14 August 1917, and was posted as a supply officer (a.k.a. quartermaster) to the American flying school at Issoudun. The camp was located near Bourges, on a clay plain sixty-five miles south of Orleans, and consisted of little more than half a dozen tents and not many more men. The base was pleasant enough in the summer, but going into the autumn, heavy rains turned all of Issoudun into a cold, muddy swamp. In winter there was nothing, one graduate recalled, but frozen mud. "Wretched flying equipment. . . . The flu. A hell of a place, Issoudun."[1]

Among those stationed at Issoudun were not only Quentin's Groton pal Hamilton Coolidge but also Cord Meyer, another old friend. The engineering officer was Lieutenant Eddie Rickenbacker, the leading American ace. Rickenbacker became the most popular man around camp when he designed a fender that kept the airplane wheels from throwing up mud against propellers and breaking them. Another notable Issoudun veteran was Major Carl Spaatz, who ran the camp for several months and in World War II would command the Strategic Air Force.

For most new American fliers trained in the United States on antiquated Curtiss "Jennies," the first task at hand was to learn the French-built pursuit ship called the Nieuport-28. These were machines cast off by the French, who had moved up to the sturdier Spad XIII. Unlike the newer Spad, the Nieuport had a reputation for fragility and a tendency to shed its upper-wing fabric in a dive. However, it was highly maneuverable and fully up to battling German Fokkers.

Over the course of the first few weeks at Issoudun, Quentin and Ham Coolidge progressed from dual flying to soloing and formation flying. The closest they came to any form of combat training, however, was the loopty-loop acrobatics that taught them the moves they would need to survive dogfights.

The acrobatics were treacherous. French instructors showed the students on the ground how to handle their sticks for dive-bombing tail-spins and other tricks. Then the fliers were sent up to try their luck. Occasionally a novice would crash. It was a tragic cost of warfare, but could not be avoided. Without the practice in acrobatics, none of them would stand a chance in battle. Toward the end of the war, the development of "camera guns" would permit more formal instruction of combat flying, but for now acrobatics was as close as Quentin and his colleagues could come.

Ironically, this was just the type of flying that had been frowned upon at the field in Mineola where Quentin had received his first training. "The French monitors make us do all the wild flying stunts that were considered tom fool tricks back home," he wrote his mother. He added that formation flying, however, was even more challenging than stunt flying. "It looks fairly easy . . . but when you get up in the air trying to keep a hundred and twenty horse power kite in its position in a V formation with planes on either side of you, you begin to hold different ideas as to its easiness."[2] Eventually, Quent and his friends would have to go through additional training in the French aerial gunnery school at Cazaux. There they would become practiced at the art of firing live ammunition while flying, a skill they had not yet begun to master.

Like so many U.S. fliers, Quentin was at the end of a long queue not only waiting for training at Cazaux, but also for viable aircraft. At the start of the war, the U.S. armed services (army, navy, and marine corps combined) boasted a total of approximately 300 obsolescent aircraft. The French, by comparison, had 1,700 state-of-the-art Spads at the front and maintained a total force of some 4,700 training and combat planes.

In the first weeks after the declaration of war, French Premier Alexandre Ribot suggested that air power was the best contribution the United States could immediately make to the Allied war effort. The optimistic Ribot requested the construction of 2,000 airplanes (along with 4,000 airplane engines) each month during the first six months of 1918. In July, just as Quentin was departing for France, Congress made a large appropriation for the construction of new aircraft, most of which—as it turned out—would not be ready to fly until after the armistice. In fact, during the month Quentin shipped out, only 78 new fighter airplanes were built in all the United States.

Quentin was to wait some time for his turn to fly in combat. When he finally did so, it would be in a French plane.

ॐ ॐ

Once his course at Issoudun was finished, Quentin, with no place to go, simply continued there as quartermaster. He also picked up extra duties as a supervisor of mechanics.

Every morning, promptly at seven o'clock, a gaudily painted Nieuport could be seen circling the camp. The plane featured a unique insignia on its fuselage, the character of Doc Yaak from Rube Goldberg's *Godbert* comic strip. This was, of course, Quentin "trying out the weather" before the students ascended. Sometimes the plane ducked in and out of low-hanging clouds, at other times it dove, twisted, and rolled in what Ham Coolidge remembered as "extravagant demonstrations" of nice handling.

Although an average pilot at best, Quentin was a first-rate administrator. Under his management, classes—taught by more able fliers than he—took off and returned with more and more precision as weeks progressed. Quentin's forte was order and exactness. Under his friendly command, the mechanics snapped to and worked diligently. Planes were ready on time; and whenever not in the air or in the garage, they were lined carefully on the white chalk line, their sides and undercarriages meticulously cleansed of oil and dirt.

Unlike some other officers, Quentin won the devotion of the mechanics, remembered Ham Coolidge, "by simply not being the type . . . who tried to impress his authority by an abrupt manner and speech." He made a point of showing he respected his men and the work they did; and he went out of his way to see they were rewarded. When the day's work was done, Quentin occasionally led the mechanics on clandestine nighttime raids to neighboring supply depots, there to "borrow" necessary supplies that might otherwise never make it to the flying school. When one enlisted man's 12-year-old daughter became ill with asthma back in Kansas, Quentin, unasked, arranged for the most famous asthmatic in the world, Theodore Roosevelt, to write her a letter of encouragement.

"Everyone who met [Quentin] for the first time expected him to have the airs and superciliousness of a spoiled boy. This notion was erased after the first glimpse . . ." remembered Eddie Rickenbacker. "Gay, hearty, and absolutely square in everything he said or did, Quentin Roosevelt was one of the most popular fellows in the group. We loved him for his own natural self."[3]

A New York policeman, Crain A. Gardiner, sent Theodore Roosevelt a copy of a letter from his son, Sgt. Crain A. Gardiner Jr., one of Quentin's mechanics. "All those bum deals I spoke of are plumb gone now," wrote Gardiner Jr. "We have a real man commanding us now, just like his father I guess, one of Colonel Roosevelt's sons. We have only had him a short while but would do more for him than all the time we knew the other man."[4] Roosevelt was also sent a letter, published in an Indiana paper, from another of Quent's mechanics who said they would follow him anywhere and "he always sees that his men are taken care of before he thinks of himself."[5]

ॐ ॐ

In order to escape the grim camp life at Issoudun, Quentin and Hamilton Coolidge kept rooms ("also a bathroom with a civilized porcelain tub") off base in the home of an affluent French family whom Quentin had befriended. The home of the Norant family at Romorantin was just a short way from the camp; and it was to this civilized retreat Quentin and Ham would go on those weekends when Quent did not prefer the idea of Paris.

"I used to sit there in speechless wonder while Quent rattled away in French and kept the whole family . . . in roars of laughter," remembered Ham. "He seemed just as much at home using French as English, and used his hands so advantageously in explaining things."

When at Romorantin of a Sunday, they often had a French breakfast served in their rooms by the Norant family maid. "A hot bath and the very congenial dinner were great luxuries—but the real luxury was the one that sticks in my mind as more intimately associated with Q.— the Sunday morning French breakfast at ten thirty—no, more about ten it was. The invariable system—almost tradition it grew to be, was this:— Up at 9:45, wash hands, face, and brush hair, put on white wrappers— breakfast in studio at ten—afterwards bath and dress. I shall never forget those Sunday mornings. We used to sit there in that little studio in our wrappers very pleased with ourselves and everything in general after our long night's sleep in civilized surroundings. The windows were wide open to the fresh spring air and clear sunlight and there was no hurry or worry about anything." After breakfast, "which by degrees had changed from the cafe-noir variety to real ham and eggs," they each brought out a handful of letters and a favorite book. Quentin would smoke his pipe, leaf through his mail, and talk about Flora.[6]

ॐ ॐ

"Lord, what a good time we'll have when we are all together again!" Roosevelt wrote Archie. "How many, many things there will be to talk over! I feel just as you do about this war; I doubt whether it will be quite as long as you think; but of course I don't know; and at any rate, long or short, at whatever cost, we must see it through. It is a very hard thing on you four to go; but it would be infinitely harder not to go, not to have risen level to the supreme crisis in the world's history, not to have won the right to stand with the mighty men of the mighty days. . . . It is becoming the custom for families with members at the front to put out flags with a star for each one of the household who has thus gone; and we have hung out our flag with four stars."[7]

While his sons prepared to fight, Roosevelt frustrated and fumed over a host of things. He was exasperated that he was not allowed to raise his own regiment and go over, exasperated at the slow pace of arming and training by the Wilson war cabinet even after war was finally declared, and exasperated at the way the American people seemed unable to share his outrage at the staggering inefficiency with which the war was executed. He was exasperated, too, over his own personal infirmities, which began, more and more, to limit his strength and therefore—in his opinion—his usefulness.

"I often feel fairly sick with impotent rage . . ." he wrote Archie during a moment when he was down, "at my inability to make the authorities show wisdom and efficiency; and the people are so foolish and uninformed that I am obliged continually to hold myself in because if I tell anything like the whole truth they simply do not believe me and I do harm rather than good. I think that they are beginning to wake up; but it is very, very late. It was curious to see how the people for many months refused to realize facts [evidence of inadequate supplies] before their very eyes, such as wooden cannon and dummy autorifles; and under such circumstances it was easy to fool them about less self-evident shortages, such as shoes and warm clothing."[8]

Soon Roosevelt was horrified further when Wilson's secretary of war, Newton Baker, admitted "difficulty, disorder, and confusion in getting things started," but called it "a happy confusion. I delight in the fact that when we entered this war we were not, like our adversary, ready for it, anxious for it, prepared for it, and inviting it. Accustomed to peace, we were not ready."[9]

Roosevelt had always been a bundle of nervous energy: a brilliant man of action—easily bored, rarely satisfied. Throughout late 1917 and most of 1918, his temperament fluctuated. His mood and outlook oscillated, often in step with his personal health, between a pessimistic despair and an optimistic hope that he could indeed educate the public and thereby pressure the Wilson administration to step out of character and act swiftly and decisively.

The ability to proselytize was the one (to his mind, limited) use he saw himself as having; and when he occasionally despaired of his effort, he despaired personally also, looking toward the grim fate he anticipated for himself in those dark moments: that of useless old man. "There is nothing for me to tell you," he wrote to Archie. "I can only gabble and scribble—not satisfactory substitutes for action. . . ."[10] "I almost break my heart over the slowness in preparation; and of course I am powerless," he wrote in another note. "I do not dare to try to tell you anything of real importance, lest the censor take umbrage. Of course I am doing everything I can to make our people put the fight through until overwhelming victory comes. But I am not at all sure that my voice carries any distance, under existing conditions."[11]

Ten years before, his voice had been the loudest in the land. Then he'd been at the height of his political power, and perhaps the height of his physical power as well: taking regular workouts in the White House basement, sparring three times a week in an improvised ring with a professional trainer. Now, while the war raged and Roosevelt kept his name in the papers by chronicling the failures of the Wilson administration, he took steps to restore not just his political health but also his personal health with an eye toward a run at the White House in 1920. Three years since his nearly fatal illness in Brazil he had once again grown obese. His doctors told him he absolutely had to lose weight.

In mid-October of 1917, Roosevelt visited a health camp in Stamford, Connecticut, run by former boxer Jack Cooper. "I have come here for a fortnight to see if I couldn't get into somewhat better condition," he told Archie. "I lead a life of irksome monotony, and the exercises bore until I feel as if I should scream; but I am losing weight, a little; and the people of the house amuse and interest me. Jack Cooper is a retired welter weight skin-glove fighter, with an intimate knowledge of the underworld and an impartially friendly attitude towards both it and the upper world from which his sporting patrons come. The rubber [masseur], Gus Nowke, came here when a year old from Germany, but was in the Spanish war and 'hasn't got no use for them Holzenhollerns,' being pure New York; . . . Margaret Walsh, the housekeeper, chambermaid and waitress must be of Irish descent, but is straight American, and shows me the easy friendliness of an efficient equal. The cook, Rose Hoffman, is a Hungarian lady; her husband was a German. But her son is in the regular army; when I went in to shake hands with her she wept."[12]

At Cooper's, Roosevelt hiked three miles every morning before breakfast, submitted to a daily massage, and then gave himself to exercises under the supervision of professional coaches. All of this led to a minimal waist reduction. When he returned to Sagamore on 22 October, Edith thought he looked more tired than fit. "I fear it was too much a strain on his nerves," she wrote. "I had hoped that since he felt that he could do it, it would be the right thing."[13]

Still, he was robust enough to have some enthusiastic play with Ted and Eleanor's three children when they came for a stay of several days. "This afternoon I took the three down to that haven of delight, the pigpen. I trundled Cornelius in his baby carriage while Gracie and Ted alternately carried and did battle over my long walking stick. We fed the pigs with elderly applies, then we came to a small pile of hay down which I had to slide each of them in turn until I finally rebelled, then halted so that each might get a drink of water."

Roosevelt's letter continued with a revealing passage. "Ted's memory was much clearer about the pigs than about me. He greeted me affably, but then inquired of a delighted bystander—Mary [Mary Sweeney, the maid], I think—'What is that man's name?' At supper, in pure friendliness and from a desire to encourage closer intimacy, he put the question to me direct, in a deep voice. Gracie explained that I was

Grandfather (adding that she had two grandmothers, who were twins) and that Ted was Theodore Roosevelt 3rd. I endeavored to explain that I was the first of that name, but the effort was a failure."[14] The colonel was not the first of that name. His own father, the avoider of Civil War conscription who now went unmentioned, had borne it before him.

ॐ ॐ

The exciting word at the very end of the month was that American troops were finally in the trenches. "We have no idea whether your regiment was among the first, but we are sure that you will soon be there . . ." he wrote Archie. "We are very eager, with an interest both proud and painful, to get news."[15]

He was proud. But he was also realistic enough to be fearful. Knowing his sons as he knew himself, he made a point of cautioning against unnecessary heroics and at the same time urged a retreat to positions of safety in due course. "Of course we wish you to get into the fighting in the line," he wrote Archie. "That is the first thing to be done; you would never be happy if you hadn't done it, and neither would I in your place. If *after* you have been in the fighting line—whether for a long or short-time matters not—you are offered a staff place *in which you can be more useful*, it would then be foolish to refuse it merely because it was less dangerous."[16] He would say much the same thing again a few months later, asking that "a weak minded elderly father . . . be excused for writing that *after* enough fighting I simply can't help hoping that if honorable and useful work is requested of you by your superiors in staff places you will not refuse merely because it is less dangerous."[17]

While his sons fought the war of bayonets and bullets on the line, Roosevelt continued his war of words aimed at revealing the grave inefficiency with which the new draft army was being trained and armed. "I receive on average 15 to 20 invitations to speak a day," he wrote Archie. "About one in a hundred is reasonably worth accepting . . . and yet in a certain number of cases the quality of the persons asking, or the nature of the object, makes my refusing on the whole a trifle worse than my accepting. Even where I am right in speaking the speech is itself, under existing conditions, a matter of extraordinary difficulty. The last half dozen years have shown that the American public can be easily misled, easily puzzled, easily persuaded to acquiesce in folly and not merely forget but applaud tricky duplicity. . . . But the only appeal that will really lift it to the heights of wisdom and strong effort for good must come from the man at the head of affairs; and at present it becomes bewildered and disoriented with the mental effort necessary to understand that the war *must* be speeded up, and that it cannot be speeded up unless there is sharp public reprobation of governmental inefficiency and delay . . . [It is necessary to] deal severely with the pro-Germans and pacifists, [and hold to account] the government officials responsible for any failure to get masses of trained men, airplanes, field guns, auto-rifles to the front. . . ."[18]

"I have *some* effect in hurrying up the war," he wrote with little self-satisfaction. "They [the administration] are afraid of me, and they do endeavor to hurry up the troops, to hurry the building of ships, guns and airplanes, and to make ready for reasonably serious effort, just in order to neutralize what I say. My constant pounding does, in this roundabout fashion, produce some small results—better than nothing."[19]

He had come to despise making speeches, but he continued because "*somebody* has to tell our people the truth; and accordingly I do so—as I am not allowed to act. The country is becoming more warlike, more anti-German, but it is very, very late. Even in Wisconsin I found a hearty response; and the bulk of the Americans of German blood are entirely loyal."[20]

ॐ ॐ

For information about the dismal state of affairs vis-à-vis supplies and training, Roosevelt relied heavily on his sons, his son-in-law, and their friends.

After finishing basic training at Camp Oglethorpe, Dick Derby attended the accelerated officers' training school established at Harvard by the French army. In September, he reported to Yaphank, Long Island, where a new training camp for draftees had just been established. From Yaphank, Dick wrote his father-in-law outraged reports of drafted men arriving to find a great shortage of blankets, uniforms, and rifles.[21]

Shortly, Dick's brother Lloyd was posted to Yaphank as a lieutenant of artillery. During a visit to Sagamore Hill, Lloyd gave Roosevelt precise details on the many shortages and inefficiencies of the camp. Lloyd's men had only two guns, no rifles, and a few borrowed horses with which to train. They had received their cold-weather gear only a few days before Christmas, and the cold weather on the Long Island shore had arrived mid-October. As for shoes, half of them were practically barefoot. And that was not the worst of it. The men's training was inhibited by the fact that Lloyd was forbidden—for reasons unknown—to use the intensive methods of instructions taught at the accelerated officers' programs at Harvard and Yale. Given the inadequate supplies and the sleepy pace of training, Lloyd anticipated an "outburst of weary discontent" once his bored and distracted men realized they might have to wait eight or ten months before being sent abroad.[22]

Roosevelt himself visited a training camp for draftees near Cincinnati and was horrified at the conditions. "They have wooden cannon, and have just begun to get their rifles—mostly old-style krags . . . ," he wrote Archie. "It is just as you say; in spite of the men high up we shall do as the English did under a similar handicap and finally develop a first-class fighting army—just as in the War of 1812 we finally developed reasonably efficient fighting forces. . . . But it is exasperating to think that even a minimum of common sense and forethought would have assured our ending the war with complete triumph last summer. . . ."

Some of the ammunition that Roosevelt's family and friends gave him to use in his speeches and columns backfired. At one point Archie reported that the army in France had been sent thousands of coffins but an insufficient supply of shoes in winter weather. Roosevelt was quick to see Wilson's hand in such morbid preoccupations. "I do not believe that Congress was to blame; all our shortcomings have been due to executive action," he wrote.[23] Roosevelt used Archie's report in a piece he published in the *Kansas City Star*, and there was hell to pay when the information proved wrong. "[Archie] got Father into real trouble by telling father about coffins being sent instead of food & it wasn't true!" wrote Ethel to Dick. "All the casket makers in America protested I believe!"[24]

Soon there was another flap when Roosevelt quoted Archie yet again. Roosevelt wrote to Ted to apologize when both Ted and Archie were rebuked by their colleagues after it was rumored they'd asked their father to use his influence to prohibit the sale of liquor to enlisted men. "I am both angered and mortified at my folly in having quoted— although quite properly, as an abstract proposition—Archie's statement about having become prohibitionist—*which I gather was an overstatement, any way!* At the time, there was a strong movement here to stop the sale of liquor round the encampments. Gen. Pershing's order [against liquor sales at training camps domestically] was nullified. And in backing it, and the moment, I mentioned that one of my sons had said that his experience in the war had made him a prohibitionist. There could be no real criticism of this, and none was made. Nevertheless I ought to have kept my head shut. . . ."[25]

In the midst of all this, Flora was a frequent guest at Sagamore Hill. She stopped by regularly from her parents' home in Westbury. Letters from Quentin were always a good excuse; she shared the less romantic ones with Edith. Sagamore seems to have been something of a refuge for the quiet, contemplative Flora who sought meaning and substance among the Roosevelts. "I have just returned from spending the afternoon at your place," she wrote Quentin. "And how I loved it and hated to leave to come home to a wild house party and an unsympathetic family."[26]

Dick Derby sailed to join the American Medical Corps in France on 12 November 1917. Shortly after, Roosevelt and Edith took Ethel and Flora with them to Canada where Roosevelt was to speak on behalf of the war-bond effort at the invitation of the Canadian prime minister.

In bringing Ethel along, Roosevelt and Edith hoped to distract her after the departure of Dick. In bringing Flora along, they hoped to signal their approval of her as a new recruit to the family.

Ethel, who was used to the crowds and the excitement with which her father was routinely surrounded during public occasions, found the trip both exhilarating and relaxing. Flora, who had never before been part of the whirlwind that was Roosevelt's political life, found it terrifying. She wrote Quentin from Hamilton, Ontario, that she was frightened all the time Roosevelt was making his speech. All she could think of was what an easy target he would be.

At Toronto, the party was driven in a motorcade through streets thronged with cheering people. Roosevelt spoke in the enormous armory downtown. Among the thousands of people who came to hear him were many in uniforms and, remembered Ethel, "legless ones wearing their crutches with great pride in them." Ethel also noticed "women in black but with heads high. . . ." All around were posters saying things like: "If money will bring your boy back, give all you can" and "Over the top with your dollars."[27]

Roosevelt reported to his son Ted that he had been received in Canada "with frantic enthusiasm. It was one of the rare occasions when I did not mind speaking, for it was ad hoc. They are raising a new loan, and are in the throes of an election to decide the question of conscription and I was anxious to do anything which they thought would help them. Flora was a dear. It was, naturally, the first thing of the kind that she had ever seen, much less taken part in, and she was absorbedly interested and was a great companion for Ethel. . . ."[28]

Flora and Ethel were, in fact, beginning a friendship that would span a lifetime. Ethel wrote to Quentin saying of Flora that "the family were all perfectly devoted to her and thought her a very fine person."[29] The girl passed muster. Only one formality remained before she would be an official Roosevelt.

Chapter 14

PATER FAMILIAS

$\mathscr{A}$ few days before Christmas of 1917, Eleanor sent her mother-in-law, Edith, a nostalgic note from war-torn France. She said she could think of nothing but Christmas at Sagamore Hill. Poignantly, she detailed all of her fondest memories: going out to select the tree in the woods behind the house, the sound of Roosevelt chopping, and later Roosevelt's annual Christmas visit to the children at Cove Neck School, for whom he played Santa Claus. There was also the recollection of the huge roaring fire in Sagamore's wide hearth, and everyone trooping up to bed but Theodore, and Edith wrapping his gifts for him. Her memory of Christmas mornings was of the whole family sitting on Edith and Theodore's bed opening their stockings. Then there were the presents, the roast pig dinner, and the requisite game of Hearts in the evening. "Well," wrote Eleanor, "this year the 'lonely lights are shining on the ocean far away,' but we must keep on thinking hard of the time when we will have it all again, and we will all sit down around the fire and you will knit, and there will be someone stretched out on the lion [the lion-skin rug], and we will all be happy again."[1]

There was a coal famine in New York that December. As a result, several days before Christmas, Eleanor and Ted's three children were scheduled to leave the Manhattan apartment of their maternal grand-mother for an extended stay at the Westchester home of a maternal great-aunt. Thus, on Friday 21 December, a trainload of commuters on the North Shore branch of the Long Island Railroad were treated to the sight of a rotund ex-president moving gingerly down the train aisle balancing a plethora of gifts for his soon-to-be-evacuated grand-children.

For his granddaughter Gracie he brought three boxes of doll's fur-niture. For Cornelius he carried "a very meritorious and brilliant duck on wheels." And there was a set of toy trains for Ted III. Roosevelt was delighted with how Gracie, in a real "little girl way," at once sat down, made the covers of the three boxes into three rooms (which she explained were the dining room, drawing room, and bedroom), dis-tributed the furniture accordingly, and paid no attention to the toys of the little boys.[2]

Later in the day, return passengers on the railroad were amused to see Roosevelt once again, this time juggling even more packages. He'd done more shopping while in Manhattan. What he carried now in-cluded several dozen small packages that he would distribute to his "little oysters," as he called the children at the Cove Neck School. Then there were the presents for his Derby grandchildren, who were spending Christmas at Sagamore, and a few things for the children of his groundskeeper, Gillespie.

On Christmas morning Richard Derby Jr. opened his stocking in his grandparents' bedroom, and after breakfast received his big presents in the parlor. "Little Edie, smiling and crowing, in a white dress with pink ribbons, was brought down to the latter ceremony and I was allowed to hold the darling, cuddling thing most of the time," recalled Roosevelt. After breakfast, he walked through rain which turned to wet snow to give the Gillespie children their presents. "These included a globe of goldfish for the smaller-girl, which I had carried out in the train from New York with considerable agony."[3]

ॐ ॐ

Quentin spent Christmas on medical leave in the house on rue de Villejust with Eleanor. He'd been sick for more than a month—tended by an old friend of Flora's from her days at the Foxcroft School, a nurse with the Red Cross stationed at the 3rd Aviation Instruction Center. Her name was Irene Givenwilson.

Hamilton Coolidge came back to Issoudun after a leave in early December to find Quentin quite ill, though still at his duties. Coolidge tried to convince Quentin to go to bed, but he would have none of it. Several other officers were already down with the grippe and someone needed to stay on his feet and see that things got done. "He said he couldn't leave his work, and went right ahead," recalled Coolidge. "That is when he really did become sick." While his fellow officers had the grippe, it turned out Quentin had pneumonia, which Ham and a few others contracted as well.[4]

All during the fall he had—like everyone else at Issoudun—lived through a horrible time of mud and cold compounded by no decent quarters and a grueling work schedule. "[Quentin] was terribly sick with pneumonia and so were Ham Coolidge and Seth Lowe, to a lesser degree," Irene Givenwilson recalled. "I would not let any of them go to the camp hospital. You can guess what such places are like, so I just nursed them in their own bunks, and finally Eleanor came down and carried Q. off to Paris . . . He was away from here for three weeks, and when he came back, he seemed very thin for him."[5]

At Eleanor's house Quentin gradually regained his strength. When he felt up to it, he and Eleanor went walking about town buying gifts to send Ted and Arch, who were spending Christmas with their unit. Shortly after Christmas, Quentin left Eleanor in Paris and went by train to spend a few days by himself on the French Riviera, where he did a fair bit of gambling and losing, before returning to Issoudun.

ॐ ॐ

That January, Roosevelt delighted in a glowing portrait of Ted written by Heywood Broun, war correspondent for the New York *Tribune*. Broun described Ted as alert and efficient and emphasized how the young officer had overcome the initial prejudice against him among regular officers. Roosevelt wrote Ted to say how proud he was. But even as he basked in pride, he also fretted about the conditions his sons and other people's sons were being made to endure. "The accounts of the arctic weather in France have of course given us constant anxiety about you and Archie. We know the hardships you and your men are encountering. Here the zero weather has caused us a discomfort which was comic rather than serious—altho [sic] it has been serious enough for the poor people, and a good many who were not poor, in New York."[6] Roosevelt took the coal famine as a sign that not only was the administration criminally inefficient in matters of war, but in domestic affairs as well.

He traveled to Washington in mid-January, installed himself at Alice's house, and began lobbying for the assembly of a War Cabinet (modeled after the special War Cabinet active in Great Britain) to take the management of the military out of the inept hands in which it now resided. Only then, said Roosevelt, would the country see an end to chronic arms shortages at the front, unsanitary conditions and sickness at training camps, and the rampant inefficiency that seemed to manifest itself everywhere throughout the military bureaucracy. George E. Chamberlain (chairman of the Senate Military Affairs Committee) introduced a bill to create just such a War Cabinet comprised of "three distinguished citizens" who would take responsibility for directing and planning all war-related activities.

On the heels of this, Roosevelt held a press conference in Alice's living room. Speaking to thirty-three reporters, he criticized not only the inefficient implementation of war plans thus far, but also Wilson's recently enunciated "Fourteen Points," which Roosevelt remarked were nothing more than "fourteen scraps of paper." This master plan for peace, with its aim of "peace without victory" and the formation of a "league of peace," represented, said Roosevelt, not the unconditional surrender of Germany but the conditional surrender of the United States to the overriding sovereignty of the international league.

Privately Roosevelt had little hope a War Cabinet would be formed or, if it was formed, that he would be awarded a seat. His real ambition, for the moment, was purely rhetorical. His real sights were on a Republican sweep in the Congressional elections to take place the following autumn. There was a good chance of this. Wilson's popularity was in decline. He'd won reelection over Hughes by only a narrow margin of electoral votes the previous year. Assuming victory in 1918, Roosevelt had hopes that he would then be able to seize the Republican presidential nomination—and, indeed, the White House itself—in 1920.

A year before, he had been viewed by many as nothing but an angry, bitter old man lusting for a war in which the young might die. But now he was viewed as someone who'd spoken with a prophetic voice of reason. The more horrible the state of U.S. military preparedness appeared, the more correct and wise, in retrospect, Roosevelt seemed to have been. His stock climbed higher and higher with every new revelation of soldiers without guns and pilots without airplanes. "If we'd only listened to the warnings of Roosevelt!" editorialized the *Herald*.

At Alice's house, Roosevelt subjected himself to a grueling, nonstop round of conferences and interviews going on for several days. A steady string of Republican operatives came to see him—progressives and conservatives, senators and congressman, army and navy officers, and representatives of labor unions—all smelling Democratic blood and looking for just the right shark to send in for the kill. Very few doubted that the man to lead them was Roosevelt.

One day, in the middle of a meeting, Roosevelt felt a sharp pain in his stomach that he described to Alice as "severe indigestion." He took to his bed, but was well enough the next morning to hold a breakfast conference with eighteen supporters and follow that up with a full day of meetings. When he left Washington at the end of the month, he was feeling confident.

ॐ ॐ

The pains, however, continued. What he'd thought was indigestion turned out to be something else entirely. The first week of February 1918 found the colonel in Roosevelt Hospital—the Manhattan establishment endowed by his distant cousin, James Henry Roosevelt. The situation was grave. Poisons were spreading throughout his body from unhealed abscesses in his right leg (remembrances of the River of Doubt) and two more abscesses in his ears. The doctors feared the poisons were affecting the functioning of Roosevelt's intestines, and he was already quite weak after several hemorrhages.

In an hour-long operation, the doctors punctured Roosevelt's ears, found the abscess in each, and dissected and removed a fistula with a long sinus.[7] At first this small operation seemed to remedy the problem, but then signs of aural infection returned and the doctors recommended a mastoid operation, a procedure that in those days had a high mortality rate. There was a very good chance Theodore Roosevelt might die. Reporters crowded the lobby of the hospital.

Edith moved into a room adjacent to that of her 59-year-old husband and stayed there, refusing to go home. Alice and Ethel shared duty with Roosevelt's secretary, Josephine Stricker. Spelling each other, the three women answered the telephone beside Roosevelt's sickbed (which never seemed to stop ringing) and handled such correspondence as Roosevelt was able to gather himself to deal with. He focused most of his little energy on seeing that his hand-picked candidate, a progressive from Indiana named Will Hays, secured election as chairman of the Republican National Committee.

One of the first things Hays did in his new capacity was to announce that the nomination of Roosevelt for the presidency in 1920 was a virtual certainty. Even William Barnes Jr., the Republican boss who'd dragged Roosevelt into court for libel in 1915, was now a supporter.

When another politician told Barnes that Roosevelt would likely be nominated in 1920 by acclamation, Barnes answered, "Acclamation, hell! We're going to nominate him by assault!" Not only would the party ask him, it would not countenance anything but acceptance of the nomination.[8] From his hospital bed, Roosevelt commented to Alice that all he need do now was live to claim his prize.

"I hated to have you worried in any way, but I loved your sending the cable of inquiry," Roosevelt wrote to Archie. "Mother has written you about my sickness. I hope I need not tell you that all I thought about in connection with it was to wish that it were in my power to guarantee the safety of one of you boys by any such trivial business as this. Really I have been as comfortable as possible, everything clean and with the devoted attention of the doctors and nurses, and Mother staying in the hospital and sister [Alice] and Ethel in every day. I tell you I would give anything in the world if I could feel that half as much would be done for each of you. . . . My trouble is merely due to some complications concerned with the abscesses and fever that have lasted over since the Brazilian trip four years ago. Curiously enough I seem to have had most trouble from a side show in the shape of abscesses that started in both of my ears. The hearing in the left one seems to have gone, but I guess the other one will come through alright and I shall practically be as well off as ever."[9]

By the end of the month, he was feeling well enough that Edith left him to spend three days at Sagamore Hill with Ethel and the children. Roosevelt was looking forward to going home himself shortly, at the start of March. Although feeling much better, he reported to his daughter-in-law Eleanor that his left ear had gone deaf. With the loss of the ear he'd also lost much of his equilibrium, so that he walked "more like a lunatic duck than anything else." The doctors told him it would be two or three months before he was free from dizziness and able to move around "without considerable care."[10]

ॐ ॐ

Roosevelt was still in the hospital when word came that Archie's wife, Grace, had given birth to a baby boy in Boston. The boy was named Archibald B. Roosevelt Jr. Archie himself was to get the news from a notice published in the Paris *Herald*, the newspaper most often distributed to men in the line. "Well, think of little Archie being born with his father just promoted to a Captaincy and in the trenches," Roosevelt wrote to Archie. "He will have every right to be proud of his parents!"[11] The grandchildren were beginning to add up: There were Ted's three, Ethel's two, and Belle Roosevelt had given birth to a second son, Joseph Willard Roosevelt, that January at the home of her parents in the American Embassy, Madrid.

Just a few weeks after the birth of Archie Jr., and not long after Theodore Roosevelt was released from the hospital in early March, Archie Sr. was severely wounded by flying shrapnel, which shattered a kneecap. Another piece of shrapnel broke one of his arms and severed the main nerve. For this he was awarded the Croix de Guerre. A friend wrote Grace Lockwood Roosevelt with a vivid description of the unconscious Archie lying in bed while "the Cross lay on the pillow to his right. . . ."[12] Archie was to remain in Blake's Hospital, Paris, for four months.

The news of Archie came to Sagamore Hill in spurts all day on 13 March. Roosevelt was the one who answered the door early that morning, when newspapermen knocked to tell the colonel that Archie had been awarded the French Cross, and to ask for a comment. Roosevelt said he was of course proud, but made no further statement as he had no information and no idea of the circumstances surrounding the medal. Then an understated telegram came from the War Department saying Archie was slightly wounded. This was followed by a cable from Ted giving the full details of Archie's extensive injuries.

"I hope dearest Eleanor is with you now," Roosevelt wrote his Archie. "Ethel called up darling Gracie on the phone; naturally her pride and anxiety were even greater than ours. Fortunately your letter to her, saying that you had seen in the Paris *Herald* about the birth of your small son, had just come—what became of our various cables I have no idea. Thank Heaven, Ted's cable was not similarly delayed! . . . At lunch [with Ethel and a guest] Mother ordered in some Madeira; all four of us filled the glasses and drank them off to you; then Mother, her eyes shining, her cheeks flushed, as pretty as a picture, and as spirited as any heroine of romance, dashed her glass on the floor, shivering it in pieces, saying 'that glass shall never be drunk out of again'; and the rest of us followed suit and broke our glasses too."[13]

In a letter written the same day to her husband, Ethel Roosevelt Derby filled in a portion of the scene that the colonel did not sketch for Archie. "At lunch we drank Archie's health & broke the glasses. And there were tears in Father's eyes."[14] The Madeira, as Archie would have known, was from a rare, reserved store kept in the basement at Sagamore Hill and broken out only on the most special occasions. This was one of the very last of a few choice bottles once belonging to Edith's grandfather, Isaac Carow, whose wine cellar, fifty years before, had been considered the finest in New York state after that belonging to the Vanderbilt family.

Ethel Derby had a keen sense of how her brothers constantly competed with one another in all aspects of life. She knew that the competition would be no less fierce when it came to wounds, scars, medals, and other tokens of war. She told her father she could imagine how Ted felt after Archie's brush with death. He was probably "a very sad and envious bunny." He could stand Archie having either the wound or the medal, but that he should have both would seem to Ted unfair.[15]

Ethel said much the same to General Leonard Wood when he visited Sagamore a few days later. Wood was just back from an inspection trip at the front. He had not run across Archie, but he'd seen Ted and Quentin, both of whom he said were looking very well. Quentin, Wood reported, was quite happy to have finally got to spend a few weeks at the French aerial gunnery school before returning to Issoudun. Wood went on to say Ted's battalion had a reputation that surpassed all others in the army. But the General also had plenty of bad news to report—news of the scarcity of field guns, machine guns, and aircraft. Wood told Roosevelt he needed to step up his rhetoric as regards the lax schedule for the manufacture of arms. Indeed, Wood criticized TR's most recent comments on war-planning as being "moderate to the verge of timidity."[16]

Wood's commendation of Ted and his comrades was seconded less than a month later when G.T.M. "Tom" Bridges—a British general who'd recently lost a leg in the war—came to lunch at Sagamore Hill. He told Roosevelt the First Division was the only American unit the French and English considered to be fully up to battle requirements.[17] Ted in particular won praise from Brigadier General George B. Duncan, who wrote that the process of training for and then engaging in combat against the Germans "resulted in the relief of some older officers and placing responsibility upon more ambitious youngsters." Ted Jr., said Duncan, was an exceptional example of the latter. "I have never known a harder working, more conscientious leader," wrote Duncan.[18]

૱ ૱

If Ted was perturbed about Archie's Croix de Guerre, then he was probably even more put out to learn Kermit had received the British War Cross for gallantry in command of a light-armored motor battery.

Kermit saw his first real fighting in January at Tikrit, Iraq, during a major phase of the British offensive against the Turks. His armored LAM Rolls-Royce, moving in formation with dozens of others like it, seemed not only out of place geographically, but also displaced in time as it moved past the ancient mountains and settlements that skirted the banks of the Tigris and Euphrates. (After the war, when he wrote a book about his exploits with the British, Kermit titled it *War in the Garden of Eden*.)

The armored car did not have the firepower of a tank (in fact it had but one mounted machine gun), but it was excellent for fast moves across country and swift, startling attacks. In the staggering Middle Eastern heat, Kermit's men usually rode on the LAM car's running boards until it came time to engage the enemy, at which moment they jumped inside, slammed the steel doors shut, and began firing out the rifle holes. The armor provided only limited protection, however; at least one of

Kermit's men was hit in the face by enemy fire while inside the car and later died of his wounds.

What Roosevelt would call Kermit's finest hour—and what the candid observer must call not his finest but his luckiest hour—came during the battle for Baghdad.

In his book, Kermit would write that whenever he thought of this fight, the memory of a terrible, sickening stench accosted him like a scent put up from hell. It was the smell of hundreds of Turkish camels and men, killed in the battle, going quickly bad in the dry desert heat. In the midst of this macabre landscape, Kermit came upon the wounded remnant of a Turkish platoon holed up in a house. Foolishly, he kicked open the door and ran into the building in front of his men, forgetting to draw his revolver. Before he knew what he was doing, he pointed his swagger stick (one of several British affectations he'd picked up) at the commander of the Turkish group and demanded they surrender. Either the stars or the gods were with Kermit; the heavily armed Turks complied. The episode won Kermit his Cross.

చ౩ చ౩

"At last Mother and I have seen darling Gracie and the blessed wee son," Roosevelt wrote to Archie on 31 March. "I had to speak in Maine, and had been obliged to argue with the doctors to let me go. So last Wednesday (this is Sunday) Mother and I went to Boston, where we stayed with Sturgis Bigelow. Thursday I went to Portland, accompanied by Joe Alsop, while Mother stayed in Boston; and the next morning I rejoined her. In the forenoon I went to 111, and Gracie showed me little Archie in his bath; and then I held him for about half an hour while I talked with Gracie and Mrs. Lockwood and told them stories about you when you were a small boy. . . . The baby is a darling little fellow, and certainly does look like you. He is very sturdy and smiles continually."[19]

Addressing members of the Maine Republican Party on 28 March, Roosevelt gave a speech that was meant to serve two functions. First, it was to be the keynote for Republicans looking toward the autumn

Congressional elections. Second, it was a preview of Roosevelt's 1920 presidential platform. In these connections, the speech was seen in advance and approved by such conservatives as Root, Taft, and Lodge, the progressive Republican Hiram Johnson, and several members of Congress whom Roosevelt described as "labor Republicans."[20]

Pledging the Republican Party "to war to the hilt," Roosevelt cast the G.O.P. as a distinct alternative for any and all voters unhappy with Woodrow Wilson's hopes for a mediated peace. In his sermon to the Republicans of Maine, Roosevelt said the G.O.P. must take pains to position itself as the party of absolute victory in Europe: the party of unconditional German surrender. Then looking forward, to after the war, Roosevelt said Republicans must endorse a strong defense infrastructure (thus avoiding the danger of unpreparedness in the future). Building upon this one cornerstone of stability, he went on to walk a rhetorical tightrope between the various conflicting interests that he recognized must form the coalition behind any Republican success in either 1918 or 1920.

Calling for industrial reform, he sketched a program meant to reconcile the interests of both labor and capital. He said he meant for the federal government to take an activist stance in arbitrating the divisions between unions and industrialists, lest the working class become easy prey for "the sinister demagogues and loose-minded visionaries who preach red folly . . ." and lest capital become indentured to the "tyranny of the mob." There must, he said, be a basic level of "economic justice and well-being or no high moral standard can be permanently maintained." Business could not be permanently successful nor could the commonwealth itself permanently stand on a safe basis unless the nation as a whole conscientiously strove to make the working man in some real sense a partner in the businesses in which he worked.

Along with protection and economic justice for industrial workers, so too, he insisted, must there be the same for small farmers. "It is a mere truism to say that the property of the farmer stands as basic to the prosperity of the nation," he said. "On the whole, in every great crisis in the past, the farmer has stood as preeminently the arch-typical [sic]

American, who in peace and in war took the lead in the work without which the republic must succumb. In our country the typical farmer has been the man who owned the land which he himself, with his own hands, assisted by his sons and by one or two hired men, tilled—and this is the farmer of whom I especially speak. We cannot afford to have him supplanted by the man who merely holds his land as a tenant for an absentee owner. We cannot afford to have his land absorbed by a big landowner."

While he called for activist federal regulation of industries and agriculture, Roosevelt nevertheless insisted that such regulation must be balanced and restrained. For example, he foresaw no federal limits on production, no federal price-fixing, no undue meddling with the marketplace whatsoever. "Our aim must be to help business, not hamper business," he proclaimed. "We should accept the fact that big business deserves fair treatment and should not be penalized; but that it should not be left unregulated, uncontrolled. The nation must be the master of the corporation; not in the least to destroy the corporation; on the contrary, to help it and to see that an ample reward comes to those who invest in it and who manage it; but to see also that no injustice is done competitors, that the public is served, and that the labor men, the workingmen, are treated as in effect partners who must have their full share of the prosperity."

In this spirit—in lines of the speech that must have received enthusiastic approval from many conservative Republicans—the old trust-buster Roosevelt implied that the day for rigid, strenuous enforcement of the Sherman Anti-Trust Act had passed. "The Sherman law at first did good for it stopped the uncontrolled riot of the big businessmen who wished to be a law unto themselves and to absorb all business, and it definitely established the supremacy of the federal government over them," he declared. "But for the last ten years it has done serious mischief, far more mischief than it has done good. It is foolish to object to large scale business. The telegraph and telephone, steam and electricity, have rendered large scale business an absolute necessity."

Returning to Sagamore after the Maine trip, Roosevelt and Edith found it a lonesome, somber place—even with spring approaching. One step they took to cheer up the mansion was finally, after years of procrastination, to install electricity. Then, to further dispel the gloom of the house that had previously been lit by the presence of so many fresh young faces, Ethel and her two children were invited to come and stay for a number of months.

Ethel routinely scolded the doting grandfather, telling him he must not continually pick up his granddaughter Edith and hug her, because— reported Roosevelt—"of the damage it does her moral character." For his grandson Richard, he repeatedly read "the book about the nice horsey," which, said Roosevelt, was "the excessively inappropriate ti-tle" the boy had chosen for a South African hunting book in which most of the pictures depicted the hero on horseback.[21]

Richard provided a wealth of distractions. When Edith asked the boy to call his grandfather to supper, he flew to the window and called loudly, "Theodore." Then he looked roguishly at his mother and said, "I'm going to call you *Efful*!" When asked what his father was doing in the army, the boy answered, "He's trying to be a soldier." Ethel told Dick she thought there was a tone of accusation in the word "trying."[22] When Roosevelt tucked Richard into bed at night, the boy insisted Grandfather sing him "Onward Christian Soldiers," which his father had always sung to him.[23] After Ethel gave Richard some tiny china bunnies to play with, saying they were from Dick, he tried to telephone his father to say that he loved them. "He takes off the receiver and says that he wants 'War.' This is how he insists on getting you," wrote Ethel.[24]

For about a month, starting at the end of April, Grace and baby Archie lived at Sagamore Hill as well. The baby, Roosevelt reported to his son, "is such a sturdy mite, with an absurd resemblance to you when you were small. I am allowed to hold him, as I am an expert in holding small babies."[25] He said he did not want Gracie to leave. "I wish she would stay here until the war is over—and as long afterward as you and she desire! Whenever I get permission I pick up wee, solemn Archiekins and carry him round in my arms, and croon to him."[26]

The grandchildren added an air of activity to the otherwise quiet household; and so did the work of installing the electricity. "All over the house I hear the electricians calling imploringly, always for more cable," wrote Ethel. "It's almost as bad as a piano tuning. But my, won't it be nice to have it in? I wonder now why Mother never had it done before."[27]

Late in April, the naturalist Theodor Roosevelt reported to Archie that the weather was still "bleak and cold, but spring draws on. Near the frog spring the hillside across the hollow is ablaze with blood root. Many other birds are beginning to join the chorus of the robins."[28] He wrote something very similar to Kermit, who by now was tired of deserts and hungry for descriptions of what he called "green things."

Kermit was anxious to get out of the Middle East. By mid-April the season for active operations in Mesopotamia was closing. Kermit hoped to join the American army in France, and his father sought to pave his way. He wrote General William March, Chief of Staff, to find out whether Kermit could be transferred to the A.E.F.[29] General March obliged. Kermit was transferred to the U.S. army as captain of artillery within a matter of weeks. "By permission," Roosevelt wrote Ted, "I have called [Kermit] to go at once to Madrid, where his orders will reach him, so he will get a glimpse of Belle and the babies. I am exceedingly glad that he should now be in American uniform."[30] From Madrid, Kermit was to proceed to Paris, there to attend a French artillery school before beginning active duty with the A.E.F.

༝ ༝

He slowly regained his strength after leaving the hospital at the beginning of March. He was riding again by mid-May, though on what he described to Kermit as "a clergyman horse of the safest-type, one which Ethel also occasionally rides." Still, the tame beast enabled Roosevelt to "go about the country and see the woods and wildflowers. Soon mother and I will begin to go out in the little rowboat."[31]

༝ ༝

Early in the war, Theodore and Edith were greatly amused by an advertisement appearing in a local Long Island newspaper:

MEN ATTENTION!

You are going to the front. Have you made arrangements to have your home defended during your absence? I make a specialty of defending homes during the duration of the war. I guarantee to keep the Hun from your threshold or will make no charges. My terms are as follows:

To defending one home and one wife, $25 per month.
To defending one home and one dearly beloved wife,
$40 per month.
To defending one home and one dearly beloved wife
and one child of either sex, $50 per month.
An additional charge of $10 per month for each child.
Reduced charges to Rooseveltian families.
Telephone Westbury 139

J.C. Cooley
Maple Avenue
Westbury, L.I.[32]

Clipping the advertisement from the paper with a grin, Roosevelt turned serious when he told Edith *he* would look after the Rooseveltian families, despite the promised discount.

In addition to seeking company for himself and Edith by having the grandchildren about, Roosevelt was also seeking to provide shelter, insurance, and comfort for his family generally—whether they happened to be under his roof at the moment or not. He let them know in no uncertain terms that all Roosevelts and Derbys had a place at Sagamore Hill while the men were away, just as they would after the men returned.

To Eleanor he wrote: "If I had plenty of money I'd build rambling additions to this house, connected with it by galleries, each addition being practically a little house by itself: one for the Ted Jr.'s, one for the 'little Derbys,' as Mother calls them, and so on . . . and all to be kept for visits at any moment and for any length of time by those for whom they were designed—all the beloved little families."[33]

Likewise Roosevelt sought, during this time when U.S. forces were still suffering from chronic lack of supplies, to include as members of his extended household those who served with his sons. "Remember," he wrote Archie, "if you must have shoes for the men get them in Paris and I'll pay for them."[34] In addition to shoes and boots, Roosevelt also funded the purchase of blankets, food, and even ammunition.

He was earning $25,000 annually writing a weekly column for the *Kansas City Star*, and an additional $5,000 annually for a brief monthly editorial published in the *Metropolitan*. He did not need any of the money for himself, since his substantial inheritance from his father still sustained him. All his writing income he therefore earmarked for the support of his sons' men, Eleanor's work with the Y.M.C.A., the civilian training camps, and other such endeavors.[35]

An additional inflow of cash in early 1918 was Roosevelt's Nobel Peace Prize money from 1906 ($36,734.39, which with interest had mushroomed to $45,482.83 by 1918). This money was returned to him at his request after Congress failed to use the money for the purpose he had prescribed so many years before (the formation of an industrial peace foundation). Roosevelt took the windfall and distributed it to enhance both the morale and efficiency of the Allied effort. He made twenty-eight different donations of various amounts. A few of the gifts included $6,900 to the Red Cross; $5,000 to Eleanor[36] for her Y.M.C.A. project; an additional $4,000 to the Y.M.C.A. National War Work Council; and $1,000 to Edith's sister, Emily Carow, a volunteer with the Italian Red Cross at Porto Maurizo, Italy.

Roosevelt made large block grants to the Jewish Welfare Board ($4,000), the Salvation Army War Fund ($4,000), and the Y.M.C.A. War Work Council's Negro division ($4,000). He sent Herbert Hoover $1,000 to aid his work with Belgian war refugees. He gave the Japanese Red Cross $500 and the same amount to an Australian friend in Nairobi, Leslie Mo Tarlton, "as a token of my admiration for what has been done in this war by the Canadians, Australians, New Zealanders

and Africanders, both of Boer and British blood." Roosevelt also provided various gifts for relief of Romanians and Montenegrins. Finally,
he widened his extended family even further when he made random
gifts of $500 to families of wounded Allied soldiers around the globe.
He wanted to take care of all of them, all of them.[37]

Chapter 15

DARK HARBOR

*I*n December of 1917, while Quentin was suffering from pneumonia, his brothers Ted and Archie let him know that he was not getting to the front fast enough to suit them. They told him point-blank that he was the *embusqué* member of the family—a slacker. Did he realize he was the only Roosevelt son not spending his days within range of enemy fire? At his remote supply and training outpost in Issoudun, Quentin had no way of knowing that the recrimination voiced by his brothers did not emanate from Sagamore Hill itself. When he was at Eleanor's Paris home recuperating over Christmas, he said nothing to her about the rebuke.

Ted and Archie's condemnation was followed by a long silence from Quentin, who refrained from writing letters to the demanding family he felt was now unhappy with his performance. The silence was born not of anger, but rather shame.

Quentin easily fell into the trap of feeling unworthy of the name *Roosevelt*. He had always suffered from low self-esteem. And he was used to his brothers' habit of challenging him to come up to their mark. "I have often thought that the best thing about me was the people I earned for [friends]," he wrote Flora. "I am a very, very ordinary person I am afraid. . . ."[1] It is important to remember that in Quentin's family being ordinary was a cardinal sin; and it seems to have never quite gotten through to him that his kin, or at least his parents and sisters, did not think him ordinary at all. The poems he published in the literary magazine of Groton often spoke of many inadequacies he detected in his personality and manners. Thus he accepted the verdict of his brothers despite the injustice of it. He did not argue. He did not put it to them that again and again he had requested combat, and again and again he had been informed that the scarcity of available aircraft meant an overabundance of fliers.

At Sagamore Hill, the situation between Quentin and his brothers came to light only when Quentin responded candidly to Ethel, the sibling to whom he was closest, after she wrote to demand an explanation as to why he was not writing his parents.

"This morning came a letter from Quentin which just *finished* me," wrote a stunned and enraged Ethel to Flora during the last week of February. "I am so angry with Ted, & I do feel he put Archie up to it."[2] In the same mail came a letter from Ted complaining about Quentin's lack of action. "So we had it straight from the source," wrote Ethel, "no exaggeration on Q's part. Mother was very angry."[3]

So was Flora. "Your letter just received," she telegraphed Ethel from Fort Worth, Texas, where her brother Sonny was training as an aviator. "Am perfectly furious—will never forgive Archie and Ted—writing—Flora."[4] A letter quickly followed. "If you knew how I felt," wrote Flora. "I did not know I could be so mad. I got your letter this morning and have just sent you a telegram. I'm boiling with rage. It's too much. I shall never *never* forgive Archie and Ted! . . . I can't understand how they can say such things, and why anybody should have such a peculiarly developed imagination to invent such untrue things. I can't write any more and you must forgive this strange disjointed epistle but I have never been so angry in all my life. . . . *I'm miserable.*"[5]

Reading Quentin's letter, the colonel was equally annoyed. Ted and Archie's stern injunction was too much for Roosevelt, who cabled

Quentin immediately: "Have just read your letter to Ethel. Shocked by Ted's and Archie's attitude. If you have erred at all it is in trying too hard to get to the front. You must take care of yourself. We are exceedingly proud of you."[6] *We are exceedingly proud of you.* This was the message Quentin needed to receive; and it came from the one source that mattered—the old lion himself. He was, he told Flora, "renewed" by his father's words.[7]

ॐ ॐ

In early March, Quentin was "very well but longing to get out to the front." As immediate action was still unlikely, he thought briefly of bringing Flora over to France so they might be married.[8] He thought she could work with Eleanor at the Y.[9] In the end, however, Flora was stopped from going overseas by an arcane regulation that said sisters of servicemen must remain stateside.

Roosevelt blamed Wilson for messing up his son's love life, just as he blamed him for virtually everything else that went wrong with the war. "Under the idiotic ruling about the sisters of soldiers poor Flora was not allowed to go across," wrote Roosevelt. "It is wicked. She should have been allowed to go, and to marry Quentin; then, even if he were killed, she and he would have known their white hours. It is part of the needless folly and injustice with which things have been handled."[10] The colonel wrote to Archie at the end of June to say, "As yet the War Department has positively refused to let poor Flora go abroad; she is a trump, and her father and mother have behaved splendidly; I hope she can get over sooner or later." He added pointedly that "It has been very hard on Quentin not to get to the front; the complete breakdown in the airplane program fills me with impotent rage."[11]

Quentin and Archie, meanwhile, enjoyed a rapprochement. Eleanor was arranging her days so as to transact all her business for the Y in the morning, when Archie was busy getting physical therapy. Then she would devote afternoons to entertaining him at Blake's Hospital. When he was in Paris, Quentin joined her in the errand. "I was up in Paris for five days," Quent wrote his father in May, "to rest up and as I was staying at Eleanor's, saw a lot of Arch. I wasn't awfully satisfied with the way he looked and neither was Eleanor. I think what it is more than anything else is that he is frightfully nervous." In fact, he was battling depression.

When Archie tired—or grew too morose for guests—Eleanor and Quentin would leave him and give the remainder of the day to enjoying Paris, doing everything from visiting Notre Dame to shopping for dresses. "She is making up a regular trousseau for Ted's leave," Quentin wrote the colonel. "It's really too amusing. She feels that she must have everything that is absolutely the prettiest and nicest for those wonderful seven days when Ted is there, so she has bought a whole flock of new dresses and new shoes and new everythings."[12]

It perhaps helped Quentin, with nothing to combat except feelings of loneliness and inadequacy, that if he did not have Flora near him, he at least had her good friend, the nurse Irene Givenwilson. There was no flirtation here; no wartime romance. Quite the contrary. Quentin hardly ever spoke to Irene of any topic other than Flora. Whenever he received letters from his fiancée, he would burst into Givenwilson's quarters at Issoudun "like an avalanche . . . and dance round the room waving them aloft," she recalled. "Then he would sit down & read me little bits of news out of them, & we would discuss you & the old times & be very happy. . . ."

In fact, the presence of a close associate of his fiancée seems to have inspired—or at least enforced—a measure of constancy in Quentin. Under Givenwilson's watchful gaze, Quentin avoided imitating Ham Coolidge and other friends who often romanced the local women. This self-control was duly reported to Flora. Irene Givenwilson assured Flora she was "enshrined" on Quentin's heart; she was his "guiding star" that kept him straight when other boys were off "doing fool things."[13]

On one memorable evening, Quentin spoke to Irene of what would happen if, as he expressed it, he got "bumped off." He said he did not care for himself, but that he would be sad for Flora being left behind. "But Fouf has so much spunk," he said, "and she knows just how I would want her to act. Life is such a wonderful thing, that she must live, and if she must drink the cup, then drink it with thankfulness for what we have already had, and then she must live on again. Life is glorious."[14]

జ్ఞ జ్ఞ

It was mid-June when Quentin, and Ham Coolidge along with him, finally got orders to report for combat flying. The colonel was glad Quentin was getting into action, but at the same time he was concerned, acknowledging darkly that "Now he too is where he may pay with his body for his heart's desire."[15]

Quentin stopped a day or two in Paris, going there on his motorcycle and staying with Eleanor, before reporting for his new duty. "Arch was quite amusing," he wrote Flora, "for when he found that I really was going he became most affectionate,—he evidently felt that he was saying a last fond farewell to me. I was amused, for at the moment Arch, who isn't at all well, feels that no one of us are going to get back, and that our one interest now should be how soon we are going to die. As a matter of fact, casualties in this group aren't so terribly big. Out of the last two squadrons—there are four in a group—the losses for a month and a half of hard work, with wonderful weather, were only six killed, and they brought down twenty, which is a pretty good record. . . ."[16]

Quentin's departure from Issoudun was touching. All the mechanics lined up outside the hangars to say good-bye. A sergeant yelled to Quentin, "Let us know if you're captured and we'll come get you." It was nice to know, he wrote his parents, that his men had liked him.[17]

They not only liked him; they were worried about him. Unlike his colleague, the precise and pragmatic Eddie Rickenbacker, Quentin was a daredevil who courted risk and glory. His men at Issoudun knew him well enough to understand that once he got into combat, he would be both selfless and voracious in his search for victory. They had seen his kind before. And they hoped they were wrong in guessing that Quentin's combat career, once launched, would be poignantly brief.

Quentin and Ham were sent to Orly Airfield, near Paris. Quentin was assigned to the First Pursuit Group of the 95th Aero Squadron (popularly known as the "Kicking Mule" squadron), and Ham to the 94th. Yet they still saw much of each other, as the two squadrons had adjoining barracks.

"I took a half hour ride yesterday to get used to my plane, and somewhat to the sector," he wrote Flora. "Then later on I went out on a patrol just up along the lines, to, as they put it, get used to being shot at by the Archies. It is really exciting at first when you see the stuff bursting in great black puffs round you, but you get used to it after fifteen minutes."[18] It was all just sport to him. He felt indestructible. Indeed, he wrote his mother he believed his Issoudun training had groomed him for survival. The flying he learned there would be a "revelation" for any "Mineola-trained" pilot. "When I first got over here I wondered why every flier was not killed within the first three months of his flying. Now I have changed so far the other way that I feel as though a man could hardly drive one of these machines into an accident, short of completely losing his head."[19] He was more than confident. He was overconfident.

He experienced his first dogfight on 6 July, while flying pursuit aircraft in a squad escorting a photographic reconnaissance plane. "You get so excited," he exclaimed with boyish enthusiasm in a letter to his mother, "that you forget everything except getting the other fellow, and trying to dodge the tracers, when they start streaking past you."[20]

It was five days after his initial mission that he downed his first and last German. "The press dispatches have just carried the account of Quentin's fight with three German airplanes, of which he downed one and escaped from the other two," gloated the colonel in a letter to Ted. "The last of the lion's brood has been blooded!"[21] A note Roosevelt wrote to Ethel was more fatalistic. "Whatever now befalls Quentin he has now had his crowded hour, and his day of honor and triumph."[22] Although excited by the news of Quentin's triumph, Flora, with a sense of foreboding, responded to it with just one plaintive little thought: "Oh, how I wish it was all over."[23]

On the same day Quentin killed his German, Theodore Roosevelt served as pallbearer for John Purroy Mitchell, a former New York City mayor (elected in 1913 at the age of 25, and called "the boy mayor" up till his defeat in a 1917 reelection bid) whom Roosevelt considered a casualty of war.[24] After the administration refused Mitchell a commission to command troops, Mitchell tried to qualify as an aviator and was killed in an accident. "Such a death, before ever having had the honor and glory of facing the foe in battle, is peculiarly hard," he wrote. "I think the possibility of such a fate was one of Quentin's nightmares during the many months when he was unable to get to the front."[25]

Quentin's kill was genuine. But it was also lucky, for Quentin was very nearly the victim rather than the victor. Writing to Flora, he explained how a comedy of errors led to his triumph.

He was returning from patrol and was suddenly separated from his group by a billowing wind that swept him up and away from them. Coming back down out of a cloud ceiling, he saw three planes below him, just north of Château-Thierry, which he took to be his squadron. He was almost in their midst before he realized they were German. "I was scared perfectly green," he wrote, "but then I thought to myself that I was so near I might as well take a crack at one of them, so I pulled up a little nearer, got a line on the end man, and pulled the trigger. . . . My tracers were shooting all around him but I guess he was so surprised that for a bit he couldn't think what to do. Then his tail shot up and he went down. . . ."[26]

Still confined to Blake's Hospital in Paris, Archie cheered up a bit with news of Quentin's success. Quentin came to visit his brother on 12 July, supremely proud of having made his first "kill." On his way to Archie's bedside, Quentin stopped at the Paris Y.M.C.A. headquarters where he picked up Eleanor. Then the two of them went off in search of wild strawberries and Normandy cream with which to surprise Archie—Eleanor all the while telling Quent excitedly of her lunch with Edith Wharton several days earlier. (Wharton was a distant cousin of Edith's and an old childhood friend of Theodore Roosevelt. She was living in France where she was deeply involved with war refugee work and was just finishing a novel about the 1914 Marne fight.[27])

During their visit at the hospital, Archie entertained Eleanor and Quentin with the story of how he had "destroyed" Secretary of War Newton Baker during the secretary's recent stop at Blake's. Followed by a large body of reporters, the secretary could not ignore the severely wounded son of a former president. When Baker stopped by Archie's bed and asked what he could do for him, Archie—after first making sure all the reporters were listening—replied dryly that he did not need anything but would love some guns and ammunition for his men, if that was not asking too much.

Quentin and Eleanor dined at Ciro's after leaving Archie. Then they retired to Eleanor's house. Augusta fed him breakfast on the morning of 13 July, after which he left on his motorcycle to return to Orly.

"Quentin blew in yesterday . . . ," Archie wrote Flora that morning. "[He] looks very well. But of course one can't help being worried. You now know, of course, that he is in an American Squadron on the front, and, like everything else in our army, we have had to take cast off machines from the Allies, so that they have had added dangers. It's not very pleasant to go into war unprepared! And with so many of our family over here, I confess, since I have been in the hospital, that I never take up the paper without a tremor."[28]

ॐ ॐ

On the morning of 14 July—Bastille Day—Ted Jr. and his men were up to their necks fighting in what would prove a critical moment of the second battle of the Marne. As usual, Ted was driving himself too hard. He should probably not have been in the field at all. He was still getting over the effects of a severe gassing he'd suffered seven weeks earlier, near Cantigny. Immediately after the gassing he'd insisted on continuing to lead his battalion as it advanced through a heavy bombardment. Today, south of Soissons, Ted's and four other American divisions, along with some French troops, were not only trying to blunt a German attack but also to turn the Germans around and rout them from the Château-Thierry salient.

Looking up at the sky in the midst of the fight, Ted may have noticed a group of Nieuports running fast in the direction of Orly, pursued by a cloud of red-nosed German Fokkers. And he may well have seen the "tail-end Charlie" of the Nieuports—a plane that he could not have realized was piloted by his brother Quentin—break off, kick its rudder, and bravely rise, alone, to meet the oncoming Germans.

Whether or not Ted spotted the unlikely move, the Germans certainly did. The confident young men of the famous Flying Circus were flying this day under the command of young Hermann Göring. Their friend and guru, Rittmeister Manfred von Richthofen (the Red Baron), had been killed seven weeks earlier. Still, they remembered his genius and the great dogfight strategies his genius produced. "Let the customer come into the store," he'd always told them. And now they did.

ॐ ॐ

Theodore and Edith pursued a relatively tranquil summer throughout the early weeks of July 1918. Occasionally he trotted off to make a speech—but never when he could avoid doing so. He appeared at Passaic, New Jersey, on the fourth of July. The colonel wrote Ted that he talked "straight-out Americanism of course, which was most enthusiastically received." Roosevelt was pleased the German mayor's two sons were serving in the navy. "The war-spirit of our people has steadily risen. One amusing result is that the President has announced that he intends soon to come out for universal military training!" Better late than never, said Roosevelt, but *much* better early than late.[29]

Theodore and Edith were alone now at Sagamore Hill, except for the staff. Ethel was at a rented summerhouse in Isleboro, Maine, with her children. Archie's wife, Grace, was in Boston with her parents and the infant Archie Jr. And the children of Ted and Eleanor remained with their maternal grandmother in Manhattan. In the mornings, Roosevelt worked at his enormous and ever-growing pile of mail, dictating letters to his secretary, Josephine Stricker. In the afternoons, he more often than not took Edith for a row before dinner. Then it was reading and conversation until bedtime.

On Tuesday, 16 July, Roosevelt was in his study dictating when he was interrupted by Phil Thompson, the Oyster Bay correspondent for the AP with whom he was friendly. Standing in the doorway of Roosevelt's study, Thompson showed the colonel a cryptic telegram sent to the New York *Sun* from a reporter at the front. "Watch Sagamore Hill for—" The telegram had no conclusion. The rest of the message had been wiped out by the censor. After reading the wire, Roosevelt pulled Thompson into the study and closed the door. "Something has happened to one of the boys," whispered Roosevelt, anxious that Edith not hear.

Then Roosevelt calmly and methodically ran through the probabilities and possibilities with Thompson. It could not be Archie, who was still at Blake's Hospital. Nor could it be Kermit, who'd been delayed on his journey from Mesopotamia to Madrid when he came down with malarial fever in Rome. He was due in Paris at any moment, from there to report to the Artillery School at Saumur.[30] Nor could it be Dick Derby, who was in Paris recovering from a bout of influenza. That left Ted Jr. and Quentin. Roosevelt told Thompson one of them must be either wounded, captured, or dead.

Very early the next morning, the 17th, Thompson again knocked at the door of Sagamore Hill. He carried a dispatch, unofficial, announcing Quentin had been shot down over enemy lines. There was no further information. It was not to be known for three more days whether Quentin was alive or dead, although Roosevelt seems to have instantly assumed the worst.

The colonel held the dispatch in his hand, walking back and forth across the length of the piazza in the early morning sunshine. "But Mrs. Roosevelt!" he told Thompson. "How am I going to break it to her?" After more pacing, Roosevelt went into the house, from which he did not emerge for thirty minutes. When he came out, he held in his hand a brief statement. "Quentin's mother and I are very glad that he got to the front and had a chance to render some service to his country, and show the stuff that was in him before his fate befell him."[31]

Roosevelt spent the remainder of the day indoors, tending to business. He dictated the mail to Stricker, who remembered "his voice choking with emotion . . . and the tears streaming down his face."[32] Later in the day, while Roosevelt exorcised his grief by waging war on his mail, Edith came to speak to Thompson, who was keeping a vigil outside the house. Her eyes were red, but she bore herself with dignity. "We must do everything we can to help him," she said, referring to Roosevelt. "The burden must not rest entirely on his shoulders."[33]

On the following morning, she accompanied Roosevelt to the Republican State Convention at Saratoga, New York, where he had long been scheduled to speak (along with Taft and Root) on the topic of speeding up the war.[34] Isaac Hunt, a friend who was in the audience for Roosevelt's Saratoga speech, told Hermann Hagedorn later he had never seen a face marked by such extreme human misery as was Roosevelt's when he mounted the convention dais. The audience to whom Roosevelt spoke did not yet know about Quentin; and he would not be the one to tell them. Nevertheless, Quentin was present in the speech.

"The finest, the bravest, the best of our young men have sprung eagerly forward to face death for the sake of a high ideal. . . ." he said. "When these gallant boys, on the golden crest of life, gladly face death . . . shall not we who stay behind, who have not been found worthy of the great adventure . . . try to shape our lives so as to make this country a better place to live in . . . for the women who sent these men to battle and for the children who are to come after them?"[35]

The family was tortured for several days by conflicting reports and cables on the fate of Quentin. Both Eleanor in Paris and Alice in Washington heard rumors that Quentin had been able to land his plane safely. This meant he could well be alive, though perhaps a prisoner. In France, Quentin's cousin Phil Roosevelt, another army aviator, borrowed a plane and went looking for him, with no luck. In England, Rudyard

Kipling wrote Kermit a note telling him to take heart—if Quentin had been taken prisoner, he would be treated well since the Germans now realized the war was turning against them. Back and forth this went on until early 20 July, a Saturday, when the flier was confirmed dead by a German news release. Flora, who had slept over at Sagamore Hill on Friday night, was with Theodore and Edith when definitive word arrived.[36] The German announcement was followed shortly by a sympathetic cable from President Wilson. Kermit, having just arrived in Paris, was with Eleanor when the news came to the house on the rue de Villejust.[37]

The German government's semiofficial Wolff Bureau press release contained many details. Quentin, said the Germans, valiantly and bravely made "repeated attacks" on seven German planes, deflecting them from the pursuit of his squadron. "This culminated in a duel between him and a German noncommissioned officer, who, after a short fight, succeeded in getting good aim at his brave but inexperienced opponent." Quentin died from two bullets in the back of the head, after which his plane crashed into a field near Chaméry, several miles west of Rheims. He was buried with full military honors near the spot where he fell. His belongings, said the Wolff release, would be forwarded to his parents through neutral parties.

It was later discovered that a civilian photographer among the Germans had photographed Quentin in death. The image he captured was of a battered, grimacing mask of pain. Eventually, prints of the picture, in the form of a postcard, would find their way to Sagamore Hill.

Theodore and Edith went to church that Sunday (attending the early service to take Holy Communion), but spent the rest of the day in seclusion save for an hour or so when W. Sheffield Cowles Jr.—a lieutenant in the Marine Corps on leave from Quantico—stopped by to tender his condolences. "Mother has been wonderful as she always is in a great crisis," the colonel wrote to Kermit. "She has the heroic soul." In the afternoon they went out for a row on the still, glassy water of Oyster Bay, through a slight haze, "and it all soothed her poor bruised and aching spirit." Then they took a swim. "As we swam she spoke of the velvet touch of the water and turning to me smiled and said, 'there is left the wind on the heath, brother!' "[38]

She was being brave for him; but she could not fool him. "Mother," he told Kermit, "will carry the wound green to her grave."[39] And so would he. Replying to a letter of condolence from Edith Wharton— who had suggested that he write a book about Quentin—Roosevelt answered that he could not, "for I should break down." (Roosevelt would shortly be writing Wharton a letter of condolence. Newbold ["Bo"] Rhinelander, the son of Wharton's first cousin Thomas Rhinelander, was shot down over German territory on 16 September.) A few days later a maid found Roosevelt alone in his bedroom, moving back and forth in a rocking chair on which he'd rocked all his children, muttering to himself over and over again: "Poor Quinikins! Poor Quinikins."[40]

"Little Flora is broken hearted, but very brave," he wrote Archie, "and Mother suffers as much and is even braver; for Mother has the true heroism of heart. Well, it is very dreadful; it is the old who ought to die, and not fine and gallant youth with the golden morning of life still ahead; but after all he died as the heroes of old died, as brave and fearless men must die when a great cause calls. If our country did not contain such men it would not be our country. I bitterly mourn that he was not married and does not leave his own children behind him; but the children's children of his brothers and of Ethel will speak of him with pride as long as our blood flows in the veins of man or woman."[41] In a similar vein, Roosevelt soon suggested to his surviving sons that the next born Roosevelt male be named Quentin—thus unwittingly setting off yet another round of competition between them, to see who would be first to father just such a namesake.[42]

ॐ ॐ

Within days after Quentin was confirmed dead, Theodore and Edith—harried by their grief, by memories of Quentin with which Sagamore was saturated, and by the press—sought refuge at Dark Harbor on Islesboro Island, Maine, where Ethel and her children were summering. Located in the middle of Penobscot Bay, approximately three miles off the coast from Camden, Islesboro is fourteen miles long north to south: a rocky swath of land spotted with pine trees, surrounded by other small islands just like it. "It is a lovely place," wrote Roosevelt, "the . . . rocky islands covered with the northern forest. I can see the moose, caribou and black bear in the glades or by the little pools—ghosts all!"[43]

Uncharacteristically, Roosevelt did little else than stare out at the ocean for hours on end. He wrote few letters. He made few telephone calls. He did not speak of the future. Occasionally he went out for a row. Edith spent days walking the beach alone, going up and down the craggy shoreline, sitting on a rock for a time, then moving on. The long, brooding silence of the household was interrupted infrequently. One night the group tried, without much success, to celebrate Edith's fifty-seventh birthday.[44] Only the children who were too small to be conscious of the tragedy enjoyed the party; in turn it was only they who provided any real solace.

Edith, unable to sleep, wandered the rooms of the house for hours until she finally settled down on a bed beside her little grandson Richard, Quentin's favorite nephew who reminded her so much of Quentin when young. With her arm draped protectively around the toddler, she finally drifted off.

The next day, writing to a friend back on Long Island, she commented that one could not bring up boys to be eagles and then expect them to be sparrows. Everything was always for the best, she wrote. And as a Christian she looked forward to the reunion with her son she knew would one day come. Possessed by a faith just as strong, Ham Coolidge wrote her, "Death is not a black unmentionable thing. I feel that dead people should be talked of just as though they were alive. . . . To me Quentin is just away somewhere. I know we shall see each other again and have a grand old 'hooshe' talking over everything . . . his personality or spirit are just as real and vivid as they ever were."[45]

Quentin's last letters arrived. He sounded so alive and optimistic in the warm and loving notes written just hours before he died. The letters served as a reminder of the extent of their loss, and the grieving at Dark Harbor began anew.[46]

Writing to Ted from Islesboro, the colonel channeled some of his emotion into a barrage of abuse for Henry Ford who, after having "added to his uncounted millions because of this war," secured an exemption for his son on the ground that he was "needed in the business." Roosevelt found reprehensible the idea of Ford using his wealth to exempt his son from the draft. In the same note, Roosevelt wrote, "The country has accepted gallant Quentin as standing in this war as young Shaw and young Lowell and young Winthrop stood in the Civil War."[47] It is fascinating that, in his grief, Roosevelt compared Quentin to Robert Gould Shaw and other upper-class martyrs of a war that, as Roosevelt was acutely aware, his own father had dodged just as surely as Edsel Ford had dodged the fighting of 1918.

He sent a note to his old Rough Rider colleague Bob Ferguson in which he seemed to regret nothing. "It is bitter that the young should die," he wrote, "[but] there are things worse than death, for nothing under Heaven would I have had my sons act otherwise than as they acted. They have done pretty well, haven't they? Quentin killed, dying as a war hawk should . . . over the enemy's lines; Archie crippled, and given the French war cross for gallantry; Ted gassed once . . . and cited for 'conspicuous gallantry'; Kermit with the British military cross, and now under Pershing."[48]

Theodore and Edith stayed at Dark Harbor for a fortnight. Shortly before they departed, Flora came up, intending to stay with Ethel once Roosevelt and Edith headed home. Arriving at Sagamore Hill on 15 August, Quentin's parents found Alice waiting for them.[49]

They also found letters of condolence from King George, Clemenceau, Balfour, and Lloyd George, along with two thousand additional letters and telegrams from across the country and the world—from presidents and butlers and novelists and coal miners. Some of the letters were from men who had served with Quentin. "I wonder if his dad is anything like him," a corporal wrote Edith. "If he is I would vote for him . . . he was sure a prince." And an Italian barber from Brooklyn, who had known Quentin at Issoudun, told the colonel that Quentin "was afraid of nothing . . . the goodest kid I ever saw."[50]

Each person who wrote—whether corporal or president or banker or blacksmith—received a personal response.[51] Among the many stacks of mail was the very last letter Quentin ever wrote. But it was not addressed to his parents. The final communication penned by Quentin Roosevelt before he died was a jovial birthday greeting for the family maid, Mary Sweeney.

Slowly, in the succeeding weeks, Roosevelt started to vaguely resemble himself again, even though he would never again be as he had been before the loss of Quentin. Despite his affable good humor and energetic need to continue to contribute to public life, his old exuberance had left him, never to return. No one was more attuned to this fact than Edith. "Quentin's death shook him greatly," she wrote Kermit. "I can see how constantly he thinks of him and not the merry happy silly recollections which I have but sad thoughts of what Quentin would have counted for in the future."[52]

ॐ ॐ

Sitting on the porch of Ethel's cottage overlooking Penobscot Bay, Flora Whitney read the letters of condolence that came quickly to her. "That you, or any one of my family or friends should have to face this, makes me long to put an end to it all, and turns all the humanity & kind-heartedness I once was reputed to have into steely blood-thirstyness," wrote Joseph Clark Baldurio from France on the letterhead of the War Work Council of the Army and Navy Young Men's Christian Association. Too old for the service, he'd gotten himself over the best way he could, with the Y, administering aid to men in front-line trenches. The only address printed on the letterhead read *With the Colors.* "Every day my desire to kill Germans [is] increasing, & I vow that whenever the chance comes the enemy shall pay in inverted proportion for the death of each one of my friends taken. . . . If we direct our imagination the right way, if we conjure up the true picture of *content*[ment] that belongs to death on the field of honor,—refraining from that *false* and horrid vision which jingoists love to paint,—that of a fearful death,—and if we call on the superb comfort and assistance of God & religion, we can turn our mourning from the gruesome into the *inspiring*, and say with the good old conviction: 'It's a great life, if you don't weaken.' If Quentin has died, he has given his life for the greatest of all causes,—the advancement of civilization. In one brief section he has accomplished that which all fine men consecrate their lives to,—leaving this world better than they found it,—and knowing Quentin as I did,—and what a true philosopher he was,—I am confident that, could he come to us now it would be with a smile on his face, the *satisfied* smile of sacrifice."[53]

In Baldurio's rhetoric, Quentin, by dying, had achieved the most vigorous life, a life that escaped the trivial and was blessed with a higher meaning: a dedication to a greater good rather than a dedication to self. For Baldurio, Quentin Roosevelt had not been cut down but rather fulfilled, by the German pilot's bullets.

Others echoed the sentiments expressed by Baldurio. "Q. was such an energetic, alive and wonderful person that it seems hard indeed that he should be among the first to fall," wrote Elizabeth Peabody—wife of "the Rector," Endicott Peabody, headmaster of Groton. "He was so keen though to strike a blow against the enemy, and he hated them, and all they stood for so utterly, that I know he gave himself gladly for the freedom of the world."[54] Henry Cabot Lodge wrote Flora to mourn in appropriate terms a heroic young man of his class. Quentin, wrote Lodge, was "very clever, very able, full of promise, brave and gallant like all his race. . . ."[55]

But the evidence suggests that Quentin did not, if he knew it was coming, welcome death gladly. He may well have rejected Baldurio's heroic metaphors and Mrs. Peabody's platitudes. Like other men he was a tabernacle of hopes, ambitions, and loves he earnestly sought to fulfill.

"He wanted to live," wrote Irene Givenwilson to Flora. "He told me he only wanted to go to the front for a month or two, & then he would do as all his superior officers wanted him to do—settle down in this camp as instructor & commander of one of the outlying fields. He wanted to live for you, he said; he used to dream of going home next year & marrying you, & then coming back again to finish the war. Sometimes the tears would gather in his eyes & he would put his head on my knee & talk of you & his mother. And Flora dear, you will never realize how deeply he loved you. It was the truest & most wonderful kind of love which deepened him & made him in a few months a real man. . . ."[56] (Interestingly, Quentin's own mother made a similar observation *exactly* one year before Givenwilson wrote her letter. "His love for you has made a man of Quentin," Edith wrote Flora. "Before it came to him he was just a dear boy. . . ."[57])

He wanted to live, but he nevertheless went to the brink. As Givenwilson was quick to point out, inside the love-struck Quentin there also lurked a thoroughly Rooseveltian warrior: boisterous, impudent, confident. There were more than a few moments when he plainly emulated his father. "I have seen several of the boys who were in the same squadron," wrote Irene, "& they all say the same thing, that he was absolutely recklessly brave & an inspiration to all the men with him. He would have made a wonderful leader of men, if he had lived."[58] In suggesting that leadership is often founded on the romantic, inspirational (albeit impractical) example of reckless bravery, Givenwilson unwittingly hit the Rooseveltian nail right on its head.

Chapter 16

THE CAPITAL OF
THE WORLD

$\mathcal{A}$t about the same time that Quentin's death was confirmed, word also reached Oyster Bay that Ted Jr. had been shot behind the left kneecap.

Eleanor was at her house on 19 July, upstairs reading, when the maid walked in and announced, "Major Roosevelt is here!" Rushing to the front door, Eleanor found Ted being lifted out of a car. He smiled up at her and announced cheerfully, "I got wounded this morning, and here I am!" A tag reading "GUNSHOT WOUND SEVERE" was tied to a button on his shirt.

"If only I could have got hold of a horse," he said as the driver of the car and another man carried him up the stairs. "I could have gone through the day at least. The fighting [at Ploisy near Soissons] was so hot there were no ambulances around or they'd have taken me to a field hospital, but I came out on a Field Artillery limber and got away from them." He rode for some time in the sidecar of a motorcycle, bumping at high speeds over shell-cratered roads. Then he met an old friend, Colonel Lawton, who lent him his car for the remainder of the journey to Paris.

Eleanor suggested he see a doctor immediately, but Ted refused. He told her he'd had first aid and received a tetanus shot; no further medical attention was necessary. Sitting in a big chair, his leg propped up on a hassock, he announced: "I want a hot bath! Then I want my dinner! I haven't eaten anything since yesterday morning. I would like some black bean soup, broiled live lobster, steamed clams, wild duck and hominy, rare roast beef and browned potatoes, and buckwheat cakes with maple syrup, but I'll settle for whatever French food you have in the house. You can start by bringing me a quart of champagne!" Eleanor suspected—probably correctly—that Ted was giddy from loss of blood and lack of food. What else could explain his joviality in the face of his wounds and the loss of Quentin?

Luckily, Dick Derby chose just this moment to drop by the house. He was about to be returned to his post as chief surgeon with the 2nd Division after having recovered from his bout of Flanders Flu, and he had come to say good-bye to Eleanor. Despite Ted's laughing protests, Dick examined the leg, which seemed to be paralyzed. The wound was full of bits of cloth and dirt. Dick announced that if it were not opened and thoroughly cleaned right away, it would get infected and Ted would probably lose the leg. "We are going to the hospital *now*," insisted Dick, lifting his brother-in-law out of the chair. "At least let me have my dinner," chortled Ted. "You'll have nothing," answered Dick, realizing Ted was going to be on an operating table very shortly. "Be thankful you've had a pint of champagne."

Eleanor and Dick took Ted in a taxi to Blake's Hospital—the same institution where Archie was a bored and depressed convalescent. Colonel Joseph Blake himself operated on Ted. The leg was saved, though Ted had no feeling in his heel for the rest of his life. Dick watched the operation while Archie and Eleanor sat outside the operating room, both saying frankly they hoped the wound would prove enough to send Ted home. When one of the nurses came out of the operating room to reassure them Ted would soon be almost good as new, Archie astonished her by responding, "Gee, that's tough."[1]

Finding the nerve in Ted's leg to be all right, Blake was able to excise and sew the wound up tight. "I must admit that I was disappointed when we saw the nerve was intact," wrote Dick. "Poor Eleanor felt the same way."[2]

৵৵

Endicott Peabody, rector of Groton School, eulogized alumnus Quentin Roosevelt in the *Boston Transcript* of 22 July 1918. "It is a striking instance, this, of the difference between the two systems involved in this world conflict," wrote the rector. "The Kaiser's sons are placed ex-officio in command of great bodies of troops whether they be worthy of their offices or not. They remain in comparative safety, well behind the line of battle. They must be kept to rule over the nations which will be bequeathed to them to govern. They are superior to ordinary beings by reason of their descent from this man. Germany bows to them as to their over-lords. With us, the sons of one who has held the highest office in the gift of the people come forward promptly, eagerly, to take their part as equals with all-comers, accepting conditions imposed upon all, competing with others in enduring the hardships and meeting the dangers of modern warfare."[3]

Within four weeks of Quentin's death, another Groton boy— Quentin's classmate Bill Preston—hammered together a makeshift cross with Quentin's name and dates and went in search of the grave. The Germans had retreated and the site was now within Allied lines. Preston was joined by two others: Colonel McCoy, a friend of the Roosevelt family who had been an aide to Roosevelt as president, and Father Duffy—the Roman Catholic priest and regimental chaplain with "the fighting 69th" who is commemorated with a statue in New York's Duffy Square.

The three men found the grave in a field eight hundred yards east of the town of Chaméry. The mutilated wreck of Quentin's plane lay just a few feet away. Parts of it had been stripped. Hundreds of soldiers, first German and now American, had helped themselves to pieces of the aircraft as souvenirs. The plane's four-blade propeller remained intact where the Germans had placed it, serving as a cross to mark the grave. "Roosevelt" was scratched on it.

"We put our cross in place and the Father said a brief prayer," wrote Preston to Flora. "Some men who were around said that earlier in the afternoon the Bishop of New York had held a service. There is not much else I can tell you. The grave is an ordinary soldier's grave similar to hundreds of others that cover this part of the battlefield. Its coordinates on the map are Latitude 54°.6575. Longitude 1°.4315."[4]

Visits to Quentin's grave by advancing American troops became so frequent in early August that commanders erected a *cordon sanitaire* around it, for German guns were still ranging at movement in open fields. One doughboy of the 32nd, when asked why he had paused at the grave, replied that he felt as if he and the rest of the men were *all* sons of Teddy Roosevelt, brothers of Quentin.

꙲ ꙲

Picture a beautiful summer morning in late July in Paris, on the Champs-Elysées. Imagine a nervous-looking woman in a Y.M.C.A. uniform walking beside two lunatics. The woman, plainly overwhelmed by her mischievous charges, exhorts the two deranged men in a loud stage whisper, begging them not to misbehave. But the two ignore her. One, who stands to the side on crutches, a wire splint on one leg, takes out a large handkerchief, wipes invisible tears from his eyes, and cries loudly over and over again, "boo hoo hoo." The other, whose left arm and shoulder are in a large plaster cast, frantically chases about the street reaching up and closing his good right hand on invisible butterflies that he then pops into his mouth, fiendishly cackling between bites.

The two lunatics were Ted and Archie, after a bottle of champagne. The Y.M.C.A. attendant was of course Ted's wife, Eleanor. It would be amusing, the brothers thought, to pretend to be mental patients out for a stroll. Another day, on the Metro, Ted and Arch played the parts of two boorish Americans trying to pick up Eleanor, a refined and innocent French girl.

After the battle of Soissons, the 1st Division was withdrawn to rest billets. The casualties at Soissons had been enormous; every single officer of the 26th Infantry was either killed or wounded. Ted's command, the 1st Battalion, came out of the line under a second lieutenant after Ted was evacuated. Luckily, they sustained minimal losses. It was not long after being assigned to rest billets that a half-dozen officers from the Division came to visit Ted at his quarters on the rue de Villejust. Ted broke out champagne and made the two customary toasts. The first: "Gentlemen, the Regiment!" And the second: "Gentlemen, the dead of the Regiment!"

Kermit and his wife, Belle—who had arrived in town the day Quentin's death was confirmed—were frequent visitors to Ted and Eleanor's house during the last weeks of July, a period of time when the three surviving brothers did a lot of drinking and a lot of bonding. "We believed this might well be the last time we would all be together," remembered Ted's wife. "Quentin, the youngest, was gone. No one knew how long the war would last. No one knew whose turn would come next. We played around with the feverish high spirits felt only in the shadow of death."

The convivial joviality among the three brothers was, of course, forced. They endeavored to pour a liniment of Rooseveltian bravado over the raw and painful wound of Quentin's loss. All three brothers rose to the occasion, each thinking it was his job to be cheerful and buck up the other two. They also, as Eleanor suggested in her perceptive comment, shared a newly heightened sense of the fragility of life— and the necessity to live it to the fullest just as their parents had always taught them, and just as Quentin would want them to. For this they were well positioned: They cared deeply for one another, they were young and affluent, and they were in Paris, the capital of the world.

One Sunday they all lunched at the Petit Durand. All three brothers drank their share of wine, but Kermit, as usual, had rather more than anyone. Toward the end of the meal, Kermit announced that Belle was pale and could be restored only by some good red wine. When Belle insisted she did not want any, Kermit laughingly grabbed her by the back of the neck and tried to feed her from the bottle, while his brothers looked on laughing. At this both Belle and Eleanor rose, saying Kermit's behavior was inappropriate and they were being made "conspicuous." Promptly, the two women started for home while the men behind them decided to show them what the term *conspicuous* really meant.

Clutching the bottle of wine, Kermit led his brothers out to the street. Arch was still in his cast, and Ted was still on his crutches. Nevertheless, Belle and Eleanor soon heard the men behind them, singing "Hail, Hail, the Gang's All Here" at the top of their lungs. Attracting great attention, Ted shouted, *"En avant, mes braves!"* to four wounded *poilus* who immediately fell in rank behind them. Kermit passed the new recruits some wine. Ted exhorted civilians to join in the procession as well, which some did. A man with a pushcart shouted *"Vive l'Amérique!"* Kermit, climbing up onto the pushcart, waved his cap and returned the salute: *"Vive la France!"* As Eleanor remembered it, by the time they turned into the conservative, upper-class rue de Villejust, there was quite a crowd following her and Belle as they walked with nervous dignity and blushing faces, pretending nothing out of the ordinary was going on.

Through escapades such as this, the house on the rue de Villejust gained a strange reputation in some circles. Months later, after the Armistice, when Ted was with the Army of Occupation in Germany, Eleanor got to learn with what wry speculation she was viewed by her neighbors. Coming to attend a dinner party Eleanor was hostessing, Lord Hartington (later the duke of Devonshire) startled his French chauffeur when he instructed that he be taken to 39, rue de Villejust: Eleanor and Ted's house. This could not be the right address, said the chauffeur. There must be some mistake. There was no mistake, replied Hartington. "But that's where a young American woman lives—with several officers! It is shocking!" said the chauffeur. "And the way they carry on! The whole neighborhood is talking about it!"[5]

ॐ ॐ

September of 1918 found Ted still laid up but restless, eager to get back to combat. He told his wife he disliked sitting around while others did his fighting for him. The wound on his leg had almost healed, but the leg was still paralyzed in places and the muscles had shrunk. To expedite the process of reviving his leg, Ted did special exercises, took a rigorous daily massage, and walked as much as he could (relying heavily on not one but two canes). During one of his walks, he bumped into his father's old friend Georges Clemenceau. After surveying Ted's medals and realizing he'd not yet been awarded the Croix de Guerre for his conspicuous bravery so many weeks before near Catigny, Clemenceau arranged for the situation to be remedied immediately.

Eleanor, who did not want her husband going back into action, was relieved to hear a pronouncement from the doctors that it would be at least two months before Ted could walk half a mile, and probably four months before the full use of the leg would be regained. Realizing the war would probably end before he could get back to it, Ted pestered his doctors until they finally, in exasperation, certified him fit for limited duty. He could not go back to combat yet, of course. Therefore, returning to the 26th Infantry was not a possibility. Instead, he was ordered to Langres both as instructor in the Army Line School and a student at the General Staff College. He left Paris on his thirty-first birthday, 13 September 1918. Three days later, his promotion to lieutenant colonel came through.

"Your services in this Division," wrote General Charles P. Summerall (commander of the 1st Division) in a citation that was part of the paperwork of promotion, "have been conspicuous for efficiency, energy and leadership. It would be difficult to convey to you my appreciation of the manner in which you led your battalion in the Soissons fight, and of the great assistance rendered by you in moving boldly ahead of the line, thereby greatly facilitating the general movement that followed on 19 July. The corps commander was present when the report was received of your enterprise in gaining ground under the most difficult circumstances, and he shared with me the relief and confidence that your conduct inspired. I think no one who has been a member of this Division occupies a higher place than you in the esteem of your comrades, and you will receive a warm welcome whenever it shall be our good fortune to have you return to us."[6]

This was just the kind of praise Ted Jr. would love to have his father know about, but he would not be so brash or boastful as to send it along to Sagamore. Ted's wife, Eleanor, knew this; but she also knew the old lion could use some good news. Thus a copy of Summerall's glowing letter found its way to Oyster Bay. "You have made *the* great success of all our family in the war," Roosevelt wrote Ted, "for you have had the biggest and most responsible job, particularly delicate as you [despite being a mere reservist] were [made] a Major of the Regulars, and you have won really remarkable testimony to your success."[7]

In October, while Ted was at Langres, Bulgaria capitulated. The war was slowly winding down. His leg would not be fully restored for at least another six weeks; nevertheless he reported to his old regiment. A friend who had been with Ted at Langres explained his sudden rejuvenation to Eleanor. "[Ted] was doing all right there, getting a lot of useful knowledge and also teaching a lot of people. He should have had sense enough to stay put and not keep fretting like an idiot because he thought he was in a soft job. General Frank Parker is now commanding the First Division. He called Ted on the telephone and asked how his leg was. Of course Ted said it was entirely well, the liar. The General said his old regiment needed a commanding officer and Ted could have the job if he was able to come at once. Ted was off like a shot. He still walks with a cane and is certified for limited duty only, and now he's AWOL. I hope he gets court-martialed!"[8]

Chapter 17

THE OLD LION
IS DEAD

*A*utumn came to Sagamore. The dogwood berries reddened
and the maple leaves blushed. The goldenrod and asters flaunted their
beauty. And, as in the past, log fires burned and crumbled every evening
in the North Room—but the crumbling ashes now had a new poi-
gnancy. Theodore Roosevelt spent part of the autumn helping Joseph
Bucklin Bishop edit a collection of letters he'd written to Sister, Ted,
Kermit, Ethel, Archie, and Quentin during their childhoods. It was, of
course, a labor of love. He would not live to see the book in print, but
Theodore Roosevelt's Letters to His Children was to be a best-seller in 1919
and a much-loved classic for generations of American readers.

Archie returned from Europe that fall and spent a few weeks at
Sagamore Hill with his wife and infant son. "Archie has come," the
colonel wrote Kermit in early September. "Of our four hawks one has
come home, broken-winged, but his soul as high as ever. Never did
four falcons fly with such daring speed at such formidable quarry . . .
He is in far better shape than I expected."[1]

But the colonel was acutely aware of Archie's depression. He noted
the signs: Archie's remoteness, the veiled eyes, the foggy and half-

hearted interest in anything that was not war. Roosevelt was particularly startled by Archie's lack of interest in his new baby son, whom Archie would hold for a few moments when coaxed, and then, distractedly, pass off to Grace. Roosevelt told a friend it was easy to see the negative direction Archie's dislocated mood and spirit were taking. It seemed his mental wounds were more severe than the physical ones.

In particular, Archie was obsessed with the idea that career officers, jealous of Ted's successes, were involved in a conspiracy to sabotage the career of his elder brother. Before Archie left Paris, Ted wrote his father to warn him of Archie's delusion. Archie, Ted wrote, was in an "excited condition [and] at this moment he will probably make unguarded statements about things he thinks have happened to me unjustly. Don't pay any attention to him . . . A lot of this seems cryptic but I'm sure you'll understand when you see Archie."[2] On the 21st of September came word that Pershing had just promoted Ted to lieutenant colonel—a sure sign there was no conspiracy, said Roosevelt.

In addition to emotional ups and downs, Archie had ongoing physical problems to contend with. In mid-September a fragment of shell was discovered working out through his knee. An operation was performed, after which Archie and his family moved out of Sagamore to a small apartment in Manhattan not far from the American Museum of Natural History. "I think it an excellent thing," wrote the colonel, "but darling Mother felt very sad at her returned boy leaving home, and poor Mary Sweeny actually cried!"[3]

While Archie tried to pull himself together and adjust to life with his family, Theodore Roosevelt busied himself making speeches for the Liberty Loan program. A ten-day tour in October took him from Newport, Rhode Island, to Billings, Montana. In addition to making speeches, he personally purchased $60,000 in bonds.[4] He did not, however, care for the tour. "How I loathe it!" he told Kermit.[5] One of the few highlights of the trip was in Montana, where some old Rough Riders turned up as they always did whenever he was in the area. "It is really very touching to see how eagerly they come to greet me, to live again the times of long ago, with the certainty that they are the sharers of any fame or distinction which I may at the moment have."[6]

At Newport, Grace Vanderbilt (Flora's aunt) protested directly to Roosevelt when she found herself seated far away from him at a banquet being held in his honor. She believed her status demanded that she sit at Roosevelt's side, in the spot reserved for the governor of Rhode Island. Roosevelt, however, had other ideas. He'd been annoyed by news that Grace's husband had pulled strings to get their son a military chauffeur's job safely behind French lines. When Mrs. Vanderbilt reminded Roosevelt somewhat haughtily that her husband was a General, Roosevelt "explained that the situation was gravely complicated, by her being also the mother of an enlisted man, a chauffeur; and that I thought the only solution was for her to sit in the Governor's lap during the early courses of dinner, but, as mother of a chauffeur, to eat her dessert in the kitchen."[7]

ᢌ ᢌ

Quentin was not far from any of their thoughts. Ethel and Flora, already close friends, became still closer in their grief over Quentin. "Archie brought home Quentin's trunk," Ethel wrote Flora. "He did not want Mother to know. Eleanor & Kermit & he went over some things in Paris, I believe. I have put all your letters & your pictures together for you. I kept his uniform & his dear jaunt cap, for someday they will be very precious for the children. And there was little else but his pistol, a compass, an aeronautical instrument, & the letters from Father & Mother. I have put my letters away for Richard [Derby Jr.]. Someday he must read them. . . . Did you know that his field [at Mineola] has been named Roosevelt Field? And today father had a cable saying that a French destroyer had been named after him. So often we hear from people who have been at his grave. It has become a sort of place of pilgrimage, both for our people & the French. We have a wonderful picture of it. . . ."[8]

Through that long last autumn after Quentin's death, the colonel remained convinced of the justice of the war. He nevertheless was anxious to have the war conclude with the earliest possible victory, so as not to put his boys—or anyone else's—at more risk than was absolutely necessary. "Josh Hartwell [a young physician who included the Whitneys among his patients and was a friend of the Roosevelts] has just returned," he wrote, "having just seen Ted and Kermit and Dick [Derby] at the front. They are all well. I wonder when they will be brought back; I especially wonder when Sheffield will return."[9] In an uncharacteristically emotional closing of a note to his sister Anna, Sheffield's mother, Roosevelt wrote "Good bye, gallant sister—gallant mother of a gallant boy!"[10]

His brother-in-law Douglas Robinson—husband of his sister Corinne—died on 12 September. At Robinson's funeral, held at the family home in Orange, New Jersey, Roosevelt pulled his niece Eleanor aside to insist once again, as he had on several occasions, that Franklin resign his position as assistant secretary of the navy and personally get into the war. She wrote later that she was surprised Quentin's death had not softened him. Instead, he seemed even more rigid and uncompromising. It was Franklin's obligation, said Roosevelt, to put his life on the line. For once, Roosevelt's favorite—and usually docile—niece actually became annoyed with him. Red with anger, Eleanor informed her uncle that Franklin had applied for a naval commission but was told by the president to stay where he was. The colonel's view, of course, was one that put emotion over logic; he was not being reasonable. Niece and uncle were never to see one another again.

There was another loss on 27 October, the day Roosevelt turned 60. Hamilton Coolidge was shot down by a direct hit from a German antiaircraft battery. He was leading a patrol of six planes just east of the village of Grand Pri at the northern end of the Argonne Forest. His plane fell on the bank of the little river Aire, where he was buried.[11] He had been promoted to the rank of captain just a few days before he died. A week later, the issue of *The Grotonian* in which Coolidge's obituary appeared also carried a front-page article headlined: "Military

Training: Instruction in boxing and bayonet. Advance guard problem. Attack on Brownloaf Hill."[12] As Roosevelt observed somberly to Edith, the boys of Groton were still preparing for battle.

In late October, though afflicted with constant, severe attacks of inflammatory rheumatism, Roosevelt dragged himself into Manhattan to speak for more than ninety minutes from the stage of Carnegie Hall, urging a Republican victory in the upcoming Congressional elections. He noted that the Germans—crushed that autumn in the second battle of the Marne—had leapt at Wilson's "ill-timed" proposal for a negotiated peace. What were needed now more than ever, said Roosevelt, were strong Republican majorities in both the House and Senate to compel the president to force the Germans into unconditional surrender. Nothing else would do. Nothing else could bring to heel a president who asked for the defeat of prowar Republicans more stridently than he asked for defeat of the Kaiser. When Roosevelt paused after an hour and a half and apologized for taking up so much time, the crowd shouted, "Go on! Go on!" [13]

Roosevelt's final public address was delivered in the same hall a week or so later on 2 November. He spoke under the auspices of the Circle for Negro War Relief on the topic, "The American Negro and the War." After summoning memories of the black colleagues who had shared his "crowded hour" in the Spanish-American War, he spoke at length about "the honors won and the services rendered" by black troops in Europe. Making a veiled allusion to the obvious racial bias in the Wilson administration, with its many Southern white-supremacist appointees, Roosevelt insisted, "I don't ask for any man that he shall, because of his race, be given any privilege. All I ask is that in his ordinary civil and political rights, in his right to work, to enjoy life and liberty and the pursuit of happiness, that as regards these rights he be given the treatment that we would give him if he was an equally good man of another color."[14]

Roosevelt disobeyed doctor's orders on election day, venturing out to vote even though he could barely walk. He said going a mile to the polls was the least he could do, with Kermit having just distinguished

himself as an artillery commander in the battle of the Argonne, and
with Ted and Dick still out there with thousands of their comrades
chasing the Germans back to the Rhine.

All the effort—his tireless campaigning as well as the trip down to
the voting booth at Cove School—proved worthwhile when the elections yielded Republican majorities in both the House and Senate. The
stage was set for Republican victory in 1920. Wilson, who had called
the election a referendum on negotiated peace, was clearly rebuked.
Although Roosevelt would not live to see it, these same Republican
majorities would ultimately defeat the proposal for United States membership in Wilson's cherished League of Nations. "We did an unpar-
alleled thing," the colonel wrote delightedly to Rudyard Kipling, "and
took away Congress from [Wilson] on the issue that we stood for,
forcing the Germans to make an unconditional surrender."[15]

Roosevelt was heartened by the election. He was also heartened by
rumors that Quentin's death had led to dissension in the German ranks.
Evidently, not a few German soldiers shared the same view Rector
Peabody enunciated in his editorial about Quentin: The son of a great
American president had been killed, yet the German emperor's six sons
were protected from the violence and bloodshed the Kaiser prescribed
for others. Roosevelt took comfort to think that in some small measure
the fallout from Quentin's death—along with, of course, the Republican sweep of Congress on 7 November—helped prompt Wilhelm II's
abdication on the 9th. This was followed by the Armistice (including
unconditional German surrender) on the 11th.

He went back to Roosevelt Hospital on Armistice Day. Officially,
he was there for treatment of the rheumatism he now found crippling
as well as for treatment of concurrent fever, anemia, and vertigo. In
addition to those ailments, the old infectious devils from the River of
Doubt were still with him, along with their complications. To some
close observers, it seemed that the timing of his hospitalization was no
accident. It was whispered he had been holding himself in check, refusing to surrender to his pain until after the German military beast was
crushed. Then, his mission accomplished, he collapsed.

There were moments when he was fatalistic. He reminded his sister Anna of a youthful promise he'd made to live "and work up to the hilt" until the age of 60. Now he'd kept that pledge. To Dick Derby he wrote, "It is in the nature of things we must soon die anyhow—and we have warmed both hands before the fire of life."[16] At other moments, however, he was still full of plans. When a newspaper article announced that Roosevelt was too sick to run for president in 1920, he roused himself to threaten a lawsuit over the "unjust" and "inaccurate" report. The journalist William Allen White, denied access to Roosevelt's sickroom, left a note saying that General Wood was likely to declare himself a candidate for the Republican presidential nomination. If Roosevelt was interested, he should speak up. Insisting that White be brought to him, Roosevelt told the editor he planned to announce in June. He even let White look at a penciled platform draft incorporating an eight-hour workday, Social Security, and old age pensions.

He was in the hospital forty-four days. Once again, Edith stayed with him. Her room was connected to his by a shared bathroom. When not contending with rheumatic attacks and often-agonizing treatments for his various maladies, Roosevelt dictated letters and articles and entertained visitors. When Cabot Lodge came, Roosevelt surprised him by endorsing Wilson's idea for a League of Nations with one caveat: The United States should sign no agreement that would deny the country either the right or the resources to defend her national interests with force whenever necessary. His endorsement of the League was not, however, an endorsement of Wilson. "If this left wrist were a little better," he told his doctor, "I would like to be left alone in this room with our great and good President for about fifteen minutes, and then I would cheerfully be hung."[17]

His daughter-in-law Eleanor—having arrived back in the States on 16 December—came to visit him after first stopping for a reunion with the three children she'd not seen in eighteen months. She told Roosevelt that eight-year-old Grace remembered her, five-year-old Teddy

pretended to, and three-year-old Cornelius (called Sonny) had no idea
who she was. Sonny didn't remember Ted either, although he addressed him each night before going to bed as "Our Father Who Art
in France." Years later, Eleanor recalled that the "solemn" Roosevelt
"almost laughed" when told how Sonny, pointing to the animals on
the wall at Sagamore, asked if his father would bring home the stuffed
head of a German to add to the collection.[18]

Shortly before Christmas, Roosevelt's doctors told him they could
do nothing to improve his condition. In the near future he would
probably find himself confined permanently to a wheelchair. Roosevelt
was philosophical about the verdict: Others were shouldering afflictions
far worse. He thought of all the dead boys, one of them his own, who
would probably delight in the prospect of life in a wheelchair. He said
as much in Christmas notes to both Ted and Kermit, each letter bearing
one thousand francs with which the sons were instructed to buy Christmas dinners for their men.

Just as would another presidential aspirant with the name Roosevelt,
the colonel sought to hide his invalidism from the press. Leaving the
hospital on Christmas Day, he objected when a doctor tried to take his
arm and steady him as they rode the elevator. Roosevelt pushed the
doctor's hand away. "Don't do that," he whispered. "I am not sick,
and it will give the wrong impression." When the elevator door
opened, a wobbly Roosevelt gritted his teeth and walked quickly, by
himself, through a small crowd of reporters to the car that waited for
him. Then he fell into the back seat, exhausted. It was a sign of how
ill he was that he had already decided not to partake of a decades-long
Christmas tradition: playing Santa Claus for the children at the Cove
Neck School.

"I'm afraid it won't be a very merry Christmas at Sagamore," Kermit
wrote his wife, "there will be too many ghosts around." Kermit was
right, even though a determinedly happy company waited to greet
Roosevelt on his homecoming. Alice was there. So were Ethel, her
two children, and Archie, Grace, and the baby. They all tried to throw

themselves into the day. Roosevelt picked at his Christmas dinner and spent a few minutes watching his little granddaughter Edie scamper amid her new toys, but then he tired and retreated to his bed.

Roosevelt took breakfast in bed for several days after Christmas. He came downstairs for lunch and then would lie on the sofa in his library, reading and dictating letters. On the 29th and 30th, he seemed well enough that Edith took him out for drives in the car; but he was less well on New Year's Eve and New Year's Day. The mood of the house was made darker when Quentin's official citation arrived in the mail on 31 December. The same day saw publication of an Associated Press report detailing Quentin's death from the perspective of the German pilot who brought him down.[19] As of 1 January, Roosevelt spent most of his days upstairs on a sofa in the old nursery, where a window facing south made it one of the warmer rooms in the otherwise drafty house. On the second of the month, Edith wrote Kermit that his father was "having a horrid painful time."[20]

A rheumatic specialist from Roosevelt Hospital came and checked him on 3 January. Josh Hartwell also stopped by to give his informal assessment: Roosevelt would eventually recover, but no time soon. Eleanor came. "You know, Father," she said during the visit, "Ted has always worried for fear he would not be worthy of you." Roosevelt shook his head. "Worthy of me? Darling, I'm so very proud of him. He has won high honor not only for his children but, like the Chinese, he has ennobled his ancestors. I walk with my head higher because of him."[21]

He felt somewhat better on the 5th, but still kept to the couch in the nursery, beside which was now placed a worktable loaded with letters and books. Flora dropped in for a visit, as did several other people including the prominent British poet Alfred Noyes. None of them had appointments; Roosevelt announced he was only well enough to see Flora. After she left, he dictated a letter to Kermit and then worked straight through for eleven hours on a variety of things: correcting proof of a *Metropolitan Magazine* article, finishing an editorial for the *Kansas City Star* on the League of Nations (which, having thought about it more since speaking to Lodge, he now denounced), and reviewing a book by his friend Henry Fairfield Osborne of the American Museum of Natural History.[22]

Edith remembered that as dusk came on, Roosevelt put down his reading and "watched the dancing of waves, and spoke of the happiness of being home, and made little plans." When Edith momentarily rose from her game of solitaire, he suddenly looked up and said, "I wonder if you will ever know how much I love Sagamore Hill." This, Edith told her son Ted, was the beautiful conclusion of what had been a "happy and wonderful day."[23]

But not quite so. The actual conclusion of the day came a few hours later. At about ten P.M., while still lying on the nursery sofa, Theodore anxiously asked Edith to help him sit up. He'd just had a terribly odd feeling, he said. He did not know quite how to describe it, but he felt as if his heart and breathing were about to shut down. "I know it is not going to happen," he assured her, "but it is such a strange feeling."[24] She gave him *sal volatile* and then woke the nurse who came, checked his pulse, and pronounced it normal. To be on the safe side, a doctor was summoned who in turn said Roosevelt seemed stable. A shot of morphine was administered to make sure he slept well. Then James Amos—his loyal valet of many years—put him to bed at about midnight.

At four A.M. Amos, sleeping in the chair next to Roosevelt's bed, woke suddenly and realized Roosevelt was breathing oddly. The sound was a death rattle. Amos ran to wake Mrs. Roosevelt and the nurse, but when the two women got to the colonel, he had stopped breathing. Roosevelt had died of an embolism in the coronary artery. The date was January 6: the Feast of the Epiphany. On his bedside table lay a last scribbled note reminding himself to tend to some urgent business with Will Hays, the Republican National Committee chairman who was helping mastermind Roosevelt's presidential comeback.

On the brisk afternoon of the 6th, Edith walked the shoreline near Sagamore with Roosevelt's sister Corinne. As they returned to the house—walking through the pet cemetery where all the family animals were buried including Little Texas—the horse Roosevelt rode during his famous charge of 1898—they heard the unfamiliar sound of numerous small aircraft overhead. Pilots from the Mineola field where Quentin trained—the field now named in his honor—were dropping laurel wreaths onto the lawn of Sagamore Hill.

A cable arrived from Vice President Thomas Marshall that said in part, "Death had to take him sleeping, for if Roosevelt had been awake, there would have been a fight." Another, more parsimonious message—as cold as it was brief—arrived from Woodrow Wilson, now in Europe to attend the Versailles Peace Conference. As Edith knew, amid the president's party aboard the cruiser *George Washington* were Franklin and Eleanor Roosevelt. Among the crew was Marine Lieutenant W. Sheffield Cowles Jr. Writing from the *George Washington*, niece Eleanor said Roosevelt's death was doubly sad, for she feared her uncle's last years were "full of disappointment."[25]

Archie cabled his brothers, Kermit and Ted, together in Germany with the army of occupation, camped near Coblenz: "The old lion is dead."[26] When Alice Longworth saw the text of Archie's note, she could not help but think of some lines from the *Book of Job*: "The old lion perisheth for lack of prey, and the stout lion's whelps are scattered abroad."

Ted received Archie's cable in the early evening. He rushed over to Kermit's tent, but Kermit was out on the town somewhere. When Kermit returned much later that night, he found Ted lying on a cot, drinking from one of the bottles of wine Kermit kept stashed in his footlocker. Kermit wrote his mother:

We sat up the rest of the night and talked. Father somehow seems very near, and as if he would never be far. I don't feel sorry for him; he wouldn't want it, that would be the last thing. There never was anyone like him, and there won't be. You're the only person I feel sorry for; for now you must walk in sad loneliness, for she who has lost father, has lost all; but it isn't for long; man's life is but a span, as has been said throughout the centuries; for you it's probably even a shorter run than for me, but for none of us is it very long; and then we shall all be joined together on the other side of the last great adventure; and Quentin too will be waiting over there, with his smile. . . . It is foolish to think of oneself, but you will know how the bottom has dropped out for me; at first it was complete, but then comes the realization that father could never really die, and that even though I can't bother him about every little decision, when a really vital one comes he will be there as unfailing as ever. . . .[27]

The oak coffin, draped with the flag of the United States, stood for two days in the North Room of Sagamore Hill: the room with the hunting trophies and awards and medals of a lifetime, the room that was most completely *his*. In a short service held at Sagamore, Quentin's favorite prayer was read: "O Lord, protect us all the day long of this troublous life, until the shadows lengthen and the evening comes, and the busy world is hushed, the fever of life over, and our work done. Then Lord in Thy mercy grant us a safe lodging and peace at the last, through Jesus Christ, our Lord."

Roosevelt's stark, simple funeral took place on 8 January, at Christ Church in Oyster Bay. Five hundred invited mourners (400 personal friends and relatives, 50 children from Cove Neck School, and 50 dignitaries, including Vice President Marshall, New York Governor Al Smith, and William Howard Taft) packed the tiny church for the service that was said without music and (in Episcopal tradition) without eulogy. Observing an old tradition, Edith did not attend but instead sat with a niece at Sagamore Hill, reading the funeral service quietly to herself from the *Book of Common Prayer*. At the church, a New York police captain, in tears, took Corinne Robinson aside and said, "Do you remember the fun of him, Mrs. Robinson? It was not only that he was a great man, but, oh, there was such fun in being led by him."[28]

After the service, a large number of mourners accompanied the casket on its last journey. The place of burial was the little private cemetery owned by the Youngs family that had long ago been simply "Youngs' Woods," where Theodore Roosevelt and his boys hiked and fished. Archie, in uniform, walked behind his father's coffin. Now there was another prayer, followed by three volleys over the grave, then taps, and then the removal and passing off of the flag to Arch—who stayed when all the others had left, standing in the bitter January cold, watching the grave diggers close the hole above the old lion's final den.

The announcement of Roosevelt's death sent out by the Harvard Class of 1880 quoted words spoken by Valiant-for-Truth in *Pilgrim's Progress*: "I am going to my Father's and though with great difficulty I have got hither, yet now I do not regret me of all the trouble I have been at to arrive where I am. My sword I give to him that shall succeed me in my pilgrimages and my courage and skill to him that can get it. My marks and scars I carry with me, to be a witness that I have fought His battles who will now be my rewarder."[29]

༄ ༄

In France, Woodrow Wilson visited no battlefields and spent little time with the doughboys. It is recorded that he shook hands with only one enlisted man during his entire trip. Sergeant Alvin York was bidden to Wilson's Paris residence at the hour usually reserved for dinner. In fact, the innocent and unassuming sergeant from Tennessee—the most decorated soldier of the war—hoped he might be asked to eat with the president and his wife. But after a few minutes of conversation, an aide informed the sergeant he must be moving on, as the Wilsons were expecting guests. And so the sergeant wandered back to his Paris rooms supperless. As one observer commented, Theodore Roosevelt would not only have had York to dinner, he would have wound up in the courtyard with him taking target practice at empty wine bottles.

༄ ༄

Little more than a month after she buried her husband, Edith Roosevelt made a visit to Quentin's grave. She traveled to Chaméry on 18 February. There she met her sister Emily Carow, who had come from Italy to be with her, and walked to the grave from the village. In her arms she held huge bunches of white lilac, lilies of the field, violets, and anemones that she placed on the grave before kneeling and saying the Lord's Prayer. Before she departed Chaméry, Edith arranged to endow the building of a fountain there in Quentin's memory. She also arranged for the erection of a stone marker engraved with a phrase from Shelley's "Adonais," perhaps meant to apply to Theodore as well as Quentin: "He has outsoared the shadow of our night."[30]

Chapter 18

WAR ONCE MORE

*T*heodore Roosevelt never had any friends to whom he felt closer than the Rough Riders. Ted and Kermit and Archie had similar bonds with their comrades-in-arms after the war—most particularly Ted, who went so far as to help found the American Legion in an effort to keep kindled the flame of American brotherhood he believed had been the happiest result of the war. Wherever he traveled and whatever he did— in later years he was assistant secretary of the navy, colonial governor of the Philippines, governor general of Puerto Rico, chairman of American Express, and an executive at Doubleday Publishing—Ted always made the time for veterans' activities.

He regularly attended reunions of his old division. In the years immediately following the war, when Ted served under Harding as assistant secretary of the navy, these reunions were most often held at Walter Reed Army Hospital, where many of the more severely wounded members of the division were confined. Every year Ted joined his old wartime protégés in sharing stories and watching films of themselves in training and combat. At the end of each reunion evening, Ted would ritually, somberly, lift the last glass of the night to lead the men in a toast to those no longer with them.[1]

A few years after the end of the war, Ted attended a Memorial Day celebration at Chester, Pennsylvania. Writing in his diary at the end of the day, he made a point of commenting on a scene that particularly struck him. "In the parade," he wrote, "marching with the colors was a fine looking old boy called Frank Short, a veteran of the Civil War, and an equally good looking young fellow, his grandson, a veteran of the last war." As Ted well knew, this was a symmetry of which the Roosevelts could not boast.[2]

Most of the men he saw at events such as this he had never met before and would never meet again, but they were his friends and brothers and would be so always. They had, all of them, poured every drop of their youthful idealism into the same vital cup. He felt bound to them by honor and blood and experience and sacrifice. He had no bonds outside his family that were greater.

And his family ties were great. He is fondly remembered by his many nieces and nephews as a loyal ally, advocate, and counselor. He was also, like TR, a devoted father. He regularly traveled, camped, hunted, and played sports with his four children—Grace, Teddy, Cornelius, and Quentin II. Ted adored them, and they him. Like his father, Ted took his greatest joys and satisfactions from family life while at the same time pursuing an active public life.

In the years following the Great War, Ted became a high-minded critic of the American imperialism his father had helped sponsor. He likewise became an outspoken advocate for integration and equal rights. He took pride in the fact his father had been the first president to formally entertain a black person (Booker T. Washington) at the White House, and the first to appoint a Jew to a Cabinet post (Oscar Straus, secretary of commerce). He sat on the boards of Howard University, the N.A.A.C.P., and the Anti-Defamation League. (His brother, Archie, was on the board of the Oscar Straus Foundation.) When organizing the American Legion in the early 1920s, Ted went out of his way to recruit vets from all walks of life, all religions and ethnic backgrounds.

A joke within the family was that if one could not find Ted, the best place to look was probably the Young Men's Hebrew Association.

Admitting that he was rowing against the tide in trying to end bigotry and class hatred, Ted joked that at least it was good exercise. Shortly after the end of World War I, he wrote a book entitled *Average Americans*. The book was part memoir of the many types of men who served with Ted in Europe, and part treatise meant to depict Ted's vision of a country without race hatred or class differences. "I can remember the last war," he wrote his friend Alexander Woollcott in the late 1930s, when guns once again began to sound in Europe. "I remember that I felt when I came back that no matter what we might have failed in doing, at least we stamped out intolerance in the United States, for our common service, shoulder to shoulder for the common cause, could not help but accomplish this. [But the actual result has been] the Ku Klux Klan and bigotry, hooded and rampant." He did not think another war would go any further toward solving these, the real problems of the United States.

Thus, in the 1930s, he joined the isolationist organization *America First*, of which Sister was a founding member; and he toured the country making speeches. But he was a reluctant isolationist. His heart was not in it. From the start, he presented the agenda of America First as just another doomed good cause, much like Theodore Roosevelt's Progressive bid in 1912. War would probably come despite all their best efforts. And when it did, everyone would have to work together for victory. He abruptly severed his relationship with America First when he realized three out of every four America Firsters he met "were all for everyone refusing to cooperate, enlist or fight in case we did get into war. That in no way represents my feeling. I have fought and will fight our entrance, but if and when we are committed, then I feel that every last one of us have got to do all he can to bring the war to a successful conclusion."

In early 1941 Ted petitioned the Army Chief of Staff, General George Marshall, to take him out of the reserves and post him to active duty. At age 54, Colonel Theodore Roosevelt Jr was given command of his old unit, the 26th Infantry of the First Division. In a short time he would be promoted to brigadier general. Family members said Ted, in uniform, suddenly looked happier than they'd seen him in a long time. The opinion of one of Ted's nephews was that for several years, while fighting against intervention, Ted had been unable to feel as though he were a legitimate heir to his father's spiritual estate. Now he was ready to go to the line and fight for his country, and this was an important "emotional homecoming" for him.[3]

ॐ ॐ

On the day Ted received his commission, his brother Kermit was in England flat on his back in a sickbed. Kermit had an enlarged liver, but this was just one of his problems. Another was the latest recurrence of his malaria from the River of Doubt.

The years had not been kind to Kermit. He had helped build a great steamship company in the 1920s. He'd traveled widely, written splendid books, and enjoyed literary friendships with the likes of Gertrude Stein and William Butler Yeats. But the Depression hit him hard. Not only were his finances in poor shape, but his pen was silent now that he was in the habit of having whiskey for breakfast. In the thirties, when his fortunes were at their lowest, he compounded his problems by repeatedly leaving his wife, Belle, in order to live with his mistress, Carla Peters. After a while guilt would set in and he would return to Belle for half-hearted reconciliations laced with bourbon. Then in a few weeks he would be gone again.

He had always been happiest when adventuring—first with his father in Africa and South America, later with his brother Ted and other soul mates with whom he traveled to dozens of remote outposts around the world. In the spring of 1940, with his days as a dashing, affluent gentleman explorer long behind him, he sought to renew and rejuvenate himself once again through the adventure of war.

With the help of his friend Winston Churchill, Kermit negotiated a commission in the British army. As soon as he got into uniform, he stopped drinking. His first task was to command an expedition to repel a Soviet invasion of Finland. (Russia at this early date was still an ally of the Germans.) Before the mission could be launched, however, Finland was overrun and forced to surrender. Following this, Kermit was designated to take part in a summer raid into Norway. The enterprise proved a disaster. Dramatically outmanned and outgunned by the Germans, the British were forced to retreat. Although 50 years old and out of shape, Kermit was valiant during the evacuation, helping get men and equipment out and even carrying some of the wounded on his back.

Next he was sent to North Africa, where nothing was happening. Here he found only patrols and drills and tedium that seemed to mock the memory of his dashing deeds in this same landscape nearly thirty years before. Without a war to entertain him, without a mission to consume him, Kermit started drinking again. He soon became ill and was sent back to England at the end of 1940, where his resurging malaria complicated the problem of the enlarged liver. He was discharged from the British Army in early 1941.

Kermit was well enough to return to New York in June, after which he promptly vanished. At Belle's request, Franklin Roosevelt sent the FBI out on an extensive, albeit quiet, manhunt. When Kermit finally resurfaced in July—bruised from a fistfight with a New York cabdriver—Archie had him committed to a sanitarium in Hartford, Connecticut. He was released in the autumn, after which he disappeared again, retreating into boozy seclusion with Carla Peters. The couple stayed in New York City for several months and then traveled to California in early 1942, where Kermit's drinking grew even worse. When the FBI found him, he was "stumbling drunk"—as one agent described it—and reciting a poem written by his old friend from better days, Edwin Arlington Robinson. The poem was "Richard Cory," about the man who "one calm summer night went home and put a bullet through his head."

Kermit was returned to the sanitarium in Hartford, but his family realized he needed a commission more than he needed a straightjacket. Given good reason, he could and would be sober; given real respon-

sibility for something he believed important, he could and would live
up to that responsibility. At the request of Belle and Archie Roosevelt,
FDR and George Marshall made some arrangements.

When Marshall told Kermit he could have a job as an information
officer in Washington, Kermit refused. He insisted he did not want a
"cush assignment." He must be posted to a location where there was
at least a possibility of seeing combat. He told Belle he did not want to
be the *embusqué* member of the family. Finally Kermit was assigned to
the army airbase at Fort Richardson, Alaska, where his duties were
vague. Without any specific assigned mission, he concocted his own.
He convinced the army pilots to allow him along as an observer when
they made runs to bomb Japanese positions in the Aleutians. And he
volunteered to help his friend Muktuk Marston establish a territorial
militia of Eskimos and Aleuts—these to form the backbone of an in-
surgent underground force should the Japanese overrun the region. In
the midst of all this, Kermit began to feel himself again. He told Ted
the war was his "fountain of youth."[4]

But it was not. His liver began to act up, and in early 1943 he was
flown to a Vancouver hospital to be treated for internal bleeding. This
was followed by a medical leave in the States during which he reverted
to his old habits. He and Peters took a cross-country train trip from
Los Angeles to New York, and Kermit spent most of his time in the
bar car. At Belle's request, the War Department intervened, revoked
Kermit's leave, and ordered him back to Fort Richardson in May.

He was not at all well. His stomach was distended. His arms and
legs were sticks. He had willfully destroyed the precious vessel of his
body and he knew it. He could no longer tolerate serious liquor. Two
or three times a week he'd visit a little place in Anchorage called Nellie's
Diner and have a few glasses of wine, but that was it—all his broken
body could handle. He had little strength, and found most tasks exhausting. The most he could gather himself to do was make the rounds
and enforce the local blackout, which he did many an evening in the
company of Marston.

This is how the two men were occupied early in the evening of

June 3, 1943. When they were done, and had returned to the post, Kermit asked Marston what he was going to do next.

"Sleep," said Marston.

"I wish I could sleep," said Kermit.[5]

Nearly twenty-nine years had passed since the day, on the River of Doubt, when Theodore Roosevelt had contemplated suicide rather than become a burden to others. And nearly twenty-six years had passed since Quentin wrote a short story about suicide—a story Kermit edited and anthologized in a memorial volume after the airman's death. "A service revolver is a terrible thing," read the first line of Quentin's macabre tale. Now, in his room, Kermit put his .45 to his chin and pulled the trigger.

Theodore Roosevelt always said: "Where a tree falls, there let it lay." Kermit was buried at Fort Richardson in Grave 72, Plot-A, beneath a simple white military headstone no different from that of any other serviceman.

ৎৢ ৎৢ

In 1942, at age 48, Archie Roosevelt was still troubled by the severe wounds that had earned him a discharge with 100 percent disability in 1918. His age, combined with his physical condition, meant he would not be called to put on a uniform. Nevertheless, while others used their influence to stay out of the service, or at least to stay out of the infantry, Archie Roosevelt exerted all the pressure he could, first to get himself into the army and then to get to the front. "There may come many places and many times," he wrote his cousin Franklin, ". . . where you would like to have the son of the former President and someone with your name to share the dangers of soldiers or sailors or marines in some tough spot. . . . I would be perfect for such a job. . . . You would not be throwing away [someone] who was useful elsewhere."[6]

Commissioned a lieutenant colonel, Archie was given command of a battalion of the 162nd Infantry, 41st Division in New Guinea through 1943 and into early 1944. The fighting was heavy and largely continuous. There was one brief intermission. On the 6th of January 1944, deep in the uncharted tropical jungle, Archie insisted the Americans stop for a few moments to commemorate the twenty-fifth anniversary of the death of Theodore Roosevelt. Then they pushed on. Working together with units of the Australian Third Division, Archie and his men routed the Japanese first from Nassau Bay and then Salamauna. After the latter battle, the Australians chose to recognize Archie's hero-ism in combat by naming a key piece of battle geography after him: "Roosevelt Ridge."

He was fearless. He seemed somehow convinced that he would survive the war, no matter what risks he took. When asked to pinpoint Japanese placements, Archie did so by taking a boat out into the open, in plain sight of the enemy gunners. As the cannon boomed away at him, Archie stood calmly on the deck of his little craft with binoculars and a map, marking down the flashpoints as they revealed themselves. On one of these excursions, Archie noticed a frightened enlisted man hunkered down in the bottom of the boat saying a prayer. "Don't worry," he told the boy. "You're safe with me. I was wounded three times in the last war, and that's a lucky charm."[7]

Only a few days later, he was wounded by a grenade in the same knee that shrapnel had shattered during World War I. The wound was serious enough for the army to once more declare him 100 percent disabled. To this day, Archie Roosevelt remains the only man in the history of the American armed services to have earned that classification twice.

త్ర త్ర

Colonel Theodore Roosevelt Jr. was promoted to Brigadier General in early 1942. On 8 November 1942, he led a combat team from the 1st Division in a landing at Oran, Algeria, during the Allied invasion of North Africa known as Operation Torch. His wife, Eleanor, serving in Great Britain with the Red Cross at Salisbury, heard a story of Ted in the invasion from some of his men who wound up in her hospital. It seems that after the heights above Oran had been captured, the city still held out. The only recourse seemed to be to shell the town into

submission. Instead, Ted ordered his group to hold their fire. He and
an aide, Bill Gordon, rode into the town on a half-track, flying a dirty
undershirt as a white flag. "If I'm not back in two hours," Ted told his
men, give it all you've got." In the end, the German gunners in the
town capitulated and much destruction was avoided.[8]

Not long afterward, Ted's son Quentin was seriously wounded in
the same African campaign. Second Lieutenant Quentin Roosevelt II
was shot at Kasserine by a strafing Messerschmitt in the midst of a savage
German advance. The shell from the Messerschmitt pierced Quentin's
lung and lodged in his liver. The ambulance carrying Quentin went to
three different field hospitals before the driver found one that was not
pulling out before the German advance.

Quentin had already been awarded the Silver Star at Ousseltia. Now
he was given the Croix de Guerre as well. Among the notes he received
at the hospital was one from Flora Payne Whitney—now Flora Whitney Miller. Through the years, she'd always been a generous friend to
him. When he left for war, she gave him a copied-out prayer she'd also
given his uncle in 1917. But she exacted a promise from Quentin II
that she hadn't from her lover: that he must return safely. Now she
wrote to remind him of that promise.

Quentin was sent home—to Old Orchard, the house his father had
built at Oyster Bay just a few hundred yards from Sagamore—in June
of 1943, for a convalescence of eight weeks. His mother left her Red
Cross post in England to nurse him; his elderly grandmother Edith
walked over daily from the old home. She insisted on helping tend the
wounds of this Quentin who, unlike the first, had been spared to her.
She was disappointed at the end of July when he returned to his battery
in the 33rd Field Artillery. The battery was now in Sicily along with
the rest of the 1st Division, to which Brigadier Ted was no longer
attached.

After twenty-three days of hard fighting in Sicily, during which he
had two teeth broken by a spent fragment of mortar, Ted was transferred from the 1st Division and made chief liaison officer between the

Fifth Army under General Mark Clark and the French Expeditionary Corps under General Alphonse Juin. (Both armies were then preparing to go into battle against German forces in Italy.) This posting was a form of censure for Ted from General Omar Bradley, who had relieved both Ted and his superior officer, Major General Terry Allen, from their previous duties. They were being chastised, reports Martin Blumenson, for "letting the First Division become an undisciplined and private army contemptuous of other organizations" and for routinely— "wantonly," was the turn-of-phrase Bradley used—exposing themselves and their men to enemy fire without good cause.[9]

Form dictated that Bradley punish both Allen and his second-in-command, Roosevelt, but it is clear from Bradley's memoirs—and his subsequent actions regarding Ted—that his problem was with Allen rather than Roosevelt. According to Bradley, the trouble began in May of 1943, during the Allied assault on Tunisia, when Terry Allen "foolishly ordered his division into a completely unauthorized attack and was thrown back with heavy losses. From that point forward, Terry was a marked man in my book. . . ."[10] Things got worse at the end of May, when Allen's division, in Bradley's words, "ran amok along the entire coast of North Africa from Bizerte to Oran," behaving more like a mob than a fighting unit. "This incident," wrote Bradley, "convinced me Terry Allen was not fit to command. . . ."[11]

It was in late July, during the assault on Troina in Sicily, that Allen made his final, fatal mistake. "He miscalculated the enemy's strength and verve and was thrown back with heavy losses," recalled Bradley. "Throughout the seven days of heavy fighting that ensued, he attempted to operate much as he had in the past, as an undisciplined, independent army, unresponsive to my wishes—or in some cases, orders."[12] In the wake of this fiasco, Bradley removed both Allen and Roosevelt from command of the 1st.

Bradley kept Ted in limbo for only as long as form required, and then got him back into action. Ted held the liaison job from late July 1943 through February 1944. Then, while Allen still languished without a combat command, Bradley appointed Ted second-in-command of the Fourth Division under Major General Raymond "Tubby" Barton. In this capacity, Ted played a key role in the 6 June, 1944, D-day invasion of Normandy.

A few days before the invasion, Bradley held a conference of key command officers. During the course of his talk, Bradley said those present would have ringside seats at the greatest fight in history. "Ringside, hell!" Ted whispered excitedly to the man next to him, paraphrasing one of his father's favorite expressions. "We'll be in the arena!" As the first wave of the attack prepared to launch, Ted became more sober and jotted a letter to Eleanor:

> We are starting on the great venture of the war, and by the time you get this, for better or for worse, it will be history.
>
> We are attacking by daylight the most heavily fortified coast in history, a shore held by excellent troops. We are throwing excellent troops against it, well armed and backed by good air and naval support.
>
> We are on our transports, buttoned up, our next stop France. The Germans know we are coming, for the harbors of southern England have been crowded with our shipping and the roads choked with our convoys.
>
> I don't think I've written you that I go in with the assault wave and hit the beach at H-Hour. I'm doing it because it's the way I can contribute most. It steadies the young men to know that I am with them, to see me plodding along with my cane. We've got to break the crust with the first wave or we're sunk, for the following groups won't get in. At first Tubby Barton didn't want me to do this, but eventually he agreed after I'd written a formal letter stating my reasons.
>
> Quentin goes in, I believe, at H plus 60. That's bad enough. Frankly, it may be worse than when I go in.
>
> We've had a grand life and I hope there'll be more. Should it chance that there's not, at least we can say that in our years together we've packed enough for ten ordinary lives. We've known joy and sorrow, triumph and disaster, all that goes to fill the pattern of human existence. Our children are grown and our grandchildren are here. We have been very happy. I pray we may be together again.
>
> This will be the last for the present. The ship is dark, the men

are going to their assembly stations. Before going on deck they sit in darkened corridors to adjust their eyes. Soon the boats will be lowered. Then we'll be off.[13]

Quentin was to land on Omaha Beach with the 1st Division; Ted's command would land some miles to the west at Utah Beach. Quentin had been married several weeks earlier to a Red Cross worker from Kansas City whom he'd met in England: Frances Webb. At first Quentin was not sure whether he should take the large step of marriage before returning to combat—but his father insisted he do so. *This* Quentin would know his "white hours." At the wedding—held on 8 April in the tiny Church of Saint Peter and Saint Paul in Blandford, England—Quentin had his father as best man.

The boy was much on the father's mind when, at H-hour on D-day, two battalions of the 8th Infantry, 4th Division, landed on Utah Beach. The boat carrying Ted was the first to touch down—three-quarters of a mile to the south from where it was supposed to land. The beach was already under intensive artillery, machine gun, mortar, and small-arms fire from German forces, some of whom were little more than a hundred yards away. Quickly, Ted improvised a new plan of attack to accommodate the new position his group found itself in.

His men spoke later of the brigadier grimacing from the pain in his leg but nevertheless running from place to place, rallying them, urging them to go forward and not "turn into targets." Ted led his group in a charge over a seawall, established them inland, and then returned to the beach to orient more oncoming transports. He remained there for hours, rushing back and forth to redirect succeeding waves of troops until the last assault forces cleared the shore. For his work that day, he would be awarded the Congressional Medal of Honor. Years later, when General Bradley was asked by a reporter for a statement on the bravest act he had ever seen in over forty years of military service, he described General Roosevelt at Utah Beach.

Quentin's division met with grueling enemy fire at Omaha Beach, for a German Panzer division chanced to be on maneuvers in the vicinity when they landed. Ted was terribly worried about his boy, and unable to get news of him for more than a week. Then one afternoon, as he lay on a blanket resting in the sun, the Brigadier was surprised and delighted to see Quentin come walking into camp. He wrote Eleanor that Quentin was filthy but healthy: unscathed. A check of the record of men in the Normandy invasion reveals that Ted and Quentin Roosevelt II were the only father and son team to participate and that Ted, at 57, was the oldest of all Allied participants on the beach.

The fighting, of course, went on. Ted was instrumental in the siege of Cherbourg in late June, where he served briefly as military governor—restoring order to the great port city. Once finished with his work at Cherbourg, he pushed on.

"Well now I've got a little home in a truck," he wrote Eleanor on 10 July. "It was captured from the Germans by one of our units and given to me by them. The ordnance has done it over and I've got a desk and a bed in it. The inside is painted white. Show [the nickname for his adjutant] is having a time fixing it up. He's put a headboard on the bed, made from the back of an old French chair. He's found a place for my footlocker and bag. He's put in an electric light. I feel positively a softie. The truck arrived yesterday at a most opportune moment, for the old chassis had begun to feel the strain of these last few years of combat. I was a pretty sick rabbit, and it had been raining for God knows how long. It still is, for that matter. I got in and was dry after I'd screwed up energy to take off my drenched clothes. The Doc came and said with a little embarrassment that my troubles were primarily from having put an inhuman strain on a machine that was not exactly new. Anyhow, he gave me something to make me sleep, and this morning I was almost as good as new. It's getting late and tomorrow we attack again—as we will day after tomorrow. Artillery is firing nearby—the heavies—and every salvo shakes this paper."[14]

He was not telling the truth about the doctor. He had not seen one. He was, in fact, intent on avoiding doctors at all cost. He was not well, and he knew it. He had a serious heart condition that he kept secret from Eleanor and from almost everyone else, most especially the army doctors who would send him from the front the moment they found out about the condition.[15]

After a vigorous day on the front lines with his troops on 11 July, he went back to his little truck and, late that evening, dropped dead. At the time of his death, Bradley was in the process of promoting him. Orders giving Ted command of the 90th Division and recommending him for promotion to the rank of major general were on Eisenhower's desk to be signed the next day.

"The Lion is dead," Quentin wrote his mother. "You've already heard, of course, and I hope you got the message I sent back through press channels telling a few details. It was like the magnificent climax of a great play. . . . To me he was much more than simply a father, he was an amazing combination of father, brother, friend, and comrade in battle. Thank God I had an urge to go and see him on the night it happened. I dropped in at seven-thirty and stayed having a wonderful time until after ten o'clock. We talked about everything—home, the family, my plans, the war—having a swell time. He hadn't expected me to drop in and was terribly happy when I left him, as I was."[16]

Ted was buried in the military cemetery at Sainte-Laurent-sur-Mer, near Normandy, on Bastille Day—the twenty-sixth anniversary of the day Quentin died. An army band played "The Son of God Goes Forth to War" while the honorary pallbearers—Generals Bradley, Patton, Collins, Huebner, Barton, and Hodges—stood at attention. Enlisted men from Ted's battalion carried the flag-draped casket. The sound of artillery rumbled in the distance. Quentin II stood at attention as the firing squad let off three volleys, followed by two bugles playing taps, echo fashion.

Theodore Roosevelt Jr. was the most decorated soldier to serve in World War II. Commenting on Ted's death, A. J. Liebling wrote that that while Theodore Roosevelt had been a dilettante soldier and a first-class politician, his son had been a dilettante politician and a first-class soldier. The army, which his father had talked him out of as a career, had been his first, best destiny all along.

A year after Ted's death, Quentin was removed from his grave near

Chaméry and brought to lay beside his brother. The stone that had marked Quentin's grave at Chaméry for more than twenty-five years was at the same time brought to Sagamore Hill and placed in a spot of honor beside the flagpole on the lawn. There it remains to this day, baffling visitors, many of whom leave Sagamore believing Quentin is actually buried there.

In the autumn of 1945, when Quentin II brought his new wife home to meet his sad and failing grandmother, the old lady was confused for a moment and, looking at Quent, announced mournfully: "You were the first of my babies to die."[17]

Chapter 19

EPILOGUE

FLORA

$\mathcal{I}$n 1920, Flora Whitney married a Harvard-educated aviator and veteran who was the son of a powerful politician. Roderick Tower's father was Charlemagne Tower of Philadelphia, former U.S. ambassador to Russia and Germany and owner of a seat on the New York Stock Exchange. Roderick and Quentin had known each other Stateside and were stationed together at Issoudun.

"None of us are very happy about it," Ethel wrote when she heard the news of Flora's wedding, "though he is a nice boy. Poor child, I think she has just done it in desperation; she was so unhappy. He adores her, but otherwise is a perfectly commonplace youth, doing very well in a banking house downtown."[1]

As Ethel accurately predicted, it proved a mistake for Flora to try to marry the man she hoped Quentin would have become. The happiest results of the marriage were two splendid children, Pamela (born 1921) and Whitney (born 1923).

Flora's second marriage, to architect G. Macculloch ("Cully") Miller, was a true love match that endured. There were two more children:

Flora Macculloch Miller (born 1928) and Leverett Saltonstall Miller (born 1931).

Flora became president of the Whitney Museum of American Art after the death of her mother, Gertrude Vanderbilt Whitney, in 1942. Flora remained president until 1966. She then chaired the museum's board from 1966 to 1974 and was honorary chairperson from 1974 onward.

The museum fascinated and excited her, but it did not consume her. She had hobbies as well. She loved the races, and could often be found at Belmont track where she liked to bet on horses owned by her son Lev Miller. She also enjoyed watching baseball—most especially the Mets, which her cousin Joan Payson owned for a time. Flora's grandson John LeBoutillier (son of Pamela Tower and Thomas LeBoutillier) remembers she was a big fan of Keith Hernandez. She also liked Mookie Wilson, Gary Carter, and Darryl Strawberry. Tom Seaver, she said, was in a league of his own.

Flora's husband Cully died in the early 1970s. Flora died eleven days before her eighty-ninth birthday in July of 1986, right in the midst of the best season the Mets ever had. As John LeBoutillier watched the Mets' near-miraculous performance through the playoffs and World Series (including Ray Knight's fantastic clutch hits and the incredible comeback from certain defeat in game six of the Series), he imagined his grandmother up in heaven pulling strings and managing her team, making sure they won no matter what.

THE ROOSEVELTS

Edith Roosevelt lived for nearly thirty years after the death of her husband. Throughout that time she was a stalwart supporter of the Republican Party and an energetic world traveler. Sagamore Hill remained her home, but it was also something more than that. She meant the place to be both a living memorial to Theodore Roosevelt and a refuge and anchor for succeeding generations of the family. Intensely private, she spent the last days before her death in 1948 burning the majority of Theodore's letters to her—a task in which she was aided by her daughter Ethel.

Ted's wife, Eleanor, lived on at Oyster Bay until her death at age 75 in 1960. Her home, Old Orchard, is now a part of the Sagamore Hill National Historic Site. Eleanor's son Quentin II died in China in 1949 under suspicious circumstances. Quentin was working for both Pan Am and for the CIA, and was involved with arranging airlifts of food and other supplies to cities under siege by the communists. On a commercial flight from Shanghai to Hong Kong, under command of communist air controllers above communist-held territory, his plane crashed into the side of a mountain.

Quentin's daughter Susan later became an expert on the ancient culture Mao so successfully sought to dismantle. She is the wife of William Weld, former governor of Massachusetts. Another daughter, Dr. Anna C. Roosevelt, is a noted anthropologist associated with Chicago's Field Museum.

Quentin II was just one of four grandsons of Theodore Roosevelt associated with the CIA. Quentin's brother Cornelius, an MIT-trained scientist, had a long career with the Agency, as did their cousin Archie Roosevelt Jr., who was chief of station in Beirut and later ran agents in Turkey and Spain. After the CIA, Archie Jr. enjoyed a successful second career with the foreign division of Chase Manhattan. His wife, Selwa ("Lucky") Roosevelt, was chief of protocol for the Reagan White House.

Kermit Roosevelt Jr.—Kim—became a near-legendary figure in the CIA when he masterminded the overthrow of Mossadegh and the return of the Shah to head the government of Iran in the mid-1950s. One associate of Kim Roosevelt—another Kim, the Soviet mole in Britain's MI-5, Kim Philby—characterized him as "a courteous, soft spoken Easterner with impeccable social connections, well-educated rather than intellectual, pleasant and unassuming as host and guest . . .

in fact the last person you would expect to be up to his neck in dirty tricks."[2] Philby had dubbed Kim "the quiet American" five years before Graham Greene wrote his novel.

Kim's Uncle Archie and Aunt Grace made their home at Cold Spring Harbor, not far from Oyster Bay. Archie enjoyed a successful career on Wall Street after World War II, founding Roosevelt & Cross, a brokerage house specializing in municipal bonds. Perhaps remembering his brother Kermit's tragedy, Archie was active in supporting Alcoholics Anonymous and eventually became one of the few nonalcoholics ever to sit on that organization's board of directors. Archie's life changed forever when Grace was killed in an automobile accident in Cold Spring Harbor in 1971. He was at the wheel when their car collided with a bus. Blaming himself for Grace's death, he retreated to his winter home at Hobe Sound, Florida, and cut himself off from most business and social contacts. He died there, of a stroke, in late 1979 at the age of 85.

During the 1950s and '60s, Archie became involved with the John Birch Society and other extreme right-wing groups. As might be guessed, he was outraged by the protests against the war in Vietnam—protests in which some of his own grandchildren and many others of Theodore Roosevelt's great-grandchildren participated. Archie's sister Ethel was equally disaffected when she considered the antiwar rebellion at Harvard and other campuses. "How differently," she wrote on the fiftieth anniversary of Quentin's death, "many of [today's] young people look at duty, honor and service to your country in this strangely divided world."[3]

Ethel and Dick made their home at Oyster Bay, not far from Sagamore Hill. Dick pursued a highly successful career as a physician. Ethel became a mainstay of the Theodore Roosevelt Memorial Association (later renamed the Theodore Roosevelt Association). She was a driving force behind the opening of Sagamore Hill as a museum in 1953. When Dick lay mortally ill in the early 1970s, Ethel—ever the nurse—tended him personally. After his death in 1973, she continued to be active in the Theodore Roosevelt Association until her death at the age of 86 in 1977.

Kermit Roosevelt's widow Belle died in 1968 at the age of 76.

The eldest of her generation, Alice Roosevelt Longworth—known as "Auntie Sister" to succeeding generations of the family—remained controversial and unpredictable to the end. Like her brother Archie, she could sometimes be coaxed to support extreme right-wing points of view, but for Alice, character always outweighed politics. She personally liked Lyndon Johnson and disliked Barry Goldwater, thus she endorsed the former in 1964, politics aside. She outlived all her siblings. Well into her nineties, she still did yoga every day and could touch her toe to her nose. She died in 1981 at the age of 96.

Notes

CHAPTER 1

1. Morris, Sylvia Jukes. *Edith Kermit Roosevelt*. New York. 1980. 272.

2. Roosevelt, Theodore to Henry Cabot Lodge. Santiago. 4 July 1898. Theodore Roosevelt Collection, LOC (hereafter TR/LOC).

3. Collier, Peter. *The Roosevelts*. 96–97.

4. Typescript book of letters and poems used in the Quentin Roosevelt memorial volume edited by Kermit Roosevelt. Theodore Roosevelt Collection, Houghton Library, Harvard (hereafter TRC).

5. Morris, Sylvia Jukes. *Edith Kermit Roosevelt*. 447.

6. Longworth, Alice Roosevelt to Michael Rainey. Washington, D.C. 13 May 1968. Rainey Collection. St. Joseph's College.

7. Roosevelt, Archibald to Flora Payne Whitney. 29 July 1917. Flora Whitney Miller Papers. TRC.

8. Harbaugh, William. *Power and Responsibility: The Life & Times of Theodore Roosevelt*. New York: Farrar, Straus & Cudahy. 1961. 513.

9. Author interview with John Gable, Ph.D., executive director of the Theodore Roosevelt Association.

10. There are several death photos of Quentin in family scrapbooks contained in the Theodore Roosevelt Collection, Harvard. Goeffrey C. Ward has also come upon at least one such picture in the archives of the Franklin Delano Roosevelt Library at Hyde Park, NY, a print sent to the Franklin Roosevelts by their Oyster Bay cousins in the autumn of 1918. Author interview: Geoffrey C. Ward.

11. Author interview with J. West Roosevelt.

12. The axle is now on display at the Old Orchard House museum, adjacent to Sagamore Hill. The death mask remains in the vault.

13. Roosevelt, Archibald B. Typescript memoirs. TRC.

14. Kerr, Joan Paterson. *A Bully Father.* New York: Random House. 1995. 17.

CHAPTER 2

1. Roosevelt, Theodore to Owen Wister. 4 June 1905. Owen Wister Papers, Library of Congress (hereafter Wister/LOC).

2. Roosevelt, Archibald B. Jr. *For Lust of Knowing.* Boston: Little, Brown & Co. 1988. 4.

3. Kerr, Joan Paterson. *A Bully Father.* 28.

4. West (whose given name was James West Roosevelt) was the family physician. He delivered several of Roosevelt's children. Emlen (whose given name was William Emlen Roosevelt) was Roosevelt's financial adviser. West was the son of Roosevelt's uncle Weir (whose given name was Silas Weir Roosevelt), and Emlen was the son of Roosevelt's uncle James Alfred Roosevelt, who ran the family firm of Roosevelt & Son for many years. Like his father before him, Emlen was a shrewd man of business.

5. Roosevelt, Theodore to Owen Wister. 17 December 1883. Wister LOC.

6. Roosevelt, Theodore to Emily T. Carow. 16 August 1903. TRC.

7. Theodore Roosevelt called himself Theodore Roosevelt Jr. until his father died in 1878. Thereafter he dropped the Jr. Likewise, Roosevelt's son Ted, born ten years after the grandfather died, used Jr. until Roosevelt died in 1919, after which he in turn dropped it. Ted Jr.'s first son, born while Theodore Roosevelt was still alive, was given the name Theodore Roosevelt III and stuck to it. He lives in Maine and is referred to as "T-3" within the family. His son, who lives in Brooklyn, is Theodore Roosevelt IV ("T-4"). In short, every generation is off by one digit. Young "T-5"—the latest edition—is actually the sixth to bear the name.

8. Roosevelt, Theodore to William Sheffield Cowles Jr. 3 December 1911. TRC.

9. Van Doren Stern, Philip. *When the Guns Roared: World Aspects of the American Civil War.* Garden City, NY: Doubleday 1965. 249–50.

10. The *Alabama* stopped a total of sixty-nine vessels, one of which was released outright and eleven of which were, like the *Ariel*, bonded before being allowed to proceed on their way. The balance were burned to the waterline.

11. Williams, K. J. *Ghost Ships of the Mersey.* Liverpool: Countywise, Ltd. 1980. 8. James Bulloch is buried in Smithdown Road Cemetery, Toxteth, Liverpool.

12. Robert Barnwell Roosevelt was originally named Robert *Barnhill* Roosevelt, Barnhill being his mother's maiden name. He changed his middle name to *Barnwell* when entering politics. The change was made in anticipation of rude interpretations— "manure pile," and so on—of his Barnhill name by political opponents.

13. Years later, the children of Theodore Roosevelt had a similar collection of beasts at Sagamore Hill. The Sagamore menagerie included a set of guinea pigs named Dewey Sr. and Dewey Jr., a cat named Pershing, a pony named General Grant, a badger named Josiah, and, briefly, a foul-tempered bear that was namesake for the Puritan minister Jonathan Edwards.

14. Barnwell married his mistress, Miss Minnie O'Shea (sometimes known as Mrs. Robert J. Fortescue) in 1887, after the death of his first wife. The children of this union—all born before Barnwell married Miss O'Shea—always went by the name Fortescue.

15. The complete roster of Theodore Sr.'s generation of Roosevelts included Silas Weir (born in 1823), James Alfred (born 1825), Cornelius Jr. (born 1827), Robert Barnwell (born 1829), and Theodore (born 1831). There were no sisters.

16. Brace, Charles Loring. *The Dangerous Classes of New York and Twenty Years' Work Among Them.* New York: Scribner's. 1880. 210.

17. Roosevelt, Theodore to John Hay. Albany. 10 December 1900. Hay Papers. Brown University.

18. McCullough, David. *Mornings on Horseback.* New York: Simon & Schuster. 1981. 151.

19. Norton, Charles Eliot, ed. *Orations and Addresses of George William Curtis,* Vol. 1. New York: Harper & Brothers. 1894. 217.

CHAPTER 3

1. Roosevelt, Theodore to Theodore Roosevelt Jr. 25 April 1898. TRJr/LOC.

2. The official name of the regiment was the 1st U.S. Volunteer Cavalry.

3. Roosevelt, Archibald B. Typescript memoirs. TRC.

4. Roosevelt, Theodore to Alexander Lambert, 1 April 1898, in Elting E. Morison, ed., *The Letters of Theodore Roosevelt,* Vol. II, 808.

5. Adams, Henry to Henry Cabot Lodge. 15 June 1898. LOC.

6. Samuels, Peggy and Harold Samuels. *Teddy Roosevelt at San Juan: The Making of a President.* College Station: Texas A&M University Press. 1997. 26. (Author's note: Although I occasionally cite this volume for some facts that I have verified independently, I must mention that *Teddy Roosevelt at San Juan* is a highly unreliable work, riddled with many errors of both fact and interpretation.)

7. McCullough, David. *Mornings on Horseback.* 60–61.

8. Ibid. 58.

9. Collier, Peter. *The Roosevelts.* 33.

10. Harbaugh, William. *Power and Responsibility.* 98.

11. Collier, Peter. *The Roosevelts.* 24.

12. Mahan, Alfred Thayer. *Some Neglected Aspects of War.* Boston: Little, Brown & Company. 1907. 99.

13. deVoto, Bernard, ed. *Mark Twain in Eruption*. New York: Harper & Row. 1940. 8.

14. Hofstadter, Richard. *The American Political Tradition and the Men Who Made It*. New York: Random House. 1948. 205.

15. Harbaugh, William. *Power and Responsibility*. 101.

16. Collier, Peter. *The Roosevelts*. 96–97.

17. Kerr, Joan Paterson. *A Bully Father*. 33–34.

18. The ex-captain of the *Columbia* crew, Fish was namesake for his grandfather, President Grant's Secretary of State. He was also a cousin of the Harvard All-American, later longtime Congressman from Dutchess County, NY, of the same name.

19. Roosevelt, Theodore. *Complete Works*. XI. 8.

20. Roosevelt, Theodore to Theodore Roosevelt Jr. 15 June 1898. TRJr/LOC.

21. Roosevelt, Theodore to Theodore Roosevelt Jr. 10 June 1898. TRJr/LOC.

22. Samuels, Peggy and Harold Samuels. *Teddy Roosevelt at San Juan*. 85–86.

23. Roosevelt, Theodore to Archibald Roosevelt. 19 September 1917. TRC.

24. Roosevelt, Theodore. *The Rough Riders*. 70.

25. Harbaugh, William. *Power and Responsibility*. 105.

26. Goldhurst, Richard. *Pipe Clay and Drill*. New York: Reader's Digest Press. 1977. 76.

27. Kerr, Joan Paterson. *A Bully Father*. 37.

28. The Rough Riders arrived at Camp Wyckoff on 15 August. They were demobilized on 13 September.

29. Kerr, Joan Paterson. *A Bully Father*. 38.

30. Roosevelt, Theodore to Theodore Roosevelt Jr. 15 July 1898. TRJr/LOC.

31. New York *Herald*. 2 January 1907.

32. Hagedorn, Herman. *Roosevelt in the Bad Lands*. Boston: Houghton Mifflin & Co. 1921. 468.

33. Renehan, Edward J. *John Burroughs: An American Naturalist*. Chelsea, VT: Chelsea Green. 1992. 244.

34. Collier, Peter. *The Roosevelts*. 144.

35. Kerr, Joan Patterson. *A Bully Father*. xxi.

36. Blumenson, Martin. *Patton: The Man Behind the Legend*. New York: Quill. 1994. 407.

37. Michaels, Paul to Theodore Roosevelt. Paris. 17 June 1918. TRC.

38. Roosevelt, Theodore to Theodore Roosevelt Jr. Juja Farm, Nairobi, British East Africa. 17 May 1910. Container 3. TRJr/LOC.

39. Coolidge, Hamilton to Flora Payne Whitney. 16 July 1918. TRC.

40. "Quentin Roosevelt Wins Air Battle." *New York Sun*. 11 July 1918. Clipping in Box 91M-50 of the Flora Whitney Miller Papers. TRC.

CHAPTER 4

1. Leuchtenburg, William E. "Progressivism and Imperialism: The Progressive Movement and American Foreign Policy, 1898–1916." *Mississippi Valley Historical Review.* XXXIX (December 1952). 483–504.

2. Roosevelt, Theodore to Mrs. Theodore Roosevelt Jr. 20 March 1917. TRJr/ LOC.

3. Harbaugh, William H. *The Theodore Roosevelts' Retreat in Southern Albemarle: Pine Knot, 1905–1908.* Charlottesville, VA. 1993. 30.

4. Burton, David H. "Three Roosevelt Women." *The Theodore Roosevelt Association Journal.* Vol. XXI, no. 2. (Spring–Summer). 1996. 4.

5. Thayer, William Roscoe. *Theodore Roosevelt: An Intimate Biography.* Boston. 1919. 323–24.

6. Collier, Peter. *The Roosevelts.* 117–20.

7. Roosevelt, Theodore to Kermit Roosevelt. Oyster Bay. 27 August 1914. Kermit Roosevelt Papers. Library of Congress (hereafter KR/LOC).

8. Roosevelt, Edith to Owen Wister. 9 September 1914. Wister/LOC.

CHAPTER 5

1. Roosevelt, Theodore. "The Foreign Policy of the United States." *The Outlook,* CVII (22 August, 1914). 1011–15.

2. Roosevelt, Theodore. "The World War: Its Tragedies and Its Lessons." *The Outlook,* CVIII (23 September 1914). 169–78.

3. Roosevelt, Theodore to Hugo Munsterberg. 8 August 1914. TR/LOC.

4. Adams, Henry. *The Education.* 1103–4.

5. TR failed to mention in his autobiography that both his father and his uncle, Robert Barnwell Roosevelt, had been longtime Democrats, as were all his Hyde Park cousins. While the Hudson Valley branch of the family and "Uncle Bob" became "War Democrats" in the 1860s and remained in the Democratic Party throughout the Civil War, TR's father found in the Civil War an occasion to convert himself, and most Oyster Bay Roosevelts to come after him, to the Republican Party.

6. TR was also a naval historian. His *Naval History of the War of 1812* was written while he was still an undergraduate at Harvard, and it remains a classic to this day.

7. Mahan, Alfred Thayer to Horatio G. Dohrman. Quogue, NY. 2 September 1912. Typescript in Seager Papers. NWC. Original in Mahan Papers. LOC.

8. Mahan, Alfred Thayer to Theodore Roosevelt. Quogue, NY. 1 July 1911. Typescript copy in Seager Papers. NWC. Original in TR/LOC.

9. Mahan, Alfred Thayer to Bouverie F. Clark. New York, NY. 12 March 1912. Typescript copy in Seager Papers. NWC. Original in Mahan Papers. LOC.

10. "Admiral Mahan's Warning." *The London Daily Mail.* 6 July 6, 1910.

11. Mahan, Alfred Thayer to Theodore Roosevelt. Quogue, NY. 8 July 1913. Typescript copy in Seager Papers, NWC. Original in TR/LOC.

12. Spring-Rice, Cecil to Elizabeth Cameron. 2 July 1891. Henry Adams Papers. Massachusetts Historical Society.

13. Kipling, Rudyard to Theodore Roosevelt. 10 September 1914. TR/LOC.

14. Kipling, Rudyard to Theodore Roosevelt. 20 October 1914. TR/LOC.

15. Grey, Sir Edward to Theodore Roosevelt. 10 September 1914. TR/LOC.

16. Roosevelt, Theodore to Stewart Edward White. 31 August 1914. TR/LOC.

17. Bishop, Joseph Bucklin, *Theodore Roosevelt and His Times* (2 vols., New York, 1920), II, 370–71.

18. Coonley, Henry E. to Theodore Roosevelt. 19 September 1914. TR/LOC.

19. Roosevelt, Theodore to Leonard Wood. 31 August 1914. TR/LOC.

20. Harvey, George. "Europe at Armageddon." *North American Review.* September 1914. 321–22.

21. Hagedorn, Hermann. *Leonard Wood, A Biography.* (2 vols., New York, 1932). II, 149–50.

22. Mahan, Alfred Thayer. "Why Not Disarm?" Typescript copy of unpublished draft article. September 1913. Seager Papers. NWC.

23. Roberts, Elmer to Stephen B. Luce. Berlin. 13 May 1910. Luce Papers. NWC.

24. New York *Evening Post.* 3 August 1914. Page 1. Photostat in Seager Papers. NWC.

25. Roosevelt, Theodore to Theodore Roosevelt Jr. 10 August 1914. TRJr/LOC.

26. Mahan, Lyle Evans. *Recollections of My Father: Rear Admiral Alfred Thayer Mahan.* Typescript in folder 2 of Mahan's Presidents File. NWC. All quotes from Lyle Evans Mahan in this chapter are from this unpublished document. See chapter 1 notes for more details on this citation.

27. Mahan, Lyle Evans to Ralph Pulitzer Jr. Quogue, NY. 10 August 1914. Typescript copy in Seager Papers. NWC. Original in Mahan Papers, LOC.

28. Mahan, Lyle Evans to Josephus Daniels. Quogue, NY. 15 August 1914. Typescript copy in Seager Papers. NWC. Original in Mahan Papers, LOC.

29. Daniels, Josephus to Lyle Evans Mahan. Washington, DC. 18 August 1914. Josephus Daniels Collection, LOC.

30. Lincoln, Thomas. New York. 14 August 1914. Xerox of typed letter in Seager Papers. NWC.

31. Roosevelt, Theodore to Theodore Roosevelt Jr. 20 December 1914. TRJr/LOC.

32. Villard, Henry Serano to Edward J. Renehan Jr. 22 February 1995. Author's Collection.

33. Cowley, Malcolm. *Exile's Return: A Literary Odyssey of the 1920s.* New York. 1951. 36.

34. Howe, Mark A. DeWolfe, Compiler. *The Occasional Speeches of Oliver Wendell Holmes, Jr.* Cambridge, MA. 1962. 73–80.

35. Herrick, Robert. "Recantation of a Pacifist." *New Republic* 4 (30 October 1915). 329–30.

36. All Archibald B. Roosevelt quotes in this chapter are from Archie's typed memoirs. TRC. Lowell never made good on the threat of suspension.

37. Dos Passos, John. *The Best of Times: An Informal Memoir.* New York. 1966. 22.

38. Collier, Peter. *The Roosevelts.* 181.

39. Roosevelt, Edith Kermit to Anna Roosevelt Cowles. Oyster Bay, NY. 21 July 1909. TRC.

40. Collier, Peter. *The Roosevelts.* 126.

41. Roosevelt, Theodore to Theodore Roosevelt Jr. Washington, DC. 11 January 1904. TRJr/LOC.

42. Collier, Peter. *The Roosevelts.* 125.

43. Kerr, Joan Paterson. *A Bully Father.* 75–76.

44. Roosevelt, Theodore Jr. to Archibald Bulloch Roosevelt. 1 May 1920. Typed carbon. TRJr/LOC.

45. Kerr, Joan Paterson. *A Bully Father.* 64.

46. Roosevelt, Archie. Typescript memoirs. TRC.

CHAPTER 6

1. Kerr, Joan Paterson. *A Bully Father.* 60–61.

2. Roosevelt, Kermit to Michael Jessup. 27 June 1926. KR/LOC.

3. Roosevelt, Theodore to Theodore Roosevelt Jr. New York, NY. 23 August 1910. Container 3. TRJr/LOC.

4. Kerr, Joan Paterson. *A Bully Father.* 46.

5. *Congressional Record.* 63rd Congress. 2nd Session. p. 16747. The statement was released to the press on 15 October 1914.

6. *New York Times.* 20 October 1914.

7. Roosevelt, Theodore to Henry Cabot Lodge. 8 December 1914. LOC.

8. *Congressional Record.* 63rd Congress. 2nd Session. p. 16747.

9. Roosevelt, Theodore. Speech at Hartford, CT. 15 August 1914. TR/LOC.

10. Lodge's statement was published in the *New York Times* for 3 December 1914.

11. *The Diary of Colonel Edward M. House.* 4 November 1914.

12. Baker, Ray Stannard and William E. Dodd, eds. *The Public Papers of Woodrow Wilson.* (6 vols. New York. 1925–27. *Volume 1: The New Democracy.* 215–18.

13. *New York Times.* 9 December 1914.

14. Roosevelt, Theodore to Anna Roosevelt Cowles. 10 December 1914. TRC.

15. Roosevelt, Theodore. *Address of Hon. Theodore Roosevelt, Assistant Secretary of*

the Navy, before the Naval War College, Newport, RI, Wednesday, June 2, 1897. Washington, DC: Navy Branch, Government Printing Office. 1897.

16. Collier, Peter. *The Roosevelts.* 170.

17. After the United States entered the war in 1917, Bacon would be made a Major in the army and assigned as chief liaison officer from the Allied Expeditionary Force to British General Headquarters. Exhausted by his war efforts, Bacon would die in New York in 1919 while being operated on for an illness contracted in France.

18. Derby, Ethel Roosevelt to Theodore Roosevelt. 22 December 1915. TRC.

19. Derby, Richard to Theodore Roosevelt. 15 December 1915. TRC.

20. Derby, Ethel Roosevelt to Theodore Roosevelt. 22 December 1915. TRC.

21. Derby, Richard to Theodore Roosevelt. Paris. 23 December 1915. TRC.

22. Kerr, Joan Paterson. *A Bully Father.* 24.

23. Author interview with John Gable, Ph.D.

CHAPTER 7

1. Roosevelt, Theodore to Kermit Roosevelt. 15 March 1915. KR/LOC.

2. Foulke, William Dudley to Charles J. Bonaparte. 24 December 1914. TR/LOC. Bonaparte served as secretary of the navy for two years under President Theodore Roosevelt.

3. See "America Unready" in *The Outlook* for 30 December 1914. 997–999.

4. Roosevelt, Theodore Jr. Diaries. Dictated typescript. 6 December 1921. Container 1. TRJr/LOC.

5. Toland, John. *The Rising Sun.* New York: Random House. 1970. 58.

6. Roosevelt, Franklin Delano to Alfred Thayer Mahan. 28 May 1914. Franklin Delano Roosevelt Library.

7. Roosevelt, Franklin Delano to Alfred Thayer Mahan. 16 June 1914. Franklin Delano Roosevelt Library.

8. Mahan, Ellen Lyle to Franklin Delano Roosevelt. New York. 9 January 1915. Franklin Delano Roosevelt Library.

9. Morhart, Fred H. "Navy Marks 100th Anniversary of Admiral Mahan's Birth." Washington *Evening Star.* 27 September 1940.

10. New York *Herald.* 6 December 1914.

11. *New York Times.* 24 December 1914.

12. *New York Times.* 24 January 1915.

13. Joy, Henry B. to Theodore Roosevelt. 13 January 1915. TR/LOC.

14. *The Literary Digest.* 23 January 1915. 137–38, 162–68.

15. Wister, Owen. *The Pentecost of Calamity.* New York: Scribners. 1915. 120–22.

16. Roosevelt, Theodore to Theodore Roosevelt Jr. 29 January 1915. TRJr/LOC.

17. Thayer, William Roscoe. *Theodore Roosevelt.* 411.

18. *New York Times.* 4 January 1915.

19. O'Laughlin, J. C. to Theodore Roosevelt. 16 February 1915. TR/LOC. O'Laughlin quotes Root in the letter.

20. Smith, Page. *America Enters the World: A People's History of the Progressive Era and World War I.* 1985. 442.

21. Lodge, Henry Cabot to Theodore Roosevelt. 15 January 1915. TR/LOC.

22. House, Colonel Edward to William Jennings Bryan. 15 April 1915. House Papers. Library of Congress (hereafter House/LOC).

23. Roosevelt, Theodore to Kermit Roosevelt. 25 April 1915. KR/LOC.

CHAPTER 8

1. Harbaugh, William H. *Power and Responsibility.* 476.

2. Ward, Geoffrey C. *A First Class Temperament.* 296.

3. Harbaugh, William H. *Power and Responsibility.* 476.

4. *New York Times.* 8 May 1915.

5. *New York Tribune.* 8 May 1915.

6. *The Literary Digest.* 22 May 1915. 1134, 1201.

7. Roosevelt, Archibald to Kermit Roosevelt. Boston. 15 May 1915. TRC.

8. Collier, Peter. *The Roosevelts.* 177.

9. Baker and Dodd (eds.). *The Public Papers of Woodrow Wilson. The New Democracy*, I. 321.

10. Murdock, Victor to Theodore Roosevelt. 11 May 1915. TR/LOC.

11. Baker and Dodd (eds.). *The Public Papers of Woodrow Wilson. The New Democracy*, I, 323–28.

12. Thayer, William Roscoe. *Theodore Roosevelt.* 411.

13. Roosevelt, Theodore to Archibald B. Roosevelt. Oyster Bay. 19 May 1915. TRC.

14. Roosevelt, Theodore to Anna Roosevelt Cowles. Oyster Bay. 14 May 1915. TRC.

15. New York *Herald.* 12 June 1915.

16. Kerr, Joan Paterson. *A Bully Father.* 58.

17. Roosevelt, Edith Kermit to Anna Roosevelt Cowles. 15 October 1913. TRC.

18. Roosevelt, Theodore to Endicott Peabody. 9 September 1901. TRC.

19. *This* Ham Fish was an All-American from the famous Harvard football squad that beat the Carlisle College team (featuring Jim Thorpe) for the national championship in 1908. By the time he came to Plattsburg, he had already run successfully for the New York Assembly on the Bull Moose ticket in 1914—one of the few Bull Moose winners. Ham Fish went on to lead a black regiment and receive a Silver Star in France. After the war he served as a Republican Congressman for twenty-five years. He died on 18 January, 1991 at the age of 102.

20. Roosevelt, Archibald. Typed memoirs. TRC.

21. Roosevelt, Theodore to Kermit Roosevelt. Oyster Bay. 31 August 1915. TRC.

CHAPTER 9

1. Roosevelt, Theodore to John Burroughs. 15 August 1915. John Burroughs Papers. Vassar College (hereafter JB).

2. Roosevelt, Theodore to Admiral William Sheffield Cowles. 17 August 1915. TRC.

3. Roosevelt, Theodore to Charles J. Bonaparte. 30 August 1915. Bonaparte Papers. LOC.

4. Roosevelt, Theodore Jr. to Kermit Roosevelt. 29 August 1915. KR/LOC.

5. Villard, Henry S. to Edward J. Renehan Jr. 7 February 1995. Author's collection.

6. House Diary. 20 August 1915.

7. *New York Times.* 22 August 1915.

8. *New York Times.* 5 September 1915.

9. Roosevelt, Theodore. *Fear God and Take Your Own Part.* New York: Scribner's. 1915. ix.

10. Ibid. 27–38.

11. *New York Times.* 8 January 1916.

12. *New York Times.* 28 February 1916.

13. Roosevelt, Theodore to Archibald B. Roosevelt. 16 December 1915. TRC.

14. Lodge, Henry Cabot to Theodore Roosevelt. 1 February 1916. TR/LOC.

15. Roosevelt, Theodore to Henry Cabot Lodge. 4 February 1916. TR/LOC.

16. *New York Times.* 25 February 1916.

17. Roosevelt, Theodore to Kermit Roosevelt. Oyster Bay. 14 May 1916.

18. The event was organized by New York philanthropist Charles Sherrill.

19. Collier, Peter. *The Roosevelts.* 162–63.

20. Roosevelt, Mrs. Theodore Jr. Typed memoirs. TRJr/LOC.

21. Roosevelt, Theodore to Anna Roosevelt Cowles. 23 July 1916. TRC.

22. Roosevelt, Theodore to Anna Roosevelt Cowles. 3 February 1916. TRC.

23. Roosevelt, Theodore to Anna Roosevelt Cowles. 27 August 1916. TRC.

24. Roosevelt, Theodore to Owen Wister. Oyster Bay. 10 March 1916. Wister/LOC.

25. Wister, Owen to Theodore Roosevelt Jr. Saunderstown, RI. 14 August 1921. TRJr/LOC.

26. Roosevelt, Theodore to Cecil Spring-Rice. Oyster Bay. 27 March 1916. TRC.

27. Spring-Rice, Cecil to Theodore Roosevelt. Washington, DC. 4 April 1916. TRC.

28. Roosevelt, Theodore to Anna Roosevelt Cowles. 15 April 1916. TRC.

29. Roosevelt, Theodore. "Speech at Cooper Union." Typescript. TRC.

CHAPTER 10

1. Roosevelt, Theodore. Typescript statement on the war in Europe drafted Oyster Bay, NY, 20 March 1917. Container 3. TRJr/LOC.

2. Roosevelt, Theodore to Anna Roosevelt Cowles. 17 May 1917. TRC.

3. Gunther, John. *Roosevelt in Retrospect*. New York: Harper & Brothers. 1950. 10.

4. Collier, Peter. *The Roosevelts*. 239.

5. This story comes from Winston Churchill, who got it directly from Colonel House himself. Churchill told the tale to Belle Willard, wife of Kermit Roosevelt, who wrote it down for posterity.

6. Collier, Peter. *The Roosevelts*. 240.

7. Roosevelt, Theodore to John Burroughs. New York, NY. 14 August 1918. Photostat in collection of Edward J. Renehan Jr.

8. Harbaugh, William. *Power and Responsibility*. 502.

9. Pershing, John J. *My Experiences in the World War*. 2 Volumes. New York. 1931. 1:23.

10. Palmer, Frederick. *Newton D. Baker: America at War*. 2 Volumes. New York. 1931. 1:205.

11. Brough, James. *Princess Alice*. 242.

12. Gwynn, Stephen, ed., *The Letters and Friendships of Sir Cecil Spring-Rice*. 2 Vols. Boston: Houghton Mifflin. 1929. 2.396—97.

13. Collier, Peter. *The Roosevelts*. 198.

14. Roosevelt, Theodore Jr. to Theodore Roosevelt. Bordeaux. 2 July 1917. TRC.

15. Roosevelt, Theodore Jr. to Theodore Roosevelt. Paris. 30 May 1918. TRC.

16. Roosevelt, Theodore to Archibald Roosevelt. 8 August 1917. TRC.

17. Roosevelt, Theodore to Archibald Roosevelt. 2 August 1917. TRC.

CHAPTER 11

1. Roosevelt, Theodore to Anna Roosevelt Cowles. 26 August 1917. TRC.

2. Coolidge, Hamilton to Flora Payne Whitney. 18 September 1918. First Pursuit Group, Air Service, France. Flora Whitney Miller Papers. TRC.

3. Morison, Elting E., ed. *Letters*. 8.1276.

4. Roosevelt, Theodore to Archibald Roosevelt. 20 January 1918. TRC.

5. Roosevelt, Quentin to Edith Kermit Roosevelt. n.d. 1917. TRC.

6. Roosevelt, Quentin to Flora Payne Whitney. Telegram. 19 February 1917. Flora Whitney Miller Papers. TRC.

7. Roosevelt, Quentin to Flora Payne Whitney. "Tuesday night," April 1917. Flora Whitney Miller Papers. TRC.

8. Roosevelt, Theodore to Archibald Roosevelt. New York. 28 June 1917. Postcard with letterhead of Harvard Club written for hand delivery by Major Bert McCormick. TRC.

9. Roosevelt, Theodore to Archibald Roosevelt. 8 July 1917. TRC.

10. Book of typescript letters from Quentin Roosevelt to Flora Whitney in Box 91M-50 of the Flora Whitney Miller Papers. TRC.

11. Roosevelt, Quentin to Edith Kermit Roosevelt. n.d. TRC.

12. Roosevelt, Quentin to Flora Payne Whitney. On board ship. 29 July 1917. Flora Whitney Miller Papers. TRC.

13. Coolidge, Hamilton. Partial (three-page) TLS carbon memoir of Quentin Roosevelt enclosed in letter from Ethel Roosevelt to Flora Payne Whitney. 4 June 1919. Flora Whitney Miller Papers. TRC.

14. Roosevelt, Eleanor (Mrs. Theodore Roosevelt Jr.) to Edith Kermit Roosevelt. Paris. n.d. Attached to a letter postmarked 28 August 1918, Dark Harbor, ME, from Ethel Roosevelt to Flora Payne Whitney. Flora Whitney Miller Papers. TRC.

15. Villard, Henry to Edward J. Renehan Jr. 7 February 1995. Author's Collection.

16. Book of typescript letters from Quentin Roosevelt to Flora Whitney in Box 91M-50 of the Flora Whitney Miller Papers. TRC.

17. Roosevelt, Quentin to Flora Payne Whitney. 29 July 1917. Flora Whitney Miller Papers. TRC.

CHAPTER 12

1. Cushing, Harry C. to Flora Payne Whitney. 6 May 1918. Flora Whitney Miller Papers. TRC.

2. Roosevelt, Theodore to Archibald Roosevelt. 21 October 1917. TRC.

3. Roosevelt, Theodore to John Burroughs. 7 November 1917. Author's Collection.

4. Roosevelt, Eleanor (Mrs. Theodore Roosevelt Jr.). Typescript memoirs. TRJr/LOC.

5. Roosevelt, Theodore to Anna Roosevelt Cowles. 3 February 1917. TRC.

6. Roosevelt, Theodore to Anna Roosevelt Cowles. 26 April 1917. TRC.

7. Roosevelt, Franklin Delano. Letter to Admiral William Sheffield Cowles. 6 July 1917. TRC.

8. Roosevelt, Theodore to Anna Roosevelt Cowles. 1 May 1918. TRC.

9. Roosevelt, Theodore to Anna Roosevelt Cowles. 6 July 1918. TRC.

10. Roosevelt, Theodore to Anna Roosevelt Cowles. 5 September 1918. TRC.

CHAPTER 13

1. Coffman, Edward M. *The War to End All Wars*. Madison, WI. 1968. 199

2. Roosevelt, Quentin to Edith Roosevelt. 18 December 1917. Xerox copy of typescript, TRC. Original in Sagamore Hill Collection.

3. Toland, John. *No Man's Land*. Garden City. 1980. 314–15.

4. Roosevelt, Theodore to Flora Whitney. 7 December 1917. Oyster Bay, NY. TRC.

5. Roosevelt, Theodore to Theodore Roosevelt Jr. 10 December 1917. Container 3. TRJr/LOC.

6. Coolidge, Hamilton to Flora Payne Whitney. 18 September 1918. Flora Whitney Miller Papers. TRC.

7. Roosevelt, Theodore to Archibald Roosevelt. 8 September 1917. TRC.

8. Roosevelt, Theodore to Archibald Roosevelt. 20 January 1918. TRC.

9. Thayer, William Roscoe. *Theodore Roosevelt*. 439.

10. Roosevelt, Theodore to Archibald Roosevelt. 2 August 1917. TRC.

11. Roosevelt, Theodore to Archibald Roosevelt. 8 August 1917. TRC.

12. Roosevelt, Theodore to Archibald Roosevelt. 14 October 1917. TRC.

13. Roosevelt, Edith Kermit to Ethel Roosevelt Derby. 22 October 1917. TRC.

14. Roosevelt, Theodore to Theodore Roosevelt Jr. 27 October 1917. Container 3. TRJr/LOC.

15. Roosevelt, Theodore to Archibald Roosevelt. 30 October 1917. TRC.

16. Roosevelt, Theodore to Archibald Roosevelt. 7 October 1917. TRC.

17. Roosevelt, Theodore to Archibald Roosevelt. 20 January 1918. TRC.

18. Roosevelt, Theodore to Archibald Roosevelt. 19 May 1918. TRC.

19. Roosevelt, Theodore to Archibald Roosevelt. 23 May 1918. TRC.

20. Roosevelt, Theodore to Archibald Roosevelt. 19 September 1917. TRC.

21. Roosevelt, Theodore to Archibald Roosevelt. 16 September 1917. TRC.

22. Roosevelt, Theodore to Archibald Roosevelt. 25 December 1917. TRC.

23. Roosevelt, Theodore to Archibald Roosevelt. 18 December 1917. TRC.

24. Derby, Ethel Roosevelt to Richard Derby. 6 March 1918. TRC.

25. Roosevelt, Theodore to Theodore Roosevelt Jr. 10 March 1918. Container 3. TRJr/LOC.

26. Whitney, Flora Payne to Quentin Roosevelt. September 1917. TRC.

27. Derby, Ethel Roosevelt to Richard Derby. 26 & 27 November 1917. TRC

28. Roosevelt, Theodore to Theodore Roosevelt Jr. 29 November (Thanksgiving) 1917. Container 3. TRJr/LOC.

29. Derby, Ethel Roosevelt to Quentin Roosevelt. 20 September 1917. Oyster Bay, NY. TRC.

CHAPTER 14

1. Roosevelt, Mrs. Theodore Jr. to Edith Kermit Roosevelt. 17 December 1917. Container 3. TRJr/LOC.

2. Roosevelt, Theodore to Mrs. Theodore Roosevelt Jr. 23 December 1917. Container 3. TRJr/LOC.

3. Roosevelt, Theodore to Theodore Roosevelt Jr. 25 December 1917. Container 3. TRJr/LOC.

4. Coolidge, Hamilton. Partial (three-page) TLS carbon memoir of Quentin Roosevelt enclosed in letter from Ethel Roosevelt to Flora Payne Whitney. 4 June 1919. Flora Whitney Miller Papers. TRC.

5. Givenwilson, Irene to Flora Whitney. 23 February 1918. Flora Whitney Miller Papers. TRC.

6. Roosevelt, Theodore to Theodore Roosevelt Jr. 6 January 1918. Container 3. TRJr/LOC.

7. Derby, Ethel Roosevelt to Richard Derby. Roosevelt Hospital, NY. 6 February 1918 (Wednesday). TRC.

8. This story is recounted in several places, including Geoffrey C. Ward's *A First Class Temperament* (421), Sylvia Jukes Morris's *Edith Kermit Roosevelt* (424), and Hermann Hagedorn's *The Roosevelt Family of Sagamore Hill* (406).

9. Roosevelt, Theodore to Archibald Roosevelt. 15 February 1918. TRC.

10. Roosevelt, Theodore to Mrs. Theodore Roosevelt Jr. n.d. Dictated/typed. Container 3. TRJr/LOC.

11. Roosevelt, Theodore to Archibald Roosevelt. 25 February 1918. TRC.

12. Mason, O.H.L. to Grace Lockwood Roosevelt. 10 April 1918. TRC. Mason was a Presbyterian minister with the Y.M.C.A. He brought a piece of the shrapnel from Archie's wound back to the States and gave it to TR in April.

13. Roosevelt, Theodore to Archibald Roosevelt. 13 March 1918. TRC.

14. Derby, Ethel Roosevelt to Richard Derby. 12 & 13 March. TRC.

15. Roosevelt, Theodore to Theodore Roosevelt Jr. 18 March 1918. Container 3. TRJr/LOC.

16. Roosevelt, Theodore to Theodore Roosevelt Jr. 24 March 1918. Container 3. TRJr/LOC.

17. Roosevelt, Theodore to Theodore Roosevelt Jr. 28 April 1918. Container 3. TRJr/LOC.

18. Coffman. *The War to End All Wars*. 136.

19. Roosevelt, Theodore to Archibald Roosevelt. 31 March 1918. Typed copy. TRC.

20. Roosevelt, Theodore to Theodore Roosevelt Jr. 31 March 1918. Container 3. TRJr/LOC.

21. Roosevelt, Theodore to Mrs. Theodore Roosevelt Jr. 21 April 1918. Container 3. TRJr/LOC.

22. Derby, Ethel Roosevelt to Richard Derby. 25 August 1916. TRC.

23. Derby, Ethel Roosevelt to Richard Derby. 1 February 1918. TRC.

24. Derby, Ethel Roosevelt to Richard Derby. 22 February 1918. TRC.

25. Roosevelt, Theodore to Archibald Roosevelt. 28 April 1918. TRC.

26. Roosevelt, Theodore to Archibald Roosevelt. 12 May 1918. TRC.

27. Derby, Ethel Roosevelt to Richard Derby. 27 March 1918. TRC.

28. Roosevelt, Theodore to Archibald Roosevelt. 20 April 1918. TRC.

29. Roosevelt, Theodore to Theodore Roosevelt Jr. Oyster Bay, NY. 14 April 1918. Container 3. TRJr/LOC.

30. Roosevelt, Theodore to Theodore Roosevelt Jr. Oyster Bay, NY. 28 April 1918. Container 3. TRJr/LOC.

31. Roosevelt, Theodore to Kermit Roosevelt. Oyster Bay. 19 May 1918. TRC.

32. Copy of clipping in Ethel Roosevelt Derby Papers. TRC.

33. Roosevelt, Theodore to Mrs. Theodore Roosevelt Jr. 29 June 1915. TRJr/LOC. In later years, Ted, Kermit, and Ethel lived in Oyster Bay, and Archie in Cold Spring Harbor. So in a sense this cluster of family all living near each other eventually came to pass.

34. Roosevelt, Theodore to Archibald Roosevelt. 30 December 1917. TRC.

35. Roosevelt, Theodore to Archibald Roosevelt. 20 January 1918. TRC.

36. In the hardcover edition of Blanche Wiesen Cook's *Eleanor Roosevelt: Volume One, 1884–1933* (New York: Viking. 1992. 225), it is asserted that TR gave the $5,000 to his *niece* Eleanor, wife of Franklin. This is incorrect and was amended in the paperback edition.

37. See Archibald B. Roosevelt's article "Lest We Forget" in *Everybody's Magazine*, May and June 1919. Also see the piece "The Disposition of the Nobel Peace Prize Fund" published in *The Theodore Roosevelt Association Journal*, Vol. IX, 1 (Winter 1983), 36–37.

CHAPTER 15

1. Roosevelt, Quentin to Flora Payne Whitney. "Tuesday night," April 1917. Flora Whitney Miller Papers. TRC.

2. Roosevelt, Ethel to Flora Payne Whitney. 27 February 1918. Flora Whitney Miller Papers. TRC.

3. Derby, Ethel Roosevelt to Richard Derby. 27 February 1918. TRC.

4. Whitney, Flora to Ethel Roosevelt Derby. Undated Western Union telegram originating in Fort Worth, TX. TRC.

5. Whitney, Flora to Ethel Roosevelt Derby. Undated. On stationery of the Westbrook Hotel, Fort Worth, TX. TRC.

6. Derby, Ethel Roosevelt to Flora Payne Whitney. 27 February 1918. Flora Whitney Miller Papers. TRC.

7. Roosevelt, Quentin to Flora Whitney Miller. Issoudun. 9 March 1918. TRC.

8. Derby, Ethel Roosevelt to Flora Payne Whitney. 11 March 1918. Flora Whitney Miller Papers. TRC.

9. Roosevelt, Quentin to Theodore Roosevelt. 12 May 1918. Xerox copy of typescript. TRC. Original in Sagamore Hill Collection.

10. Roosevelt, Theodore to Anna Roosevelt Cowles. 6 July 1918. TRC.

11. Roosevelt, Theodore to Archibald Roosevelt. 2 June 1918. TRC.

12. Roosevelt, Quentin to Theodore Roosevelt. 12 May 1918. Xerox copy of typescript. TRC. Original in Sagamore Hill Collection.

13. Givenwilson, Irene to Flora Payne Whitney. 28 July 1918. Flora Whitney Miller Papers. TRC.

14. Givenwilson, Irene to Flora Whitney. 23 October 1918. Paris. TRC.

15. Roosevelt, Theodore to Grace Lockwood Roosevelt. 19 June 1918. TRC.

16. Roosevelt, Quentin to Flora Whitney. 28 June 1918. Typescript copy in letter from Flora to Ethel Roosevelt Derby. 13 July 1918. TRC.

17. Roosevelt, Kermit, ed. *Quentin Roosevelt: A Sketch with Letters*. New York. 1921. 149.

18. Roosevelt, Quentin to Flora Whitney. 28 June 1918. Typescript copy in letter from Flora to Ethel Roosevelt Derby. 13 July 1918. TRC.

19. Roosevelt, Quentin to Edith Roosevelt. 18 December 1917. Xerox copy of typescript, TRC. Original in Sagamore Hill Collection.

20. Roosevelt, Kermit, ed., *Quentin Roosevelt: A Sketch with Letters*. 60.

21. Roosevelt, Theodore to Theodore Roosevelt Jr. 12 July 1918. Container 3. TRJr/LOC.

22. Roosevelt, Theodore to Ethel Roosevelt Derby. 12 July 1918. Derby Papers, TRC.

23. Whitney, Flora to Ethel Roosevelt Derby. 13 July 1918. TRC.

24. A monument to Mitchell is located in Manhattan's Central Park near East 95th Street.

25. Roosevelt, Theodore to Theodore Roosevelt Jr. Oyster Bay, NY. 12 July 1918. Container 3. TRJr/LOC.

26. Roosevelt, Quentin to Flora Whitney. 11 July 1918. Flora Whitney Miller Papers. TRC.

27. Roosevelt, Mrs. Theodore Jr. Typed memoirs. TRJr/LOC.

28. Roosevelt, Archibald to Flora Payne Whitney. 13 July 1918. Flora Whitney Miller Papers. TRC.

29. Roosevelt, Theodore to Theodore Roosevelt Jr. Oyster Bay, NY. 7 July 1918. Container 3. TRJr/LOC.

30. Roosevelt, Theodore to Theodore Roosevelt Jr. 28 June 1918. Container 3. TRJr/LOC.

31. Hagedorn, Hermann. *The Roosevelt Family of Sagamore Hill.* New York: Scribner's. 1954. 412.

32. Stricker, Josephine. "Roosevelt at Close Range." *Delineator* (September 1919).

33. Hagedorn, Hermann. *The Roosevelt Family of Sagamore Hill.* 413.

34. Roosevelt, Theodore to Theodore Roosevelt Jr. 7 July 1918. Container 3. TRJr/LOC.

35. Hagedorn, Hermann. *The Roosevelt Family of Sagamore Hill.* 423.

36. Roosevelt, Theodore to Kermit Roosevelt. 21 July 1918. TRC.

37. Roosevelt, Theodore to Mr. and Mrs. Theodore Roosevelt Jr. Dark Harbor, ME. 4 August 1918. Container 3. TRJr/LOC.

38. Roosevelt, Theodore to Kermit Roosevelt. 21 July 1918. TRC. Edith was paraphrasing a passage from George Borrow's poem "Lavengro."

39. Roosevelt, Theodore to Kermit Roosevelt. 10 August 1918. TRC.

40. Harbaugh, William. *Power and Responsibility.* 513.

41. Roosevelt, Theodore to Archibald Roosevelt. 21 July 1918. Typed copy. TRC.

42. Roosevelt, Theodore to Mr. and Mrs. Theodore Roosevelt Jr. 29 August 1918. Container 3. TRJr/LOC.

43. Roosvelt, Theodore to Kermit Roosevelt. 28 July 1918. TRC.

44. Edith turned 57 on 6 August 1918.

45. Roosevelt, Kermit. *Quentin Roosevelt: A Sketch with Letters.* 169.

46. Roosevelt, Theodore to Grace Lockwood Roosevelt. 9 August 1918. TRC.

47. Roosevelt, Theodore to Theodore Roosevelt Jr. Dark Harbor, ME. 29 July 1918. Container 3. TRJr/LOC. TR said virtually the same thing to Kermit in a letter dated 28 July 1918, comparing Quentin to the same Brahmin heros of the Civil War. TRC.

48. Quoted in Ward, Geoffrey C. *A First Class Temperament.* 389.

49. Roosevelt, Theodore to Theodore Roosevelt Jr. Oyster Bay, NY. 15 August 1918. Container 3. TRJr/LOC.

50. Roosevelt, Kermit. *Quentin Roosevelt: A Sketch with Letters.* 235–6.

51. Roosevelt, Theodore to Mr. and Mrs. Theodore Roosevelt Jr. 4 August 1918. Container 3. TRJr/LOC.

52. Roosevelt, Edith Kermit to Kermit Roosevelt. 29 October 1918. KR/LOC.

53. Baldurio, Joseph Clark (signed "Jojo III") to Flora Payne Whitney. 22 July 1918. Flora Whitney Miller Papers. TRC.

54. Peabody, Elizabeth to Flora Payne Whitney. 27 July 1918. Flora Whitney Miller Papers. TRC.

55. Lodge, Henry Cabot to Flora Payne Whitney. 20 August 1918. Flora Whitney Miller Papers. TRC.

56. Givenwilson, Irene to Flora Payne Whitney. 28 July 1918. Flora Whitney Miller Papers. TRC.

57. Roosevelt, Edith Kermit to Flora Payne Whitney. 28 July 1917. Flora Payne Whitney Miller Papers. TRC.

58. Givenwilson, Irene to Flora Payne Whitney. 28 July 1918. Flora Whitney Miller Papers. TRC.

CHAPTER 16

1. Roosevelt, Mrs. Theodore Jr. Typescript memoirs. TRJr/LOC.

2. Derby, Richard to Ethel Roosevelt Derby. 21 July 1918. Paris. Derby Papers. TRC.

3. Peabody, Endicott. "Quentin Roosevelt." *Boston Transcript*. 22 July 1918. Copy in Flora Whitney Miller Papers. TRC.

4. Preston, W.P.T. to Flora Payne Whitney. 10 August 1918. Headquarters, 165th Infantry, France. Flora Whitney Miller Papers. TRC.

5. Roosevelt, Mrs. Theodore Jr. Typed memoirs. TRJr/LOC.

6. Summerall, General Charles P. to Theodore Roosevelt Jr. 18 August 1918. TRJr/LOC.

7. Roosevelt, Theodore to Theodore Roosevelt Jr. Oyster Bay, NY. 13 September 1918. TRJr/LOC.

8. Roosevelt, Mrs. Theodore Jr. Typed memoirs. TRJr/LOC.

CHAPTER 17

1. Roosevelt, Theodore to Kermit Roosevelt. 8 September 1918. TRC.

2. Roosevelt, Theodore Jr. to Theodore Roosevelt. Paris. August 1918. Container 3. TRJr/LOC.

3. Roosevelt, Theodore to Mr. and Mrs. Theodore Roosevelt Jr. Oyster Bay, NY. 21 September 1918. Container 3. TRJr/LOC.

4. Roosevelt, Theodore to Theodore Roosevelt Jr. 20 October 1917. Container 3. TRJr/LOC.

5. Roosevelt, Theodore to Kermit Roosevelt. 13 October 1918. TRC.

6. Roosevelt, Theodore to Kermit Roosevelt. 26 September 1918. TRC.

7. Roosevelt, Theodore to Theodore Roosevelt Jr. 20 October 1918. TRJr/LOC.

8. Roosevelt, Ethel to Flora Payne Whitney. 11 October 1918. Flora Whitney Miller Papers. TRC.

9. Roosevelt, Theodore to Anna Roosevelt Cowles. 27 November 1918. TRC.

10. Roosevelt, Theodore to Anna Roosevelt Cowles. 25 September 1918. TRC.

11. Sherry, Lieutenant Alden Bradford Sheery to Flora Whitney. 30 October 1918. Flora Whitney Miller Papers. TRC.

12. *The Grotonian.* Saturday, 9 November 1918. Vol. XXXV, Number VII. Page 1. Copy in Flora Whitney Miller Papers. TRC.

13. Roosevelt, Edith Kermit to Kermit Roosevelt. 29 October 1918. KR/LOC.

14. Roosevelt, Theodore. "The American Negro and the War: Speech Delivered at Carnegie Hall, 2 November 1918." New York: The Circle for Negro War Relief. 1919.

15. This letter is quoted in both Braugh, *Princess Alice* (248), and Ward, *A First Class Temperament* (421).

16. Roosevelt, Theodore to Richard Derby. New York. 13 November 1918. TRC.

17. Hermann Hagedorn quoting Dr. John H. Richards in the *Saturday Evening Post*, 9 December 1922.

18. Roosevelt, Mrs. Theodore Jr. Typescript memoirs. TRJr/LOC.

19. Derby, Ethel Roosevelt to Richard Derby. 31 December 1918. TRC.

20. Roosevelt, Edith to Kermit Roosevelt. 2 January 1919. KR/LOC.

21. Roosevelt, Mrs. Theodore Jr. Typescript memoirs. TRJr/LOC.

22. Roosevelt, Edith Kermit to Kermit Roosevelt. 12 January 1919. KR/LOC.

23. Roosevelt, Edith Kermit to Theodore Roosevelt Jr. 12 January 1919. TRJr/LOC.

24. Roosevelt, Edith Kermit to Kermit Roosevelt. 12 January 1919. KR/LOC.

25. Quoted in Ward, *A First Class Temperament* (423).

26. Roosevelt, Archibald Bulloch. Cable to Theodore Roosevelt Jr. 6 January 1919. KR/LOC.

27. Roosevelt, Kermit to Edith Kermit Roosevelt. Coblenz, Germany. 7 January 1919. TRC.

28. Robinson, Corinne Roosevelt. *My Brother Theodore Roosevelt.* New York: Scribner's. 1921. 345.

29. Thayer, William Roscoe. *Theodore Roosevelt.* 450.

30. Stanza 40.

CHAPTER 18

1. Roosevelt, Theodore Jr. Diaries. Dictated typescript. 25 April 1922. TRJr/LOC.

2. Roosevelt, Theodore Jr. Diaries. Dictated typescript. 23 May 1923. TRJr/LOC.

3. Collier, Peter. *The Roosevelts.* 399.

4. Roosevelt, Kermit to Theodore Roosevelt Jr. 20 December 1942. TRJr/LOC.

5. Collier, Peter. *The Roosevelts.* 413.

6. Collier, Peter. *The Roosevelts: An American Saga*. New York: Simon & Schuster. 1994. 408.

7. Ibid. 407.

8. Roosevelt, Mrs. Theodore Jr. Typescript memoirs. TRJr/LOC.

9. Blumenson, Martin. *Patton: The Man Behind the Legend, 1885–1945*. New York: William Morrow & Co. 1985. 211. Allen was replaced by Major General Clarence R. Huebner.

10. Bradley, Omar and Clair Blair, Jr. *A General's Life: An Autobiography by General of the Army Omar N. Bradley*. New York: Simon & Schuster. 158.

11. Ibid. 172–3.

12. Ibid. 195.

13. Roosevelt, Theodore Jr. to Mrs. Theodore Roosevelt Jr. 5 June 1944. TRJr/LOC.

14. Roosevelt, Theodore Jr. to Mrs. Theodore Roosevelt Jr. 10 July 1944. TRJr/LOC.

15. Roosevelt, Theodore Jr. to Nicholas Roosevelt. 30 May 1944. TRJr/LOC.

16. Roosevelt, Quentin (II) to Mrs. Theodore Roosevelt Jr. 14 July 1944. TRJr/LOC.

17. Collier, Peter. *The Roosevelts*. 424.

CHAPTER 19

1. Morris, Sylvia Jukes. *Edith Kermit Roosevelt*. 447.

2. Mosley, Leonard. *Dulles*. New York: Dial Press/James Wade. 1978. 492.

3. Derby, Ethel Roosevelt to Flora Whitney Miller. 14 July 1968. Flora Whitney Miller Papers. TRC.

Selected Bibliography

Abbott, Lawrence F. *Impressions of Theodore Roosevelt*. Garden City: Doubleday, Page & Co., 1919.

Amos, James E. *Theodore Roosevelt: Hero to His Valet*. New York: John Day Company, 1927.

Beale, Howard K. *Theodore Roosevelt and the Rise of America to World Power*. Baltimore: Johns Hopkins University Press, 1956.

Berningause, Arthur F. *Brooks Adams: A Biography*. New York: Alfred A. Knopf, 1955.

Bishop, Joseph Bucklin. *Theodore Roosevelt and His Time*. New York: Charles Scribner's Sons, 1920.

Blum, John Morton. *The Republican Roosevelt*. 1954. 2nd Ed. Cambridge, MA: Harvard University Press, 1977.

Brough, James. *Princess Alice: A Biography of Alice Roosevelt Longworth*. Boston: Little, Brown & Co., 1975.

Chessman, G. Wallace. *Theodore Roosevelt and the Politics of Power*. Boston: Little, Brown & Co., 1969.

Churchill, Allen. *The Roosevelts: American Aristocrats*. New York: Harper & Row, 1965.

Cobb, William T. *The Strenuous Life: The "Oyster Bay" Roosevelts in Business and Finance*. New York: William E. Rudge's Sons, 1946.

Cooper, John Milton, Jr. *The Warrior and the Priest: Woodrow Wilson and Theodore Roosevelt*. Cambridge, MA: Belknap Press of Harvard University Press, 1983.

SELECTED BIBLIOGRAPHY

Donovan, Mike. *The Roosevelt that I Know.* New York: B.W. Dodge & Company, 1909.

Douglas, George William. *The Many-Sided Roosevelt.* New York: Dodd, Mead & Co., 1907.

Dyer, Thomas G. *Theodore Roosevelt and the Idea of Race.* Baton Rouge: Louisiana State University Press, 1980.

Einstein, Lewis. *Roosevelt: His Mind in Action.* Boston: Houghton Mifflin Company, 1930.

Emerson, Edwin. *Adventures of Theodore Roosevelt.* New York: E.P. Dutton & Co., 1928.

Gardner, Joseph L. *Departing Glory: Theodore Roosevelt as Ex-President.* New York: Charles Scribner's Sons, 1973.

Gilman, Bradley. *Roosevelt the Happy Warrior.* Boston: Little, Brown & Co., 1921.

Hagedorn, Hermann. *Leonard Wood: A Biography.* New York: Harper & Brothers, 1931.

———. *The Roosevelt Family of Sagamore Hill.* New York: Macmillan Company, 1954.

———. *Roosevelt in the Bad Lands.* Boston: Houghton Mifflin Company, 1930.

———. *The Rough Riders.* New York: Harper & Brothers, 1927.

Harbaugh, William H. *The Life and Times of Theodore Roosevelt.* 1961. Rev. Ed. New York: Oxford University Press, 1975. The first edition was entitled *Power and Responsibility: The Life and Times of Theodore Roosevelt.*

Holme, John G. *The Life of Leonard Wood.* Garden City: Doubleday, Page & Co., 1920.

Howe, M. A. DeWolfe. *John Jay Chapman and His Letters.* Boston: Houghton Mifflin Company, 1937.

Lane, Jack C. *Armed Progressive: General Leonard Wood.* San Francisco: Presidio Press, 1978.

Leary, John J. Jr. *Talks with Theodore Roosevelt.* Boston: Houghton Mifflin Company, 1919.

Longworth, Alice Roosevelt. *Crowded Hours.* New York: Charles Scribner's Sons, 1933.

Lorant, Stephen. *The Life and Times of Theodore Roosevelt.* Garden City: Doubleday and Company, 1959.

McCullough, David. *Mornings on Horseback.* New York: Simon & Schuster, 1981.

Miller, Nathan. *The Roosevelt Chronicles.* New York: Doubleday & Co., 1979.

Morris, Edmund. *The Rise of Theodore Roosevelt*. New York: Coward, McCann & Geohegan, 1979.

Morris, Sylvia Jukes. *Edith Kermit Roosevelt*. New York: Coward, McCann & Geohegan, 1980.

Pringle, Henry. *Theodore Roosevelt: A Biography*. New York: Harcourt, Brace and Co., 1931.

Putnam, Carleton. *Theodore Roosevelt: The Formative Years*. New York: Charles Scribner's Sons, 1958.

Rixey, Lilian. *Bamie: Theodore Roosevelt's Remarkable Sister*. New York: David McKay & Co., 1963.

Robinson, Corinne Roosevelt. *My Brother, Theodore Roosevelt*. New York: Charles Scribner's Sons, 1921.

Roosevelt, Kermit (editor). *Quentin Roosevelt: A Sketch with Letters*. New York: Charles Scribner's Sons, 1921.

Roosevelt, Kermit. *War in the Garden of Eden*. New York: Charles Scribner's Sons, 1920.

Roosevelt, Nicholas. *A Front Row Seat*. Norman, OK: University of Oklahoma Press, 1953.

———. *Theodore Roosevelt: The Man as I Knew Him*. New York: Dodd, Mead & Co., 1967.

Roosevelt, Theodore. *A Bully Father: Theodore Roosevelt's Letters to His Children*. Edited by Joseph Bucklin Bishop. With a biographical essay and notes by Joan Paterson Kerr. Introduction by David McCullough. New York: Random House, 1995.

———. *Fear God and Take Your Own Part*. New York: George Doran & Co., 1916.

———. *The Great Adventure*. New York: Charles Scribner's Sons, 1919.

———. *The Letters of Theodore Roosevelt*. Edited by Elting E. Morison, John M. Blum, and Alfred D. Chandler Jr. 8 vols. Cambridge, MA: Harvard University Press, 1951–1954.

———. *Letters from Theodore Roosevelt to Anna Roosevelt Cowles*. Edited by Anna Roosevelt Cowles. New York: Charles Scribner's Sons, 1924.

———. *The Man in the Arena: Speeches and Essays by Theodore Roosevelt*. Edited by John Allen Gable. Oyster Bay, NY: Theodore Roosevelt Association, 1987.

———. *Roosevelt in the Kansas City Star: War-Time Editorials by Theodore Roosevelt*. Introduction by Ralph Stout. Boston: Houghton Mifflin Company, 1921.

SELECTED BIBLIOGRAPHY

————. *Selections from the Correspondence of Theodore Roosevelt and Henry Cabot Lodge, 1894–1918.* Edited by Henry Cabot Lodge. 2 vols. New York: Charles Scribner's Sons, 1925.

————. *Theodore Roosevelt, An Autobiography.* 1913. Reprint. Introduction by Elting E. Morison. New York: Da Capo Press. 1985.

————. *Theodore Roosevelt Cyclopedia.* 1941. 2nd Ed. Edited by Albert Bushnell Hart and Herbert Ronald Ferleger. Introduction by John Allen Gable. Oyster Bay, NY, and Westport, CT: Theodore Roosevelt Association and Meckler Corporation, 1989.

————. *The Works of Theodore Roosevelt.* National Edition. Edited by Hermann Hagedorn. 20 vols. New York: Charles Scribner's Sons, 1926.

Roosevelt, Theodore Jr. *All in the Family.* New York: G. P. Putnam's Sons, 1929.

————. *Average Americans.* New York: G. P. Putnam's Sons. 1920.

————. *Rank and File: True Stories of the Great War.* New York: Charles Scribner's Sons, 1928.

Roosevelt, Mrs. Theodore Jr., *Day Before Yesterday.* Garden City: Doubleday & Co., 1959.

Samuels, Peggy and Harold Samuels. *Teddy Roosevelt at San Juan: The Making of a President.* College Station, TX: Texas A&M University Press, 1997.

Schriftgiesser, Karl. *The Amazing Roosevelt Family.* New York: Wilfred Funk, 1942.

Seeger, Alan. *Letters and Diary of Alan Seeger.* New York: Charles Scribner's Sons, 1917.

————. *Poems.* New York: Charles Scribner's Sons, 1916.

Spring-Rice, Cecil. *The Letters and Friendships of Sir Cecil Spring-Rice.* 1929. Reprint. Edited by Stephen Gwynn. 2 vols. Westport, CT: Greenwood Press, 1971.

Taylor, Charles C. *The Life of Admiral Mahan.* London: John Murray, 1920.

Thayer, William Roscoe. *Theodore Roosevelt: An Intimate Biography.* Boston: Houghton Mifflin Company, 1919.

Tilchin, William N. *Theodore Roosevelt and the British Empire: A Study in Presidential Statecraft.* New York: St. Martin's Press, 1997.

Ward, Geoffrey C. *A First Class Temperament: The Emergence of Franklin Roosevelt.* New York: Harper & Row, 1989.

White, William Allen. *Autobiography.* New York: Macmillan Company, 1946.

Widenor, William C. *Henry Cabot Lodge and the Search for an American Foreign Policy.* Berkeley: University of California Press, 1980.

Williams, K. J. *Ghost Ships of the Mersey: A Brief History of Confederate Cruisers with Mersey Connections.* Liverpool: Birkenhead Press, Ltd., n.d.

Wister, Owen. *Roosevelt: The Story of a Friendship.* New York: Macmillan Company, 1930.

Index

abolitionism, 115
Adams, Brooks, 24–25
Adams, Henry, 18, 53, 55
Addams, Jane, 86
"Adonais" (Shelley), 225
Africa
    colonial conflicts in, 76
    Roosevelt's journey to, 6, 34, 43–44,
        134, 229
African Americans
    as Rough Riders, 29–32
    Theodore Roosevelt Jr. as advocate
        for, 227
    in World War II, 216
Africanders, 185
Agassiz, Louis, 84
Aisne, Battle of the, 70
Alabama [Confederate raider], 13–14,
    248(n10)
Alaska, 17
    Kermit in, 231–232
Albert I, King of the Belgians, 40
Alcoholics Anonymous, 244
alcoholism, in Roosevelt family, 106–
    107, 142, 208–209, 229, 230

Alexander, Eleanor. *See* Roosevelt,
    Eleanor Alexander
Alexander Hamilton (Lodge), 53
Alfonso XIII, King of Spain, 79
Alger, Russell, 31–32
Allen, Henry T., 129, 235, 266(n9)
All in the Family (Theodore Roosevelt
    Jr.), 7
Alsop, Joseph, 178
Ambulance Américaine, 83–84, 108,
    139
Ambulance Américaine Hospital, 82
America First, 228
American Challenge Cup, 140
American Defense Society, 91–92
American Expeditionary Force (A.E.F.),
    68, 130–131, 182
American Express, 226
American Hospital (Neuilly-sur-Seine),
    83
American Legion, 226–227
American Medical Corps, 166
American Museum of Natural History,
    17, 140, 213, 221
American Relief Clearing House, 83

American Revolution, 23, 95

American Rights Committee, 116

American School of Classical Studies (Rome), 63

American Volunteer Ambulance Corps, 64, 83

Amos, James, 221

Ancona [ocean liner], sinking of, 114

Andover Academy, 92

anti-intervention activists, 112–113

anti-preparedness activists, 94, 112

Arabic [ocean liner], sinking of, 113

Ardennes Forest, battles of, 100

Argonne, Battle of the, 217

Argonne Forest, 5, 149, 215

Armistice, of World War I, 5, 149, 209, 217

Army and Navy Journal [magazine], 91

Army League, 91

Army Line School, 210

Army of Occupation, 209, 222

Arthur, Chester A., 19

Artois, Battle of the, 100

Assistant Secretary of the Navy, Theodore Roosevelt as, 21, 25, 26, 42, 55

Associated Press, 60, 195, 220

Astor, John Jacob, 28

Atlantic [magazine], 84

Australia, in World War I, 184

Austria, war with Prussia (1866), 126

Austro-Americans, 115

Average Americans (Theodore Roosevelt Jr.), 228

Bacon, Robert, 82, 108, 118, 254(n)

Badlands (North Dakota), Roosevelt's visits to, 11, 22

Baghdad, battle for, 178

Baker, Newton D., 125, 128, 130, 132, 160, 193

Baldurio, Joseph Clark, 201–202

Balfour, Arthur James, Earl, 200

Barnes, William J., 99, 123, 173–174

Barrack-Room Ballads (Kipling), 25

Barry, Thomas, 131

Barton, Raymond ("Tubby"), 236, 239

Bates, Lindon, 100

"Battle Hymn of the Republic, The" (Howe), 115

"bearded lady, the", as Hughes nickname, 123

Belgium, in World War I, 38, 56, 63, 75, 91, 112, 122, 184

Bell, J. Franklin, 131–132

Bellows, George, 140

Benét, Laurence V., 83

Benét, Margaret Cox, 83

Benton, Thomas Hart, 140

Bernstorff, Count, 96

Beveridge, Albert, 57

Bigelow, Sturgis, 178

Bishop, Joseph Bucklin, 212

black persons. *See* African Americans

Blake, Joseph, 205–206

Blake's Hospital (Paris), 188, 192, 193, 195, 205

Bliss, Tasker, 131

Blumenson, Martin, 235

Bodie, Ping, 80

Bonaparte, Charles J., 62, 87, 101

Boston

  Derby family of, 82

  Lee family of, 48–49

  Lodge family of, 53

Boston Transcript [newspaper], 75, 206

Boxer Rebellion, 109

Brace, Charles Loring, 17

Bradley, Omar, 235–236, 237, 239

Brady, James, 17–18

Brahmins [American aristocrats], 24, 26–29, 53, 64, 112

Brazil, Roosevelt in. *See* River of Doubt (Brazil)

Brearley School, 140

Bridges, G.T.M. [British general], 177

Bridges, Robert, 63

British East Africa, Roosevelt's trips to, 106

British Red Cross, 83

British War Cross, given to Kermit Roosevelt, 177–178

Broadway Improvement Association, 16

Brooke, Rupert, 145

Broun, Heywood, 171

Brown, John, 115

Brusilov, Alexey, 148

Bryan, William Jennings, 38, 58, 60, 75–76, 94, 96, 102, 103–105, 109–110

Bryant, William Cullen, 18

Buchanan, James, 128

Bull Moose Party. *See* Progressive Party

Bulloch, Irvine [Roosevelt's maternal uncle], 13–14, 20, 95

Bulloch, James Dunwoody ("Uncle Jimmy"), as Roosevelt's maternal uncle, 13–14, 20, 52, 95, 248(n11)

Bulloch, Martha ("Mittie"). *See* Roosevelt, Martha ("Mittie") Bulloch

Bullock, Seth, 73

Bunker Hill, Battle of, 126

Bunyan, John, 18

Burroughs, John, 73, 111, 130

Burton, David, 42

Bwana Makuba (Great Master), as Roosevelt's nickname, 106

Bwana Merodadi (Dandy Master), as Kermit's nickname, 106

Byron, Lord, 146

Cabot family, 53

Canada, 91, 133, 184

Roosevelt speeches in, 166–167

Carow, Edith. *See also* Roosevelt, Edith Kermit

as Roosevelt's second wife, 11

Carow, Emily, 184, 224

Carow, Isaac, 176

Carter, Gary, 242

Cathedral School for Girls, 71

Central Intelligence Agency (CIA), 243

Chamberlain, George E., 88, 171

Chaméry, France, Quentin's death and grave at, 5, 7, 206–207, 224–225, 240

Chanler, Hester, 81

Chanler, Winthrop Astor, 81

Chapman, John Jay, 93, 96–97, 120

Chapman, Victor, 93

"Charge of the Light Brigade, The" (Tennyson), 25, 130

Chase Manhattan Bank, 243

Cherbourg, siege of, 238

Chicago [ocean liner], 133

Chicago Tribune [newspaper], 75

Children of the Night, The, 105

Children's Aid Society, 17

Choate, Joseph, 17

Choate School, 69

Christian pacifism, 57–58, 89, 94, 105, 112

Church, William C., 91

Churchill, Winston, 228, 256(n5)

Circle for Negro War Relief, 216

Civil War, 64, 69, 95, 128, 163, 227

Roosevelt relatives in, 13, 23, 24

Clark, Grenville, 62

Clark, Mark, 234

Clemenceau, Georges, 130–131, 200, 210

Cleveland, Grover, 140

coal famine in New York, 168–169, 171

Coastal Patrol Power Squadron, 154

Cody, Buffalo Bill, 28

Columbia University, 28, 109

commerce raiders, in Civil War, 13–14

Commoner [magazine], 75

Confederacy, the 23, 95

Confederate Navy, Roosevelt relatives in, 13

Congressional Medal of Honor, 21, 32
Ted as recipient of, 237

Conkling, Roscoe, 19

Conscription Bill of 1863, 23

Coolidge, Hamilton, 34, 139, 144, 155–159, 170, 189, 191, 199
death in World War I, 5, 215–216

Coonley, Henry E., 57

Cooper, Jack, 161–162

Cooper, Peter, 18

Cornell University, 141

Cove Neck Public School (Oyster Bay), 71, 168–169, 217, 219, 223

cowboys, as Rough Riders, 28, 29, 30, 33

Cowles, Anna Roosevelt [Roosevelt's sister], 12, 90, 104, 127, 153–154, 215, 218

Cowles, William Sheffield, 12, 111, 154

Cowles, William Sheffield Jr., 12, 153–154, 197, 215, 222

Cowley, Malcolm, 63

Crimson [Harvard magazine], 65

Croix de Guerre
given to Archie Roosevelt, 175, 177, 200, 210
given to Quentin II, 234

Croly, Herbert, 62

Cuba, Rough Rider campaigns in, 3, 29, 79, 131

"cult of cowardice", 96

Cunard Line, 96

Curtis, George William, 18–19, 53–54

Curtiss "Jennies" [airplanes], 156

Cushing, Harry, 149–150

Cushing, Harvey, M.D., 84

The Dakotas, Roosevelt and sons in, 11, 22, 73

Dana, Richard Henry Jr., 84

Daniels, Josephus, 61, 89

Dartmouth College, 69, 78, 109

Davis, Richard Harding, 3, 109

Dean, Dudley, 28

death mask of Theodore Roosevelt, 6–7

death photos of Quentin Roosevelt, 6–7, 197, 247(n10)

Declaration of War (1917), 127

Democratic Party, 18, 45, 54, 88, 100, 104, 124
Roosevelt ancestors in, 14–15, 251(n5)

Derby, Edith ("Edie") [Roosevelt's granddaugher], 169, 181, 220

Derby, Ethel Roosevelt [Roosevelt's daughter], 5, 11, 71, 83, 118, 132, 141, 150, 173, 174, 175, 176, 181, 182, 187, 198–199, 212, 214, 219, 243, 244–245
childhood of, 21, 27, 85–86
marriage to Dick Derby, 81, 166–167
as war nurse, 82, 83, 84–85, 86, 96, 168

Derby, Lloyd, 152, 165

Derby, Richard Jr. [Roosevelt's grandson], 82, 169, 181, 199, 214

Derby, Richard, M.D. ("Dick"), 132, 244
children of, 169, 175, 181, 183–184
marriage to Ethel Roosevelt, 81
in World War I, 81–86, 96, 132, 152, 164–166, 181, 195, 205, 215, 217

Dos Passos, John, 64

Doubleday Publishing, 226

draft riots (1863), 24

"Draft Roosevelt" committee, 119

Drexel & Co., 82, 83

Drexel-Harjes Bank, 83

Duffy, Father, 206, 207

Duncan, George B., 177

Dunkirk, evacuation at, 70
Dutch-Americans, 115

Edward VII, King of England, 43
Eliot, Charles W., 103
Emerson, Ralph Waldo, 84
Espagne [ship], 151
Evening Star (Washington) [newspaper], 91
Exeter Academy, 69

Falaba [ship], sinking of, 100
Farmers Loan & Trust Company, 149
Fear God and Take Your Own Part (Roosevelt), 115–116
Federal Bureau of Investigation (FBI), 230
Ferguson, Bob, 4, 200
First City Bank (Buenos Aires), Kermit's job with, 79
Fish, Hamilton, 28, 30, 118, 230(n)
Fish, Hamilton [grandson], 108, 255(n19)
Fish, Mrs. Hamilton, 118
Fiske, Bradley A., 59
"flap-doodle pacifists", 122
Flaubert rifles, 73
Florida [Confederate raider], 13
"flub-dubs", 121–122
Flying Circus, 194
Fokker airplanes, 104, 156
Force Public School (Washington), Roosevelt sons attendance of, 71–72
Ford, Edsel, 200
Ford, Henry, 200
Foreign Trade Council, 59
Fort Richardson, Alaska, Kermit at, 231, 232
Foulke, William Dudley, 88
Four Hundred [social group], 47

"Fourteen Points", of Woodrow Wilson, 171
Foxcroft School for Girls, 140, 170
France, in World War I, 38, 57, 63, 64, 100, 127, 131, 132, 148
Frankfurter, Felix, 57
Franz Ferdinand, Archduke of Austria, assassination of, 79
Frederick II, King of Prussia, 103
French Aviation School, 143
French Expeditionary Corps, 234

Gardiner, Crain A., 158
Gardiner, Crain A. Jr., 158
Gardner, Augustus P., 74–76, 87, 116, 129
Garrison, Lindley M., 88, 125
Garrison, William Lloyd, 113
gas attacks, in World War I, 85
General Staff College, 210
George V, King of England, 200
George Washington [cruiser], 222
German-Americans, 52, 57, 87, 88, 100, 105, 112, 115–116, 162, 164, 194
Germany
    in World War I, 37–39, 51, 56, 75, 76, 85, 93, 95–96, 100–104, 123, 126, 191, 197, 202, 217
    in World War II, 234, 237–238
Geronimo, 22
Gillespie, _____. [Sagamore Hill groundskeeper], 169
Girardin, Augusta, 152, 153
Givenwilson, Irene, 170, 189, 202–203
Godbert comic strip (Rube Goldberg), 157
Goldwater, Barry, 245
G.O.P. *See* Republican Party
Gordon, Bill, 234
Göring, Hermann, 194
Gosse, Edmund, 63

Graf, Abraham [Theodore Roosevelt Sr. Civil War substitute], 23–24
Grant, Ulysses S., 18
Great Britain
  involvement in Civil War, 12–13
  Kermit in army of, 133, 177–178, 229–230
  in World War I, 61, 70, 91, 97, 111, 127, 133, 148
Greater Paris Garden Club, 153
Greene, Francis V., 91
Greene, Graham, 244
Grey, Edward, 56
Griggs, John, 101
The Grotonian [newspaper], 215–216
Groton School, 5, 12, 69, 153, 215–216
  Roosevelt sons at, 5, 66, 69, 71, 73, 78–80, 105, 108, 139, 155, 187, 202, 206
Gulflight [ship], torpedoing of, 100, 104

Hagedorn, Herman, 10, 196
Hague conventions, 97
Harbord, James G., 129
Hardy, Thomas, 63
Harjes, Henry Herman, 83
Harjes, John, 83
Harper's Magazine, 66
Harper's Weekly [magazine], 18
Harriman, Edward, 83
Harriman, Mrs. J. Borden, 118, 119
Hartington, Lord, 209
Hartwell, Josh, M.D., 215, 220
Harvard Law School, 92
Harvard Medical School, 81, 84
Harvard University, 5, 51, 53, 68, 78, 81–84, 93, 112–113, 145, 241, 243
  preparedness programs of, 62–64, 65–66, 67, 69, 70, 78, 92, 165
  Roosevelt at, 20, 42, 48, 53, 63, 65, 82, 108, 141–142, 146, 224

Roosevelt sons at, 5, 65, 66, 71, 127, 131, 138, 139
Rough Riders from, 27–28
Harvey, George, 59
Hawthorne, Nathaniel, 84
Hay, James, 74
Hay, John, 17, 55, 69
Hayes, Rutherford B., 19
Hays, Will, 173, 221
Hemingway, Ernest, 133
Herald (Paris)[newspaper], 175
Hernandez, Keith, 242
Herrick, Robert, 64
Hewitt, Abram, 15
Hewitt, Marvin, 73
Hibben, John Brier, 64, 92
Higginson family, 53
Hindenburg Line, 149
Hodges, _____. [General], 239
Hoffman, Alice, 152–153
Hoffman, Rose, 162
Holmes, Oliver Wendell Jr., 24, 25, 84
Hoover, Herbert, 184
Hopper, Edward, 140
horse racing, Whitney family in, 140
Hotchkiss machine gun, 93
House, Edward M., 76, 97, 129, 257(n5)
House Military Affairs Committee, 74
Howard University, 227
Howe, Julia Ward, 115
Howe, M. A. DeWolfe, 84
Howells, William Dean, 120
Howze, Robert L., 129
Hubbard, Elbert, 100
Huebner, Clarence R., 239, 266(n9)
Hughes, Charles Evans, 123–125, 172
Hull House, 86
Hunley [submarine], 95
Hunt, Isaac, 196
"hyphenated Americanism", Roosevelt's criticism of, 115

"I Have a Rendezvous with Death" (Seeger), 145–146

"Independent Patriotic Women of America" [war banner], 118, 119

Indian Wars, 31

Influence of Sea Power Upon History, 1660–1783 (Alfred Thayer Mahan) 54, 89

influenza, during World War I, 84, 195, 205

Irish-Americans, 57, 162

Islesboro, Maine, Roosevelts' seclusion at, 198–200

isolationism, in United States, 52, 58, 105, 116, 228

Issoudun, France, Quentin at, 155–167, 189, 190, 201, 241

Italian Red Cross, 184

Ivy League schools, 64, 109
  military preparedness programs at, 62–64, 65–66, 67, 69, 70, 78, 165

James, Henry, 63, 83, 120

Japan, 56, 58, 127, 233

Japanese Red Cross, 184

Jefferson, Thomas, 16, 54

Jewish Americans, Theodore Roosevelt Jr. as advocate for, 184, 227, 228

Jewish Welfare Board, 184

John Birch Society, 244

Johnson, Hiram, 179

Johnson, Lyndon B., 245

Joy, Henry B., 92

Juin, Alphonse, 235

Kaiser Wilhelm, 38, 40, 43, 60, 74, 76, 95, 98, 104, 110, 111, 122, 151, 216, 217

Kane, Woodbury, 28–29

Kansas City Star [newspaper], 166, 184, 220

Kearney, Thomas A., 59

Kearsage [Union corvette], 13

Kettle Hill (Santiago, Cuba), Rough Rider charge up, 3, 31, 135, 222

"Kicking Mule" squadron, Quentin in, 191

King, Clarence, 55

Kipling, Rudyard, 4, 25, 56, 63, 105, 196–197, 217

Knight, Ray, 242

Knights of Jerusalem, 83

Krief-Jorgensen rifles, 63

Ku Klux Klan, 228

La Chapelle, France, medical station at, 84–85

LaFarge, John, 55

Lafayette Escadrille, 64, 83, 93

LaFollette, Robert, 58, 75, 87, 110

LAM Rolls-Royce [armored car], 177–178

Lansing, Robert, 113

Las Guásimas, Cuba, battle of, 30

Latin America, 58

Lawton, _____. [Colonel], 204

League of Nations, 217, 218, 220–221

"league of peace," 172

LeBoutillier, John, 242

LeBoutillier, Thomas, 242

Lee, Alice Hathaway. *See* Rooosevelt, Alice Lee

Lee, Arthur, 133

Lee, Robert E., 13

Lee family, 47–49

Leman, Gérard Mathieu, 38

Lexington, Battle of, 126

Liberty Loan program, 213

Liebling, A. J., 239

Lincoln, Abraham, 90, 129, 137

Literary Digest [magazine], 101

"the little White House", 90, 128

Lloyd George, David, 55, 200

Lockwood, Grace. *See* Roosevelt, Grace Lockwood

Lodge, Henry Cabot, 18, 52–55, 74, 75, 76, 81, 97, 103, 116–117, 129, 179, 202, 218

London, Jack, 80, 120

London Maritime Conference of 1908-1909, Declaration of, 95

Long, _____. [Naval Secretary], 26

Longfellow, Henry Wadsworth, 84

Longworth, Alice Roosevelt, 5, 10, 24, 78, 86, 118, 132, 143, 171–174, 196, 200, 212, 228, 245

    birth of, 11

    childhood of, 21, 27, 32

    marriage of, 46

    White House years of, 47–48

Longworth, Nicholas, 65, 78, 128, 129

    Alice Roosevelt's marriage to, 46

Loos, Battle of, 56

Louisville Courier-Journal [newspaper], 75

Louisville Times [newspaper], 75

Lowe, Seth, 170

Lowell, A. Lawrence, 63–64, 84, 200

Lowell, Guy, 63–64

Lowell, James Russell, 84

Ludendorff, Erich von, 149

Lusitania, 96, 112

    notes of protest on, 102–103, 104, 113

    sinking of, 100–102, 111, 113–114, 140

Lycée Pasteur, 82

Mahan, Alfred Thayer, 25, 52, 54, 58–62, 89, 90–91

Mahan, Lyle Evans, 60

Maine [battleship], sinking of, 26, 101

Malone, Dudley Field, 108

Mann, James, 74

March, William, 182

Maria Christiana, Queen of Spain, 79

Marne, Battles of the, 38, 70, 149, 193, 216

Marshall, George, 228, 231

Marshall, Thomas, 222–223

Marston, Muktuk, 231–232

Martin, Thomas S., 88

Masefield, John, 63

McAlexander, _____. (General), 134

McCoy, _____. (Colonel), 206

McCullough, David, 33

McKinley, William, 26, 47–48

McNair, Leslie, 134

McPharland, Margaret, 34

Merchants Association of New York, 92

merchant shipping, in wartime, 95, 97, 104, 111, 125–126

Metropolitan Magazine, 184, 220

Metropolitan Museum of Art, 17

Mexico, 38, 39, 57, 109, 127

Meyer, Cord, 155

Middle East, as war arena, 182, 195, 230

The Midwest, immigrant groups in, 52, 57, 74, 88, 112

military preparedness programs, 87, 92–94, 107–108, 117, 172

    at Ivy League schools, 62–67, 69, 70, 78, 92

    Wilson's opposition to, 76

Miller, Flora Macculloch, 242

Miller, Flora Whitney. *See* Whitney, Flora Payne

Miller, G. Macculloch ("Cully"), Flora Whitney Tower's marriage to, 242

Miller, Jim, 146

Miller, Leverett Saltonstall, 242

Mineola airdrome (Long Island), Quentin's training at, 138, 139, 156, 191, 222

Miss Comstock's School for Girls, 42

Mitchell, John Purroy, 108, 192

"mollycoddles", 122

Monmouth College, 122

Monroe Doctrine, 26, 38, 58, 75–76

Montana, Roosevelt in, 213–214

Montenegro, in World War I, 185

Montgomery, Clothier, and Tyler, Theodore Jr. as partner in, 66

Morgan, Pierpont, 17

Morgan Bank, 82, 149

Morgan-Harjes Bank, 83

Morison, Samuel Eliot, 63

morphine addiction, of Elliott Roosevelt, 106

Moseley, George Van Horn, 130

Motley, John Lothrop, 84

Mount Vernon, 72

Munn, Charles A., 62

Munsterberg, Hugo, 51

Murphy, _____. [Tammany boss], 99

N.A.A.C.P., 227

National City Bank, 93

National Defense Act, 124–125

National Guard, 124

National Security League, 91, 92

National War Council (Y.M.C.A.), 151, 184

Native Americans, as Rough Riders, 28, 30

The Naval History of the War of 1812 (Theodore Roosevelt), 14, 251(n6)

Naval War College, 25, 77

Navy League, 59, 92

neutrality policy
  of Roosevelt, 51, 57, 58
  for sea vessels, 95, 114, 117
  of Wilson, 39, 52, 58, 64, 65, 75, 94–95, 113, 116, 117

New Deal program, 45

"New Nationalism", Roosevelt proposal of, 44–45

New Republic [magazine], 62, 64, 141, 146

Newsboys' Lodging House, 17

New York Central Railroad, 139

New York Herald [newspaper], 101

New York Journal of Commerce [newspaper], 75

New York Orthopedic Hospital, 17

New York State, Roosevelt as governor of, 17, 47, 71

New York Sun [newspaper], 34, 146, 195

New York Times [newspaper], 59, 62, 74, 85, 92, 101

New Zealand, in World War I, 184

Nieuport airplanes, 6, 83, 156, 157, 194

Nobel Prize for Peace, Roosevelt as recipient of (1906), 6, 43, 184

Norant family, 159

Norris, George W., 58

North Africa, World War II in, 235

North American Review, 53, 59

Norton, Charles Eliot, 63–64, 83

Norton, Richard, 63, 83

Norton-Harjes Ambulance Service, 63

Nowke, Gus, 162

Noyes, Alfred, 220

Oglethorpe, Camp, 164

Old Orchard, Oyster Bay house of Ted Jr., 234, 243, 248(n12)

Olmstead, Frederick Law, 18

Omaha Beach [World War II], Quentin II at, 237–238

"Onward Christian Soldiers", as Roosevelt favorite hymn, 25, 181

Orly Airfield, 191, 193

Osborne, Henry Fairfield, 221

Oscar Straus Foundation, 227

O'Shea, Minnie (Mrs. Robert J. Fortescu) [Barnwell's mistress], 15, 249(n14)

Osler, William, M.D., 27

The Outlook [magazine], 40, 51, 55, 88

Oyster Bay, Long Island, Roosevelt's home at. *See* Sagamore Hill pacifism, 116, 123, 164. *See also* Christian pacifism

Packard Motor Company, 92

Panama Canal, 38, 62

Parker, Frank, 211

Parker, Theodore, 116

Passchendele, Belgium, battle losses at, 148

Patton, George S., 34, 239

Payne, Oliver Hazard, 140

Payson, Joan, 242

Peabody, Elizabeth, 202

Peabody, Endicott, 69, 202, 206, 217

"peace-at-any price people", 58

"peace without victory" [Wilson war slogan], 171

The Pentecost of Calamity (Wister), 93

Pepper, George Wharton, 108

Perry, Bishop, 108

Perry, Bliss, 84

Pershing, John J. ("Black Jack"), 29, 31, 131–132, 134, 166, 200

Persia [liner], sinking of, 114

Peters, Carla [Kermit's mistress], 229, 230

Philby, Kim, 243–244

Philippines, 62, 109

The Pilgrim's Progress (Bunyan), 18, 224

Plattsburg, New York, preparedness camp at, 78, 101, 107–109, 113, 124, 128, 132, 133, 138, 153

Plum Island, New York, preparedness camp at, 153, 154

Porcellian Club, 65

Porter, _____. (Colonel), 134

Potomac [presidential sloop], 72

Prendergast, Maurice B., 140

preparedness programs. *See* military preparedness programs

Preston, Bill, 206

Princeton University, 28, 64, 69, 78, 92, 109

privateering, 95

Progressive Party, 116, 123, 141

Roosevelt in, 37–38, 43–46, 49, 56–57, 62, 75, 87, 99, 102, 123

pro-preparedness organizations, 91–92

Prussia, war with Austria (1866), 126

Puleston, W. D., 91

Pulitzer, Ralph, 69–70

Putnam, George Haven, 91

The Race Suicide Club, 46

Race to the Sea, 70

Reagan, Ronald, 243

Red Cross, 83, 170, 184

Reichstag, antiwar sentiments in, 111

Remington, Frederic, 32

Republican Party, 44–45, 54, 56, 92, 94, 99, 104, 116, 172, 173, 216, 217

disintegration of, 87

pro-preparedness organizations of, 91

Roosevelts in, 15, 18, 19

Roosevelt speech to, 178–180

Republican Reform Club, 18

Reserve Officers' Training Corps (ROTC), 124

Rhinelander, Newbold, 198

Rhinelander, Thomas, 198

Ribot, Alexandre, 157

"Richard Cory" (Robinson) [poem], 230

Richmond News-Leader [newspaper], 75

Richthofen, Manfred von [the Red Baron], 194

Rickenbacker, Eddie, 155, 158, 190

River of Doubt (Brazil), Roosevelt's journey on, 41, 43, 79, 106, 161, 173–174, 217, 229, 232

Roberts, Elmer, 60

Robinson, Corinne Roosevelt [Roosevelt's sister], 24, 42, 47, 215, 223

Robinson, Douglas, 215
Robinson, Edward Arlington, 105–106, 230
Romania, in World War I, 185
Roosevelt, Alice Lee [Roosevelt's first wife], 10, 48, 69
    death of, 11, 42, 49
Roosevelt, Alice ("Sister") [Roosevelt's daughter]. *See* Longworth, Alice Roosevelt
Roosevelt, Anna [Roosevelt's sister]. *See* Cowles, Anna Roosevelt
Roosevelt, Anna C. [Quentin II's daughter], 243
Roosevelt, Archibald B. ("Archie") [Roosevelt's son], 7, 29, 32, 69, 70, 102, 103, 108, 116, 151, 186–189, 205, 212, 214, 219, 222, 223, 227, 231
    birth of, 5, 7
    childhood of, 21, 27
    children of, 175, 194
    education of, 64–65, 71–72, 78, 153
    marriage of, 127
    personality of, 64–65
    post-war years of, 212–213, 244
    war injuries of, 5, 175–176, 192, 193, 209, 213, 232, 233, 260(n12)
    in World War I, 34, 117, 131, 132, 133–137, 152, 159, 163, 165, 166, 170, 177, 182, 184, 187–188, 195, 200, 207, 212
    in World War II, 232–233
Roosevelt, Archibald B. Jr. [Roosevelt's grandson], 9–10, 127, 175, 178, 181, 213, 243
Roosevelt, Belle Willard [Kermit's wife], 79, 133, 143, 175, 208–209, 229, 230, 231, 245
Roosevelt, Cornelius ("Sonny") [Roosevelt's grandson], 150, 162, 169, 227

Roosevelt, Cornelius Van Schaack ("CVS") [Roosevelt's grandfather], 16, 42
Roosevelt, Edith Kermit [Roosevelt's second wife], 65, 81, 107, 117, 132, 141, 143, 144–145, 166, 180, 194, 234
    childhood of, 42
    death of, 7, 243
    devotion to husband, 41–43, 50, 168, 173– 174, 195, 196, 218, 220, 221, 223, 225
    as First Lady, 42
    later years of, 242–243
    marriage of, 55
    reaction to Quentin's death, 195–201, 203, 224–225, 240
Roosevelt, Eleanor Alexander [Ted Jr.'s wife], 78, 117–119, 132, 144–145, 162, 168, 204–205, 208, 209, 210, 211, 214, 220, 236, 238, 243
    as war volunteer, 150–153, 170, 175, 184, 186, 188–189, 192, 193, 194, 196, 207, 218, 233
Roosevelt, Eleanor [Roosevelt's niece, FDR's wife], 89–90, 106, 128, 138, 215, 222
Roosevelt, Elizabeth [Roosevelt's paternal aunt], 15
Roosevelt, Elliot [Roosevelt's brother], 106, 142
Roosevelt, Ethel, 5, 11, 71, 83, 118, 212, 214, 219. *See also* Derby, Ethel Roosevelt
    childhood of, 21, 27, 85–86
    marriage to Dick Derby, 81, 166– 167
Roosevelt, Franklin Delano ("FDR"), 45, 48, 106, 113, 231
    early political life of, 89–91, 97, 100, 128, 154, 215
Roosevelt, Franklin Delano Jr., 128

Roosevelt, George, 152

Roosevelt, Grace ("Gracie")
[Roosevelt's granddaughter], 78,
150, 162, 169, 175, 178, 194,
227

Roosevelt, Grace Lockwood
[Archibald's wife], 127, 175, 181,
213, 219, 244

Roosevelt, Hall [Roosevelt's nephew],
138

Roosevelt, J. West, M.D. [Roosevelt's
cousin], 10, 248(n4)

Roosevelt, James Alfred [Roosevelt's
paternal uncle], 16, 248(n4),
249(n15)

Roosevelt, James Henry [Roosevelt's
distant cousin], 173

Roosevelt, John [FDR's son], 128

Roosevelt, Joseph Willard [Roosevelt's
grandchild], 175

Roosevelt, Kermit [Roosevelt's son], 38,
41, 43, 49, 51, 97, 101–102, 108,
112, 197, 201, 212, 214
  alcoholism of, 106, 107, 208–209,
  229, 230, 244
  childhood of, 21, 27, 32, 85
  children of, 175, 243–244
  education of, 73, 153
  as father's confidante, 105, 106
  health of, 229, 230, 231
  marriage of, 79
  mistress of, 229, 230
  suicide of, 7, 232
  in World War I, 5, 34, 133–134, 143,
  152, 177–178, 182, 195, 208, 215,
  216–217, 219, 222

Roosevelt, Kermit Jr. ("Kim")
[Roosevelt's grandson], 133, 143,
243–244

Roosevelt, Martha ("Mittie") Bulloch
[Roosevelt's mother], 11, 13, 23,
24

Roosevelt, Nicholas [Roosevelt's
cousin], 152

Roosevelt, Oliver [Roosevelt's cousin],
149

Roosevelt, Philip [Roosevelt's cousin],
79, 152, 196

Roosevelt, Quentin [Roosevelt's son],
107, 108, 128, 132, 212, 223
  as aviator, 5, 34, 138–147, 155–159,
  191, 206–207, 222, 250(n40)
  birth of, 11
  childhood of, 21, 33, 80–81
  death in World War I, 4–5, 6, 34,
  139, 195–203, 204, 205, 206–207,
  208, 214, 217, 220, 224–225, 239,
  240, 244
  death photos of, 6–7, 197, 247(n10)
  education of, 69, 71–72, 78, 79, 80,
  141–142, 155
  fiancé of. See Whitney, Flora Payne
  health of, 138, 170, 186
  reburial of, 7, 239–240
  resemblance to father, 79–80
  in World War I, 5, 34, 117, 127, 133,
  138, 143–147, 149, 151, 152, 155–
  167, 170, 176, 186–193

Roosevelt, Quentin, II [Roosevelt's
grandson], 227, 240, 243
  children of, 243
  in World War II, 234, 237–238, 239

Roosevelt, Robert Barnwell ("Uncle
Barnwell") [Roosevelt's uncle],
251(n5)

Roosevelt, Selwa ("Lucky") [Archie Jr.'s
wife], 243

Roosevelt, Silas Weir [Roosevelt's
uncle], 248(n4), 249(n15)

Roosevelt, Theodore ("Teddy"), 89, 96,
192
  ancestors of, 13–15, 23, 52, 249(n15)
  as Assistant Secretary of the Navy, 21,
  25, 26, 42, 55, 66, 128

children of, 4, 7, 11, 12, 21, 33–34, 46, 47–48, 71–74, 85–86, 160, 187–188, 212, 248(n7 ¦ 3)
death mask of, 6, 7
death of, 6, 10, 33, 221–222, 225, 233
family names of, 248(n7)
father of, 12, 16–20
finances and generosity of, 137, 184, 213, 219
first wife's death, 11
funeral of, 33, 223–224
as governor of New York, 17, 47, 71
grandchildren of, 7, 169, 175, 178, 181–182, 183, 199, 218–220, 9162
health of, 12, 22, 40–41, 43, 50, 130, 131, 158, 160–161, 172–174, 182, 216–217, 218, 219
as hunter, 6, 7, 22, 73, 74, 79, 106, 140
letters of, 28, 212, 243, 249(n4)
libel suit of, 99–101, 124
mother's death, 11
political activities of, 172–174, 179, 194, 196
preparedness policy of, 92
as president, 33, 42, 43, 46, 47, 48, 68, 71, 72, 80, 85, 86, 90, 95, 132, 227
as presidential candidate in 1912, 42–46
as presidential candidate in 1916, 42–43, 44, 45–46
in Progressive Party, 37, 38, 43, 44
reaction to Quentin's death, 195–201
Rough Riders of. *See* Rough Riders
second wife of. *See* Roosevelt, Edith Kermit
on son Quentin's death, 5–6
speeches of, 25–26, 45–46, 77, 121, 166–167, 213, 216
as vice president, 48, 81

World War I and, 51–52, 55–58, 94–98, 110–120, 126–133, 137, 141, 143, 149, 158, 163–164, 216, 224
as writer, 14, 30, 55, 74, 114–115, 212, 220
Roosevelt, Theodore III [Roosevelt's grandson], 78, 150, 162, 163, 169, 218–219, 227, 248(n7)
Roosevelt, Theodore IV [Roosevelt's greatgrandson], 248(n7)
Roosevelt, Theodore V [Roosevelt's greatgrandson], 248(n7)
Roosevelt, Theodore Jr. ("Ted") [Roosevelt's son], 5, 7–8, 65, 94, 101, 105, 106, 108, 112, 167, 212, 221
birth of, 11
business career of, 66–67, 109, 226
childhood of, 21, 24, 27, 32
children of, 78, 150–151, 162, 169, 175, 194, 227, 237–238
death of, 7, 238–239
education of, 71, 73, 153
marriage of, 33, 78, 118, 150
war injuries of, 193, 204–206, 209, 210, 211
as war veteran, 213, 226–227, 228
in World War I, 34, 117, 131, 132, 133–137, 152, 155, 170, 171, 176–177, 186, 187–189, 194, 195, 200, 207, 208, 215, 217, 222
in World War II, 228–229, 233–238, 239
Roosevelt, Theodore Sr. [Roosevelt's father], 12, 16–20, 23, 53, 248(n7), 249(n15)
Roosevelt, William Emlen [Roosevelt's cousin], 10, 248(n4)
Roosevelt & Cross, 244
Roosevelt Field (Mineola, NY), 214
Roosevelt Hospital (Manhattan), 217, 220

INDEX

"Roosevelt Ridge" (New Guinea), 233

Roosevelt & Son, 16, 248(n4)

Root, Elihu, 82, 96, 179, 196

Rough Riders, 6, 15, 22, 23, 27–33, 48,
    59, 65, 79, 108, 200, 213, 226

    Cuban campaigns of, 3–4, 30–32, 69–
    70, 135

    proposed rebirth of, 127–128

The Rough Riders (Roosevelt), 30

Rugby School, 69

Russia, 56, 148

Russo-Japanese War, 43

Sagamore Hill, Long Island [Roosevelt
    family home], 7, 10, 21, 32, 33, 48,
    72, 79, 81, 105, 138, 139, 144,
    162, 165, 166, 174, 176, 177, 180,
    200, 221, 240, 242–243

    holidays at, 78–79, 168, 169, 219–220

    trophy room of, 6, 7, 219, 223

Sagamore Hill National Historic Site,
    243–244

St. John's Ambulance, 83

St. Paul's School, 69

Saint-Gaudens, Augustus, 55

Salvation Army War Fund, 184

San Antonio, Texas, Rough Rider
    training camp at, 28

San Juan Hill (Santiago, Cuba), 3

San Juan Ridge (Santiago, Cuba),
    Rough Rider campaign on, 3, 4,
    31, 33, 66–67, 249(n6)

Saturday Club, 84

Savoy, France, Leave Areas in, 150

Scientific American [magazine], 62

Scott, Hugh, 131

Seaver, Tom, 242

The Sea Wolf (Jack London), 80

*The Secret Service of the Confederate States
    in Europe* (James Bulloch), 14

Seeger, Alan, 64, 145–146

Shadow Lawn [Woolworth estate], 122

Shaw, Francis, 30

Shaw, Robert Gould, 30, 200

Shelley, Percy Bysshe, 225

Shenandoah [Confederate raider], 13

Sherman Anti-Trust Act, 180

Shively, Benjamin F., 88

Short, Frank, 227

*A Short History of the English Colonies in
    America* (Lodge), 53

Silver Star, Quentin II as recipient of,
    234

"Sister." *See* Longwort, Alice Roosevelt

Sloan, John, 140

Sloane, William, 151

Smith, Alfred E., 223

Social Democrats, antiwar sentiments of,
    111

social welfare programs, of Roosevelt,
    45

Soissons, Battle of, 149, 208

Somme, Battle of the, 70, 122, 148

South America, 76, 101, 108, 134, 229

Spaatz, Carl, 155

Spad XIII airplanes, 156

Spanish-American War, 63, 69, 162

    Roosevelt in, 3–4, 22, 26–27, 30

Spring-Rice, Cecil Arthur, 55–56, 121,
    133

Square Deal program, of Roosevelt, 45

Standard Oil Company, 140

Stedman, Edith, 152

Stedman, Edmund Clarence, 152

Stein, Gertrude, 229

Stern, James Van Doren, 13

Stevens, Joseph Sampson, 28

Stimson, Henry L., 91–92, 108

Straight, Dorothy, 141

Straight, Willard, 141

Straus, Oscar, 227

Straus Foundation, Oscar, 227

Strawberry, Darryl, 242

Stricker, Josephine, 173, 195, 196

Stuyvesant family, 30

submarines

    Austrian use of, 114

    early types of, 95

    German warfare using. *See* U-boats

suicide

    of Kermit, 232

    Roosevelt's contemplation of, 41, 232

Summerall, Charles P., 210–211

Sumner, Charles, 13

Sumner, William Graham, 18

Sweeney, Mary [Roosevelt maid], 162,
    201, 213

Syracuse, New York, Roosevelt trial in,
    100–101

Taft, Charles, 33

Taft, William Howard, 33, 44, 45, 46,
    82, 96, 103, 179, 196, 223

Tammany Hall, 14, 99, 100

Tarlton, Leslie Mo, 184

Tennyson, Alfred, Lord, 25

Texas Rangers, as Rough Riders, 28

Thayer, William Roscoe, 43, 103

Theodore Roosevelt Association, 245

Theodore Roosevelt's Letters to His Children
    (Roosevelt), 212

Thompson, Phil, 195, 196

Thoreau, Henry David, 18

Tiffany, Will, 28

Tikrit, Iraq, fighting at, 177

Tilden, Samuel, 15

Times [London newspaper], 63

"torpedo-boat", 95

Tower, Charlemagne, 241

Tower, Flora Whitney. *See* Whitney,
    Flora Payne

Tower, Pamela, 241, 242

Tower, Roderick, 241

Tower, Whitney, 241

Treaty of 1839, 38

Tribune [New York newspaper], 101

Tweed, William, 15

U-boats [German], in World War I, 95,
    96, 99, 110, 111, 122, 125, 133,
    143, 144, 146, 147, 154

Union League Club (New York), 118,
    119

U.S. Chamber of Commerce, 92

Utah Beach [World War II], Ted at,
    237, 238

Vanderbilt, Alfred Gwynne, 100, 140

Vanderbilt, Anne Harriman, 83–83

Vanderbilt, Consuelo, duchess of
    Marlborough, 110

Vanderbilt, Cornelius, II, 139

Vanderbilt, Grace, 214

Vanderbilt, W. K., 83

Vanderbilt family, 47, 176

Venezuela crisis of 1895, 52

Verdun, Battle of, 117, 148

Versailles Peace Conference, 222

Vietnam War, 244

Villard, Henry Serrano, 113

Villard, Oswald Garrison, 113

Wall Street Journal, 75

Walsh, Margaret, 162

Walter Reed Army Hospital, 226

war bonds, 93, 213

War Cabinet, 171, 172

warfare

    romanticization of, 24, 64

    Roosevelt's attraction to, 25–26, 34

War in the Garden of Eden (Kermit
    Roosevelt), 177

War of 1812, 23, 95, 165

Warren, Whitney, 140

INDEX

Washington, Booker T., 227
Washington, George, 72, 92, 129
Washington Post [newspaper], 75
Watson, Samuel Newell, M.D., 83
Webb, Frances. *See* Roosevelt, Frances
  Webb
Weekly, 75
Weld, Susan Roosevelt [Quentin II's
  daughter], 243
Weld, William, 243
the West, Roosevelt and sons in, 6, 33,
  73
West Point, 21
Wharton, Edith, 83, 192, 198
White, Stewart Edward, 57
White, William Allen, 218
White House, Roosevelt years at, 33, 42–
  43, 46–48, 72, 80, 85–86, 90, 106,
  137
White Star Line, 113
white supremacists, in Wilson
  administration, 216
Whitney, Barbara, 140
Whitney, Caspar, 141
Whitney, Cornelius Vanderbilt, 140
Whitney, Dorothy, 140–141
Whitney, Flora Payne, 214, 220, 234.
  marriages of, 241, 242
  as Quentin's fiancé, 139–141, 143–
    144, 146, 147, 149, 159, 166–167,
    187, 188, 189–190, 191, 192, 193,
    241
  reaction to Quentin's death, 197, 198,
    200, 201, 203
Whitney, Gertrude Vanderbilt, 84, 139,
  140–141, 242
Whitney, Harry Payne, 139, 140, 141
Whitney, Sonny, 141
Whitney, William C., 139–140
Whitney family, 215
Whitney Museum of American Art, 140,
  242

Wickersham, George, 101
Wilhelm II, of Germany. *See* Kaiser
  Wilhelm
Willard, Belle. *See* Roosevelt, Belle
  Willard
Wilson, Mookie, 242
Wilson, Woodrow, 45, 68, 89, 92, 101,
  179, 222, 224
  Declaration of War by, 127
  foreign policy in World War I, 38–
    39, 56–60, 64–65, 75–77, 94–98,
    102, 111, 113, 117
  "Fourteen Points" of, 171
  League of Nations of, 217, 218, 220–
    221
  meeting with Roosevelt, 128–129
  re-election of (1916), 125, 172
  Roosevelt's criticism of, 38, 46, 77,
    96–98, 103–104, 119, 122, 128,
    151–152, 154, 161, 166, 171–172,
    188, 216–217
  Wister's poem about, 120–121
"Wilson with whiskers", as Hughes
  nickname, 123
Wister, Owen, 10, 47, 50, 72, 81, 93,
  119–121
Wolff Bureau, 197
Wolseley, Garnet Joseph, Lord, 24–
  25
women's suffrage, 18
Wood, Leonard, 21, 26, 29, 30–31, 59,
  65, 68, 76, 78, 84, 108–109, 120,
  131, 133, 138, 176–177, 218
Woods, Arthur, 108
Woollcott, Alexander, 228
Woolworth, F. W., 122
The World [newspaper], 61
World War I, 8, 51
  American Declaration of War, 127
  American fatalities in, 148
  Archibald in. *See* Roosevelt,
    Archibald

German maneuvers in, 37–38

Kermit in. *See* Roosevelt, Kermit

land battles of, 148–149

Quentin in. *See* Roosevelt, Quentin

Theodore Jr. in. *See* Roosevelt, Theodore Jr.

World War II, 92, 150, 155

Archibald in, 34, 232–233

Quentin II in, 234–235

Theodore Jr. in, 228–229

Wotherspoon, W. W., 62

Wrenn, Bob, 28

Yale University, 28, 69, 78, 84, 92, 108, 165

Yaphank, Long Island, training camp at, 165

Yeats, Williams Butler, 229

York, Alvin, 224

Young Men's Christian Association, 150, 151, 152, 184, 188, 201, 207

Young Men's Hebrew Association, 228

Youngs' Cemetery, Roosevelt's burial in, 223–224

Ypres, Battles of, 70, 85, 100, 148

Yucatan [ship], 29